CW00926766

INTERNATIONAL POLITICAL ECONOMY SERIES

General Editor: Timothy M. Shaw, Professor of Political Science and International Development Studies, and Director of the Centre for Foreign Policy Studies, Dalhousie University, Nova Scotia, Canada

Recent titles include:

Manuel R. Agosin and Diana Tussie (*editors*)
TRADE AND GROWTH: NEW DILEMMAS IN TRADE POLICY

Mahvash Alerassool
FREEZING ASSETS: THE USA AND THE MOST EFFECTIVE
   ECONOMIC SANCTION

Robert Boardman
POST-SOCIALIST WORLD ORDERS: RUSSIA, CHINA AND THE
   UN SYSTEM

Richard P. C. Brown
PUBLIC DEBT AND PRIVATE WEALTH

John Calabrese
REVOLUTIONARY HORIZONS: REGIONAL FOREIGN POLICY
   IN POST-KHOMEINI IRAN

Jerker Carlsson, Gunnar Köhlin and Anders Ekbom
THE POLITICAL ECONOMY OF EVALUATION

Edward A. Comor (*editor*)
THE GLOBAL POLITICAL ECONOMY OF COMMUNICATION

O. P. Dwivedi
DEVELOPMENT ADMINISTRATION: FROM UNDERDEVELOPMENT
   TO SUSTAINABLE DEVELOPMENT

Steen Folke, Niels Fold and Thyge Enevoldsen
SOUTH–SOUTH TRADE AND DEVELOPMENT

Anthony Tuo-Kofi Gadzey
THE POLITICAL ECONOMY OF POWER

Betty J. Harris
THE POLITICAL ECONOMY OF THE SOUTHERN AFRICAN PERIPHERY

Jacques Hersh
THE USA AND THE RISE OF EAST ASIA SINCE 1945

The South at the End of the Twentieth Century

Rethinking the Political Economy of Foreign Policy in Africa, Asia, the Caribbean and Latin America

Larry A. Swatuk
SSHRCC Post-Doctoral Fellow
Centre for International and Strategic Studies
York University, Ontario

and

Timothy M. Shaw
Director, Centre for Foreign Policy Studies
Dalhousie University, Nova Scotia

St. Martin's Press

First published in Great Britain 1994 by
THE MACMILLAN PRESS LTD
Houndmills, Basingstoke, Hampshire RG21 2XS
and London
Companies and representatives
throughout the world

A catalogue record for this book is available
from the British Library.

ISBN 0–333–61363–5

Printed in Great Britain by
Ipswich Book Co Ltd
Ipswich, Suffolk

First published in the United States of America 1994 by
Scholarly and Reference Division,
ST. MARTIN'S PRESS, INC.,
175 Fifth Avenue,
New York, N.Y. 10010

ISBN 0–312–12128–8

Library of Congress Cataloging-in-Publication Data
The South at the end of the twentieth century : rethinking the
political economy of foreign policy in Africa, Asia, the Caribbean,
and Latin America / [edited by] Larry A. Swatuk and Timothy M. Shaw.
p.   cm. — (International political economy series)
Includes bibliographical references and index.
ISBN 0–312–12128–8
1. International economic relations.   2. International division of
labor.   3. Regionalism.   4. Developing countries—Foreign economic
relations.   5. Developing countries—Economic conditions.
I. Swatuk, Larry A. (Larry Anthony), 1957– .   II. Shaw, Timothy M.
III. Series.
HF1359.S658   1994
382'.3'091724—dc20   93–44271
                                                            CIP

Contents

PART IV   AFRICA

PART V   ASIA

PART VI   THE CARIBBEAN AND LATIN AMERICA

PART VII   CONCLUSION

List of Tables and Figures

Tables

Figures

Notes on the Contributors

Amitav Acharya is a Senior Fellow of the Centre for International and Strategic Studies at York University where he also teaches in the Political Science Department. He previously taught international politics at the National University in Singapore and was a Fellow of the Institute of Southeast Asian Studies. His major research concerns are comparative Third-World security issues, with a special focus on the Persian Gulf and Southeast Asia. His most recent publications include: *A New Regional Order in Southeast Asia: ASEAN in the Post-Cold War Era*, a chapter on Third-World regime security in Brian L. Job (ed.), *The Insecurity Dilemma: National Security of Third World States*. His articles have appeared in *Pacific Affairs*, *Journal of Peace Research*, *India Quarterly* and *Contemporary Southeast Asia*.

Robert Boardman is Professor of Political Science and Environmental Studies at Dalhousie University in Nova Scotia where he has served as Head of Department and Director of the Centre for Foreign Policy Studies as well as co-editor of the *Canadian Journal of Political Science*. His most recent books are *Global Regimes and Nation-States: environmental issues in Australian politics* and *Post-Socialist World Orders: Russia, China and the UN system*, the latter in the International Political Economy series.

Mark E. Denham is Assistant Professor of Political Science and Director of the Institute of International Relations at the University of Toledo in Ohio and a Faculty Associate with the Mershon Center at Ohio State University. He has published in *Peace Research* and is codirecting a project assembling resources on peace and conflict resolution for the US Institute of Peace.

John F. Devlin is Vice-President of N.T. Yap Environmental Systems Analysts Limited in Guelph and a doctoral candidate at Carleton University in Ottawa. His essays on environmental and developmental issues in Asia, especially the NICs and the Philippines, are appearing in *Environmental Politics* and *Third World Quarterly*. He is also preparing *Growth, Equity and Sustainability in Northeast Asia* for the International Political Economy series.

Kiaras Gharabaghi is a doctoral candidate in Political Science and a Doctoral Fellow at the Centre for Foreign Policy Studies at Dalhousie University, working towards a dissertation on regional development in Central Asia. He has contributed to the special issue of *Third World Quarterly* on 'The South in the New World (Dis)Order'.

Julius O. Ihonvbere is Associate Professor of Government at the University of Texas in Austin, having previously lectured at Bendel State, Obafemi Awolowo, and Port Harcourt universities in Nigeria. Dr Ihonvbere is coauthor or coeditor of several books on the political economy of Nigeria, including *The Rise and Fall of Nigeria's Second Republic, 1979–1984, Nigeria and the International Capitalist System* and *Towards a Political Economy of Nigeria*.

Laura Macdonald is Assistant Professor of Political Science at Carleton University in Ottawa. She holds a PhD from York University for her work on civil society in Central America and is an Associate Fellow of York's Centre for Research on Latin America and the Caribbean. She serves on the Editorial Committee of *Studies in Political Economy* and on the Executive Board of the Canadian Association for the Study of International Development.

Helen McBain holds a PhD from the University of the West Indies in Jamaica, where she is a Fellow in the Institute of Social and Economic Research. She is also Deputy Director of the Programme in International Economic Relations of the Caribbean and teaches in the Consortium Graduate School of Social Sciences. She has contributed chapters to several books on the economic development of the Caribbean.

James H. Mittelman is Professor and Chair of the Department of Comparative and Regional Studies in the School of International Service at the American University in Washington, DC. His publications include *Ideology and Politics in Uganda: from Obote to Amin, Underdevelopment and the Transition to Socialism: Mozambique and Tanzania* and *Out from Underdevelopment: prospects for the Third World*, the last in the International Political Economy series.

Julius E. Nyang'oro is Associate Professor and Director of African and Afro–American Studies at the University of North Carolina, Chapel Hill. He is author of *The State and Economic Development in Africa* and coeditor of *Corporatism in Africa* and *Beyond Structural Adjustment in Africa*. Dr Nyang'oro holds doctorates in Law and in Political Science and serves as a consultant to the All Africa Council of Churches.

Aaron Segal is Professor of Political Science at the University of Texas at El Paso. His most recent book is *An Atlas of International Migration*.

Timothy M. Shaw is Director of the Centre for Foreign Policy Studies at Dalhousie University and General Editor of the Macmillan/St. Martin's Series in IPE. He has taught at universities in Nigeria, South Africa,

Uganda, Zambia and Zimbabwe. His most recent book is *Reformism and Revisionism in Africa's Political Economy in the 1990s.*

Christopher Stevens is a Senior Fellow at the Institute of Development Studies at the University of Sussex. He was previously associated with the Overseas Development Institute in London and has served as consultant to several Commonwealth, EC, IBRD and UN agencies. Dr. Stevens has published over 250 works on ACP/EC/Lomé including six edited annual survey volumes on the *EEC and the Third World* in the 1980s.

Richard Stubbs is Associate Professor of Political Science at McMaster University in Hamilton, Ontario. He is author of *Hearts and Minds in Guerrilla Warfare: the Malayan emergency 1948–1960* and coeditor of *Political Economy and the Changing Global Order.*

Larry A. Swatuk is SSHRCC Post-Doctoral Fellow at the Centre for International and Strategic Studies at York University. He is author of *Between Choice in a Hard Place: contending theories of international relations* and coeditor of *Prospects for Peace and Development in Southern Africa in the 1990s.* Dr Swatuk holds a PhD from Dalhousie University and has undertaken research throughout Southern Africa.

List of Acronyms

ACP	African, Caribbean and Pacific (states associated with EC)
APEC	Asia Pacific Economic Community
ASEAN	Association of Southeast Asian Nations
BBC	British Broadcasting Service
BHN	basic human needs
CACM	Central American Common Market
CAP	Common Agricultural Policy (EC)
CARICOM	Caribbean Community
CBI	Caribbean Basin Initiative (US)
CCP	Common Commercial Policy (EC)
CDPSP	Current Digest of the Post-Soviet Press
CENTO	Central Treaty Organization
CIS	Commonwealth of Independent States
CSBMs	confidence- and security-building measures
CSCE	Conference on Security and Cooperation in Europe
DCs	developed countries
EAEG	East Asia Economic Grouping
EAI	Enterprise for the Americas Initiative
EC	European Community
ECA	Economic Commission for Africa
ECO	Economic Cooperation Organization
ECOWAS	Economic Community of West African States
FACS	Fundación Agosto C. Sandino (Nicaragua)
FDI	Foreign direct investment
FLS	Front Line States (Southern Africa)
FRELIMO	Liberation of Mozambique
FSRs	former Soviet republics
FSU	former Soviet Union
G-5	Group of Five
G-7	Group of Seven (Canada, France, Germany, Italy, Japan, UK, US)
GATT	General Agreement on Trade and Tariffs
GCC	Gulf Cooperation Council
GDP	gross domestic product
GNP	gross national product
IBRD	International Bank for Reconstruction and Development (World Bank)

IDA	International Development Association
IDB	Inter-American Development Bank
IFAA	Institute for African Alternatives
IFI	international financial institutions
IGO	intergovernmental organization
ILO	International Labour Organization
IMF	International Monetary Fund
INGO	international non-governmental organization
IUCN	International Union for the Conservation of Nature
LAFTA	Latin America Free Trade Association (now LAIA)
LAIA	Latin American Integration Association
LDCs	less developed countries
LIC	low-intensity conflict
LLDCs	least developed countries
MCP	Malayan Communist Party
MTCR	Missile Technology Control Regime
NAFTA	North American Free Trade Agreement
NATO	North Atlantic Treaty Organization
NEEMs	newly emerging exporters of manufactures
NGO	non-governmental organization
NICs	newly industrializing countries
NIDL/P	new international divisions of labour/power
NIEO	new international economic order
NPT	non-proliferation treaty
NTB	non-tariff barrier to trade
OAS	Organization of American States
OAU	Organization for African Unity
ODA	official development assistance
OECD	Organisation for Economic Cooperation and Development
OECS	Organization of Eastern Caribbean States
PVO	private voluntary organization
R&D	research and development
RCD	Regional Cooperation for Development Organization (Central Asia)
RSS	Regional Security System
SAARC	South Asian Association for Regional Cooperation
SADC	Southern African Development Community
SAP	structural adjustment programme
SEATO	Southeast Asia Treaty Organization
SEM	Single European Market
TNC	transnational corporation

UDEAC	Central African Customs and Economic Union
UN	United Nations
UNCLOS	United Nations Conference on the Law of the Sea
UNCTAD	United Nations Conference on Trade and Development
UNDP	United Nations Development Programme
USAID	United States Agency for International Development
VER	voluntary export restraint

Part I

Introduction

1 The South at the End of the Twentieth Century: An Overview

Larry A. Swatuk and Timothy M. Shaw

INTRODUCTION

This collection is concerned with revisiting and redefining the political economy – both empirical and theoretical – of foreign policy in the South as we approach the twenty-first century: the position of post-colonial states in the post-Bretton Woods and post-Cold War world. Neither this volume nor the interaction upon which it is based could have proceeded over the last five years without timely financial support from several funding agencies and genuine intellectual commitment and integrity from many colleagues. Generous financial assistance has been provided since the late 1980s by the Canadian Institute for International Peace and Security, the John D. and Catherine T. MacArthur Foundation, and the Social Science and Humanities Research Council of Canada for research and workshop support on 'Surviving at the Margins', 'The Political Economy of Security and Democracy in the Third World', and 'The Political Economy of Foreign Policy in the Third World in the 1990s', respectively. Amongst the products of this continuing international and interdisciplinary collaboration are Swatuk and Shaw (eds) *Prospects for Peace and Development in Southern Africa in the 1990s* (1991), Shaw and Korany (eds), 'Special Issue: The South in the New World (Dis)Order', and Shaw and Okolo (eds), *The Political Economy of Foreign Policy in ECOWAS* (1994). Together these interrelated projects on comparative regions in the South have also generated conference panels and papers at ASA, BISA, CAAS, CASID and ISA and a series of individual and joint articles. We are particularly appreciative of continuing collaboration with Henry Veltmeyer (Saint Mary's University, Halifax) and David Wurfel (previously at the University of Windsor and now International Christian University, Tokyo) and with several Dalhousie PhDs – Celestine Bassey, Cyril Kofie Daddieh

3

and Maria Nzomo – and of colleagues in the Centre for Foreign Policy
Studies and Department of Political Science, especially the indefatigable
Marilyn Langille and Susan Rolston. We anticipate further interregional
and intercontinental cooperative ventures into the next century based on
this established foundation of conceptual and professional interaction.

READING GLOBAL CHANGE: NEW INTERNATIONAL DIVISIONS OF LABOUR AND POWER

As we approach the end of the millennium, the context for understanding
Third World change has itself been dramatically altered. No longer does the
global political economy hinge on twin axes: North–South and East–West.
And while the former has been under transformation for at least two decades
(see Chapter 4 below), it has been change to the latter, that is, the end of the
Cold War, which has facilitated the mushrooming of issues and emergencies
long-stifled by the needs and discourse of superpower competition. Clearly,
the end of the Cold War and the globalization of production necessitate both
a rereading of international relations at the end of the twentieth century, as
well as a reinterpretation of what this all means for peoples of the South. As
James Mittelman points out in Chapter 2, one approach has been to focus on
the end of the Cold War as the pivotal issue for future global relations. In this
way one might perceive there to be an opportunity to create a 'new world
order', with the United States, as the sole remaining superpower, providing
leadership within any emergent postbipolar condominium. Indeed, as Robert
Boardman points out in Chapter 3, this has been the case in much of present
social science discourse, particularly that to be found in the areas of strategic
studies and US foreign policy. Hence models of bipolarity based on
Morgenthauean equations of power have given way to neorealist and neo-
institutionalist depictions of tri- or multipolarity based equally on multiple
issue areas and forms of power.

  For Boardman, this yearning for stability characterized by notions of a
new world order, emergent multilateralism and collective security is the
product of a Cold War mindset that marginalizes issues other than war.
That is, it continues to privilege the traditional security problematique,
which, by definition, marginalizes the smaller and weaker states of the
South. To be sure, the reconstruction of Eastern Europe and the Soviet
Union should be a central priority for state-makers and citizens of the West.
But, as both Mittelman and Boardman warn, to focus on the 'high political'
is to obscure a good deal of what went into ending the Cold War and
eroding the Soviet empire in the first place.

For Mittelman, what drives the world system at the end of the twentieth century is primarily economic in nature. This is captured by the term 'globalization'. However, while globalization involves the spatial reorganization of production, trade and international financial markets, it also involves elements of culture, politics and ideology. In a Gramscian sense, then, it involves the extension of Western hegemony on a global scale.

DEMOCRATIZATION AND DOMINATION

For Mittelman, what we are witnessing is an explosion of pluralism, the potential 'Lebanonization' of political life. Emergent popular pressures upon formerly repressive states have given rise to a global cry for democracy. But, as Mittelman points out and as is suggested in Gramscian analysis, this 'democracy project' has contradictory tendencies. On the one hand, multiparty democracy has historically served as a necessary agent of global capitalist development. Thus, in this case, democracy may be perceived as an ideology of domination that helps to suppress more egalitarian approaches to democratic development.

On the other hand, these more popularly conceived notions of democracy may still form the basis for an ideology of resistance and personal or communal liberation. Both of these tendencies are evident in the global political economy as state-makers throughout much of the West seek to impose political conditionalities based on limited notions of 'democracy' on much of the South. At the same time countless critical social movements have emerged in the interstices of the conventional liberal approach to state–civil society relations in multiparty democracies. This is an issue to which we will return in more detail below.

GLOBALIZATION AND DIFFERENTIATION: SOUTHS

As the country and regional case studies in this collection clearly illustrate, the coming of this new international division of labour (NIDL) has facilitated rapid economic growth in some parts of both North and South, stagnation elsewhere, and decline throughout much of the world, most acutely in Sub-Saharan Africa. In Chapter 4 Devlin describes this as a fundamental crisis of capitalism that marks a post-Fordist transition from state-based, mass production toward globalized, flexible production. So the comfortable if always over-simplified depiction of 'high-consumption' countries in the North (for example, the OECD) and 'low-consumption' countries in the South (for example, the Group of 77) no longer strictly obtains. In particular this NIDL has fragmented and differentiated the world in such a way that there are indeed many Souths. The economic dynamism of the Asian NICs juxtaposed with the downward spiral of most African economies is just one expression of this differentiation.

GLOBAL COMPETITION AND STRUCTURAL ADJUSTMENT

While some states and regions prospered via the direct and aggressive use of state policy during the last two decades of global economic restructuring, it is highly unlikely that others will follow similar paths to economic growth in the 1990s. This is so for two, closely interrelated reasons. The end of the Cold War has given rise to a general trend toward (i) less state intervention in highly indebted economies and (ii) more representative government in formerly authoritarian polities – that is, the extension of the presently dominant, Western neoconservative approach to debt and deficit reduction and (hoped for) economic growth. For most countries of the South, then, the twin conditionalities of economic and political structural adjustment make it highly unlikely that the NIC model of development (that is, strong state participation in the economy and centralized authority in the polity) is soon to be repeated. More seriously, perhaps, are the consequences of this SAP-based model for many people and states of the South.

AFRICA'S MARGINALIZATION

As discussed in Chapter 2 but most forcefully demonstrated in Chapter 5, the coming of a NIDL quite consciously marginalizes those parts of the globe that lack markets, capital, human and natural resources, knowledge and communication skills. In Stevens' case study of developing EC–ACP relations, this involves most particularly the marginalization of Africa to the south of the Sahara, as well as a general deterioration of EC–ACP links. According to him, the principal agent of these changing links comes not from a deliberate policy-level decision, but rather from generally emerging economic and political pressures: the globalization of production; the regionalization of EC politics; and the politicization of aid, trade and investment.

Many of the non-African member-states of the ACP, however, may be able to take advantage of their geographical proximity to one or the other of the three global growth poles: if not the EC, then perhaps North America or the Pacific. Indeed, as discussed by McBain, in Chapter 12, some Asian and Latin American states have been able to draw on the capital investment and technological expertise of Japan and the US so that their export profiles now resemble those of the former metropole. And, as suggested by Stubbs (Chapter 11), this process may be repeatable on a very limited regional basis, as Thailand itself now invests in Indonesia.

Sub-Saharan Africa, to the contrary, has no such links to draw on. For Stevens (Chapter 5), that North Africa may be able to blackmail the EC into preferential trade and aid packages by the threat of increased migrant labour flows is a sorry story about Africa's marginal place in the NIDL. And, with the unravelling of the Soviet empire, Africa seems nearly to have disappeared as events in Eastern Europe and the FSU in many ways loom even larger now than they did during the Cold War. Where Africa does remain on the EC agenda, according to Stevens it increasingly resembles a patron–client relationship as opposed to a partnership among equals. More-over it is everywhere informed by the EC's acceptance of the terms and conditionalities of SAP. So, with the neoconservative agenda ascendant not merely in the EC but throughout the West, much of Africa's role in the NIDL/P will be limited to its nuisance value: defined by debt rescheduling, political instability and famine relief.

COMPETITIVE DEFLATION AND THE NEW REGIONALISMS

According to Mittelman, the state no longer acts as an engine of growth. Rather state-makers, in competition with each other for scarce capital investment, seek to make their territorially based geographical and human resources more attractive to MNCs and IFIs than their competitors. The state, in Mittelman's terms, becomes less a 'determiner of' than a 'facilitator for' capitalist development. As a consequence the globalization of production has eroded state power in such a way that supra- and sub-nationalisms are proliferating in peoples' search for survival and meaning. Given the end of the Cold War, state-makers no longer have the option of containing these social pressures by appealing to the interests of one or the other global superpower. Formal state responses to the demands of local and global civil societies, irredentist pressures and changing international divisions of labour and power have come in three forms: (i) state-based responses grounded in either formal or de facto SAPs; (ii) the formation of regional security regimes based on elite's shared survivalist tendencies; and (iii) the formation of regional economic groupings that seek to take advantage of regional economies of scale.

As discussed by Acharya in Chapter 6 to date regional approaches to security and economic growth have met with limited success in the South, particularly at the macro level (for example, Arab League, OAS, OAU). However, both regional and subregional groups are proliferating, at least at a declaratory level today. For Acharya, this is so for a number of reasons. First, regionalism is being redefined: from macro groups such as those cited above to more micro units such as ASEAN, GCC, Contadora Group, the Frontline States and so on. Second, security is also being redefined to incorporate novel factors such as the environment, informal as well as formal economies, migration, food, drugs and disease. Many of these factors are most intense at the subregional level. Third, the post-Cold War world provides the opportunity for self (re)definitions of 'region' and 'regional cooperation', even if it involves, at a minimum, emerging security communities designed to keep elites safe from dissatisfied citizenries.

Nevertheless the South is rife with new regionalisms as state-makers seek to avoid or make the best of the marginalization that faces most of their peoples in the NIDL/P. In each of our country and regional case studies this notion emerges time and again. African state-makers, for example, see solutions to their de facto self-reliance within the context of an African Economic Community (AEC). The AEC seeks to foster continental cooperation through the creation of a number of subregional organizations: for example SADC, ECOWAS, and an expanded Preferential Trade Area for Eastern and Southern Africa (see Chapters 8 and 15 below).

For many policy-makers in Central Asia, the Commonwealth of Independent States appears less viable than does an Economic Cooperation Organization based on the memberships of Afghanistan, Iran, Pakistan, and Turkey, as well as the six Turkic states of the FSU (see Chapter 10). In the Pacific Rim, APEC has been advanced by Australia, among others, as a viable example of 'open regionalism' based on the successful manufacturing-for-export policies of Japan and the NICs (see Chapters 6, 11 and 12). In Latin America the Free Trade Association has become an Integration Association (see Chapter 12). And in the Caribbean, though formal intraregional trade among the member-states of CARICOM remains at roughly 10 per cent of their total trade, this regional organization continues to seek ways to retain – indeed increase – its viability in the face of an impending NAFTA (see Chapters 12 and 13).

How successful these regional projects can be seems also to be limited by the terms of ubiquitous structural adjustment conditionalities. Devlin, in Chapter 4, seriously questions the capacity of regionalism to solve the abiding problems of what he terms the 'low-consumption countries': debt, structural adjustment, stagnation, and ethnic tensions. Indeed, he points out that 'high-consumption countries' have attempted to solve their own ubiquitous problems – weak growth, increasing unemployment, debt, environmental decay, trade imbalances, problems over GATT – via the regionalization of trade. However within the equally ubiquitous context of structural adjustment, far from acting as a solution, regionalization has instead resulted in an ongoing round of competitive deflation among states. For Devlin, the peace dividend so anticipated in the post-Cold War era is nowhere to be found; instead 'competitive disorder remains the order of the day'. Somewhat cynically, Devlin states that most of the South has never enjoyed the luxury of growth cycles, be they long or short. Rather structural adjustment, in the context of much of the South means being locked into an 'international division of economic activity established during the imperialist era'. The potential for state-centred, export-based trade to act as a panacea for what amounts to systemic crisis is therefore grossly misleading. The neoconservative agenda, to the contrary, has in fact exacerbated the crisis, adding political instability to marginal or declining rates of economic growth.

McBain and Segal, in their case studies on Caribbean and Latin American economic prospects in the 1990s (Chapters 12 and 13), provide evidence corroborating Devlin's wider claims. For the former, SAPs have failed to transform the majority of Caribbean and Latin American economies into manufacturers for export. Instead they remain largely natural-resource exporters on the periphery of the NIDL. And while the Asian and Latin American NICs have dramatically increased their shares of developing-country manufactures for export, the Caribbean and parts of Latin America have failed to alter their export structures at all. For most of the Caribbean and Latin America, then, the regionalization of trade and investment has confirmed their marginality in the global economy. And even though Caribbean preferential trade access to US and European markets acts as a disincentive for change, Segal points out that the 'hard-won consensus' remains a combination of membership in both Lomé and CBI and still-to-be-proven regional integration.

In comparison with Sub-Saharan Africa or many of the new states of Asia, however, prospects for most of the Caribbean and Latin America appear quite good. For, as Gharabaghi illustrates in his chapter on prospects for Central Asian regional integration (Chapter 10) most of these former members of the Soviet Union face futures marred with economic decline, ethnic strife and ecological disaster. Nevertheless state-makers in this troubled area remain verbally committed to policies based on regional integration and economic structural adjustment.

For Devlin (Chapter 4), neither South nor North is predestined to live out such bleak futures. To the contrary, a more positive scenario may greet all members of the global political economy if a significant change occurs in present policy directions: free trade should be replaced with managed trade; deflation with reflation; patron–client relations must be replaced by partnership in North–South affairs, including debt forgiveness and the removal of structural adjustment conditionalities. Not only should such steps be taken on the basis of a 'moral imperative', states Devlin. In many ways it is in the North's self-interest that such a programme be undertaken: inward industrialization and increased markets in the South will also mean increased growth in the North.

However well-intentioned or well-reasoned is Devlin's argument, the reality so aptly demonstrated throughout our case studies reveals that states continue to move in lock-step farther down the road of competitive deflation and structural adjustment.

HUMAN RESPONSES TO STATE-CENTRED 'SOLUTIONS': NGOs AND GLOBAL CIVIL SOCIETY

The outcome for much of the South, then, is a disturbing one indeed. For if welfare states in the North are reeling under the tenets of neoconservative economic policies, then surely most people in the South, faced with no state-sponsored safety nets, confront an even more uncertain future. The well-documented legacy of structural adjustment in the South is one of failure. Each of our regional and country cases provide further testimony in this regard. Why is it, Ihonvbere (Chapter 8) asks rhetorically, that SAPs were so pervasively accepted on the African continent? In Chapter 12 McBain asks similar questions in the Caribbean and Latin American contexts. The answer, says Ihonvbere, is twofold: (i) African leaders, overseeing deeply indebted states, in need of new loans and fearing for their own political lives, had no other choice but to accept; and (ii) they hoped that SAPs would work. A third reason for SAPs' widespread acceptance is proffered by Adebayo Adedeji, former Executive Director of the UN Economic Commission for Africa: the people could not object to them (see Chapter 8). For the ECA, structural adjustment programmes are fundamentally authoritarian. Not only are they 'anti-people' in their prescriptions – as they most seriously harm the 'poorest of the poor' – but only authoritarian regimes could force such harsh medicine with such questionable effects on Africa's people.

In the Latin American case, Macdonald (Chapter 14) points out that the combined effects of the 'US hegemonic project' – that is, Cold War strat-

egy coupled with free-market ideology – was no less than a total transformation of civil society. As grassroots movements mushroomed to deal
with myriad problems brought on by civil war and structural adjustment,
international NGOs responded in 'highly personal and moralistic' ways to
the crisis in Latin America. These INGOs often forged links with the thousands of critical social movements emergent in Latin America. Yet, warns
Macdonald, 'global civil society has no natural innocence; it has no single
or eternally fixed form'.

Nyang'oro, in his chapter on NGOs and the state in Africa (Chapter
9), also discusses the implications of the increased role for civil society,
particularly indigenous NGOs and their evolving role in Africa's move
toward 'democratic development'. For Nyang'oro, a fundamental puz-
zle remains how to create and maintain space for the flourishing of
grassroots NGOs, which, by their very presence, often threaten the
state. According to Nyang'oro, 'smart NGOs' link themselves to the
state; cultivate non-adversarial relationships and only then begin to
articulate their programmes, including the needs of the poor. The basic
problem, then, for NGOs in the African case seems to be twofold:
(i) how to avoid cooptation by the state; and (ii) how to avoid the
creation of a hierarchy of privilege among NGOs. Furthermore, for
Nyang'oro, the state will remain a central if somewhat diminished
player in African development. The point, then, is not to avoid or
undermine the state (that is, exit or revolution), but rather to lobby for
inclusion (that is, voice) so that they might find themselves on the
inside of the policy-making process when resources are allocated.

For Macdonald, this might appear as somewhat naive in its 'liberal-
pluralist' formulation. She points out that not only is civil society *not*
intrinsically meritorious, but also, when viewed through a more critical
theoretical lens, civil society appears not separate from but integral to state
domination. In other words it is a 'terrain of exploitation, discrimination,
and oppression', most threatening when the dominant class is capable of
and successful in presenting its narrow political project in universalist
terms. For critical theorists, then, both civil society and NGOs become part
of the problem when articulated in neoconservative or liberal-pluralist
terms. Indeed, Macdonald argues in the Latin American case, while civil
society may at some point become the site of truly transformative, radical
democratic politics, at present it remains the site of highly contested
intellectual and personal terrain. In other words, 'global' civil society
presents two problems for critical social movements.

First, at the level of *praxis,* there are as many status quo-oriented as there
are transformative NGOs. Macdonald's Latin American study, where

(I)NGOs supported both the Sandinistas and the Contras in Nicaragua, is a case in point. Second, at the level of *analysis,* it is clear that the hegemony of Western value systems is ascendant in the NGO world as well. As a result civil society tends to be portrayed and approached in a way that seeks to complement the articulated goals of SAPs. That is to say, in its neoconservative or liberal-pluralist construction, 'civil society' is perceived to be both autonomous from and superior to the 'state'. So, as structural adjustment cuts back the perceived negative influence of states in Third World development, civil society is – at least theoretically – both freed from parochial state interests and supported by INGOs, IFIs and so on so that it might undo the harm done by state-centred economic development. This point is forcefully made by Denham in Chapter 7, where it can be seen that, in spite of criticism – over, for example, SAPs' negative effects on children and the poor – from an IBRD-sponsored committee, the World Bank continues to court and coopt NGOs active in 'adjustment-related projects'. Moreover the Bank fails to see the irony in its support for popular participation and democratic development, particularly in the African case. Whereas many Africans, among them the ECA and OAU, complain that SAP could only have been accepted in authoritarian circumstances, the Bank agrees in part that popular participation should be a precondition for economic development. (Indeed this is the central theme of Chapter 8.) Yet it is development that is to be undertaken in the context of adherence to SAP conditionalities!

Clearly, from a liberal-pluralist or neoconservative perspective, both NGOs and civil society are to play status-quo-seeking roles in Third World development. In the context of the dismantling of Third World states, Denham's discussion unfortunately suggests that far from Devlin's scenario, the rapid growth of NGOs and the emerging literature that rejects the state in favour of civil society signals what appears to us a move not toward partnership, empowerment, managed trade and democratic development in the South but toward the soup-kitchenization of the Third World; that is, a new world (dis)order that harks back to the early days of the industrial revolution and not toward a shared and prosperous post-industrial future.

Part II

Changing Structures: New International Divisions of Labour and Power

2 The End of a Millennium: Changing Structures of World Order and the Post-Cold War Division of Labour[1]

James H. Mittelman

INTRODUCTION

A valuable geopolitical pedagogy, George Bush's 1991 State of the Union Message triggered a public discourse over world order. Urging cooperative action to end aggression, he called upon the global community to 'fulfill the long-held promise of a *new world order* – where brutality will go unrewarded and aggression will meet collective resistance' (quoted in Safire, 1991). Bush envisaged an era of peace and stability in which the United States, in conjunction with the United Nations, will see that order is maintained. The Gulf War was what he called a 'defining moment', a harbinger of the new order; the Gulf crisis provided the context for the redefinition of global alignments.

True, Saddam Hussein's challenge to Western hegemony and the dénouement offered a preview of the future order, but also raised the deeper question, what drives the world system at the end of a millennium? After assessing changing configurations of global power and production, I will argue that the end of the twentieth century is indeed a period of structural transformation marked, above all, by a dialectic of subnationalism and supranationalism, simultaneous but contradictory processes of globalization arising out of economics, circumscribing the scope for state action and precipitating new forms of social struggle, which in turn are globalized. In the close of this chapter attention will return to the political and social ideals that can animate the world to come.

WORLD ORDER

To many observers the White House's image of world order is a lookalike of the old order. William Safire (1991) and other commentators noted that the phrase 'new world order' had been invoked by various US politicians, including Bush's secretary of state, James A. Baker 3rd, as well as by Mikhail Gorbachev. A former US president, Jimmy Carter, had summoned the same imagery:

> I want to assure you that the relations of the United States with the other countries and peoples of the world will be guided during my own Administration by our desire to shape a world order that is more responsive to human aspirations. The United States will meet its obligations to help create a stable, just, and peaceful world order ('Address by President Carter to People of Other Nations', 1977).

In 1974 the General Assembly called for the redistribution of wealth – a new international economic order. Three decades before, Hitler and his fascist cohorts in Portugal, the Salazar–Caetano regime, omitted the word 'world' and promulgated the idea of a new order – *de neuve ordnung* and *estado novo*, respectively.

Semantics aside, critics asked, if the United States could rescue Kuwait, why not its own poverty-stricken cities? 'The President seeks a new world order', said George Mitchell, the Senate majority leader.'We ask him to join us in putting our own house in order' ('The "New Order" Is a Tall Order', 1991). Critics also underscored the selectivity of US foreign policy – intervention to stop aggression by Iraq but not by other regional powers, such as South Africa. Observers noted a double standard: Why save a non-democratic regime in Kuwait while ignoring democratic impulses elsewhere?

Supporters of US policy in the Gulf crisis presented the action as a revival of the collective security provisions of the UN Charter. Brian Urquhart (Urquhart and McNamara, 1991, p. 13), for example, viewed the Gulf experience as 'the first comprehensive use' of Chapter VII, which is titled 'Action to Deal with Threats to the Peace, Breaches of the Peace, and Acts of Aggression'. Heralding the Security Council's application of the principles of Chapter VII in the Gulf as 'the first time in history' that 'the community of nations ... has physically expelled an aggressor from a victimized state', Urquhart (ibid., p. 9) held: 'we are celebrating the success of the United Nations as the body primarily responsible for maintaining peace in the world – although many still have doubts about this claim'.

Indeed the doubters have good reason to cast doubt on this interpretation. The authorization to deploy armed forces was not undertaken as prescribed by UN Charter Articles 43–7, which call for troops to be placed under the auspices of the Security Council and directed by its Military Staff Committee. Not only did the Security Council reject a Soviet proposal to activate this committee to unify strategic operations in the Gulf, as in the Korean War, but also Washington offered sizable financial incentives to the Soviet Union, China, Latin America and Africa; promised to turn a blind eye to certain human-rights abuses in these areas; and threatened retribution (in Yemen) in order to win multilateral support and secure the United Nations as an instrument of US foreign policy. That the United States achieved its objectives is patent: UN authorization to employ force required no bona fide means of accountability to the Security Council, and limits were not placed on the use of 'all necessary means'. Essentially abandoning multilateralism, save rhetorical flourishes, the United Nations legitimized a unilateralist, interventionist policy to which the world body was an accessory (Weston, 1991).

Leaving aside for the moment the long-term prospects for the resolution of global conflict, the debate continues over why the United States, which had armed Iraq and which had sent signals that it would not oppose the invasion of Kuwait, intervened in the Gulf. When the Iraqi attack caused oil markets to panic, did Washington decide that the dependence of the US economy on foreign oil – 50 per cent of the nation's consumption – required military action? Or as some Israeli observers believe, perhaps Washington found a convenient occasion to try to abort Iraq's nuclear-weapons programme. Or were US leaders seeking to divert attention from domestic problems and to overcome the 'Vietnam syndrome'? Did US leaders act to prove the nation's mettle in a post-hegemonic world?

Whatever the cause or causes of the Gulf conflict, it is clear that the public discourse touches the surface of the vast transformations in our lives wrought by the changing structures of world order. Manifestations of these transformations may be easily identified, but the underlying dynamics of globalization are more difficult to comprehend.

GLOBALIZATION

The manifestations of globalization include the worldwide interpenetration of industries, the spread of financial markets, the diffusion of identical consumer goods to distant countries, undocumented workers feeding a resurgence of sweatshops in the United States, Korean merchants coming into conflict with African-Americans in formerly tight-knit neighborhoods, and an emerging global preference for democracy. The term globalization is vague, and not much would be gained by trying to define it precisely. Globalization is nonetheless crucial to an understanding of world order, for it directs attention to remarkable changes underway at the end of the twentieth century.

A rubric for varied phenomena, globalization is an economically driven process. The chain of causality runs from the spatial reorganization of production to international trade and to the worldwide integration of financial markets (Griffin and Khan, 1992). Not only is economics globalized, but also politics and culture are integral to this process. The concept of globalization interrelates multiple levels of analysis – economics, politics, culture and ideology.

Beginning in the 1960s, Asia's 'four dragons' achieved spectacular economic growth by exporting not raw materials but manufactured goods. As an empirical study by Giovanni Arrighi and Jessica Drangel (1986; also see Gereffi and Wyman, 1990, pp. 8–9) shows, in the period from 1965 to 1980 the 'core' deindustrialized in terms of (i) the average percentage of the labor force employed by industry and (ii) the average portion of manufacturing in gross domestic product (GDP). By the late 1970s the 'semi-periphery' – an intermediate tier of countries – actually surpassed the 'core' in share of GDP generated by industry. Manufactures relative to export volume in East Asia jumped 13.2 per cent per year from 1980 to 1985, 19.3 per cent in 1986, an estimated 23.8 per cent in 1987, and a projected 11.2 per cent in 1988 (World Bank, 1989, pp. 148–50).

With industrial upgrading, the newly industrializing countries (NICs) transformed their structures of production from an emphasis on labor-intensive to capital- and technology-intensive goods centring on high-value-added products (see Chapters 11 and 12 below). No longer was there a dichotomy between a small number of industrial countries and a Third World providing primary products. An emerging world market for labor and production entailed massive industrial relocation, the subdivision of manufacturing processes into multiple partial operations, major technological innovations, widespread migration and the feminization of labor. From Asia's export-processing zones to Mexico's *maquiladora* programme (assembly plants as subsidiaries or subcontracting firms for the manufacture of export-oriented goods), a barometer of the changing character of the labor force is the increasing number of women employed in manufacturing. Jobs take on characteristics associated with female employment: a minimum level of skills, low wages and limited possibilities for promotion.

To explain this restructuring, scholars have devised the construct of 'the new international division of labor'. The title of a seminal study by Folker Fröbel, Jürgen Heinrichs and Otto Kreye (1980), this construct identifies the 'overriding pressure of competition' as the mainspring of a distinct set of conditions for global capital accumulation. Fröbelians hold that observable changes in the international division of labour – the transfer of plants to the Third World, the fragmentation of production processes and so on – are the result of 'the conditions for the valorisation and accumulation of capital' (Fröbel *et al.*, 1980, p. 46).

> This new international division of labour is an institutional innovation of capital itself, necessitated by changed conditions, and not the result of changed development strategies by individual countries or options freely decided upon by so-called multinational companies (ibid.).

For these authors, national strategies and the policies of multinational corporations are consequences, not causes, of new conditions, especially the need for additional industrial sites around the world.

Following Fröbel, Heinrichs and Kreye, other authors have emphasized the expansion of capital and hence production as the driving force behind an international division of labour that is new primarily in that it reverses the classical division of labour. Citing heightened competition among the developed countries in the late twentieth century, Steven Sanderson (1985, p. 9) notes that the new international division of labour restructures the relationship between former hewers of wood and drawers of water – Third World producers – and industrialized countries. To detail the new international division of labour, Frank Bonilla and Ricardo Campos (1985) locate the displacement of workers through migration in the global reorganization of production. They argue that divisions within the working class – along the lines of gender, race and ethnicity – are explicable in terms of 'the segmentation of capital itself in the cycle of its reproduction' (Bonilla and Campos, 1985, p. 202).

These are but a few of the many authors who embrace the idea of the new international division of labour, a mode of explanation that advances the scholarly literature by providing a novel way to examine the relationships between developed and developing countries. This mode of inquiry emphasizes increasing differentiation within the Third World and focuses on the spatial reorganization of production. However some of the key tenets of the concept of the new international division of labour are misleading.

As with the notion 'new world order', it is appropriate to ask, what is new about the new international division of labour? The claim that industrialization in the Third World is new overlooks the establishment of import-substituting industries in Argentina, Brazil and Mexico in the 1930s and 1940s. In fact industrial growth in some parts of Latin America stems from the interwar period (Gereffi and Wyman, 1990, p. 3). Additionally, the new international division of labour has not replaced the old international division of labour. Properly understood, they coexist. In countries such as Mexico, jobs in export industries account for less than 10 per cent of total employment. In many parts of the Third World the share of primary goods in exports is more than half of all exports. The variance in job allocation among and within regions is sufficiently large to call into question the concept of the new international division of labour. What is more, to stress that cheap labour drives the movement of capital around the globe runs the risk of a mechanical and economistic explanation. It depoliticizes production.

The state – and more properly the interstate system – may not be treated as historically incidental to labour flows, which capital shapes. In recent decades several countries adopted acts of economic nationalism: the nationalization of industries, indigenization decrees, requirements for local incorporation and so on. Today, however, the state no longer primarily serves as a buffer or shield against globalization. Rather the state seeks material gains from globalization (Cox, 1987, pp. 253–65).

It is evident that 'delinking' is not a viable strategy in an age of globalization. The scope for state autonomy – a concept that drew considerable attention from scholars in the 1970s and 1980s – is reduced in the context of economic globalization. Additionally, the drive to bring the state back in to the forefront of social theory requires fresh analysis in light of globalization (Evans *et al.*, 1985). From another perspective the state increasingly plays an integral role in facilitating globalization. In other words, the state is a mechanism and agent in the globalization process (Cox, 1987, pp. 253–65). Surrounded by impersonal forces beyond their control, leaders no longer lead (Hughes, 1990). Statecraft, tested as it is by non-state actors, is diminished in importance.

The state is at risk because of the challenges to sovereignty at the end of the Cold War. With the disintegration of socialist regimes came the eruption of subsurface tensions formerly stifled by the state. Now state borders are subject to revision (Halliday, 1990). East Germany has disappeared, former Soviet republics have achieved independence and Yugoslavia is riven by similar tensions. Separatist movements in Northern Ireland, the Basque region and Corsica are challenging the status quo. While North Korea could be absorbed by South Korea, Balkanization is always a danger in Africa, where colonizers arbitrarily drew borders without regard to ethnic distribution and natural frontiers such as rivers and mountains. Hence Ethiopia as a unified country is a dubious proposition.

This explosion of pluralism involves a renewal of historical forces – a maze of religious loyalties, ethnic identities, linguistic differences and other forms of cultural expression. As noted, the state, especially in the Soviet Union and Eastern Europe, had restrained these tensions. While globalization limits state power, there is a reassertion of historical forces. Just as globalization gives impetus to cultural homogenization (for example the diffusion of standard consumer goods throughout the world), so too does a global thrust undermine state power and unleash subterranean cultural pluralism.

This contradictory process merges with a dialectic of subnationalism and supranationalism. The polity is disrupted by substate actors and simultaneously seeks advantage in global competition through regionalization. Despite the past failings of regional groupings, regional cooperation is widely regarded as a way to achieve mobility in the changing international division of labour. Thus the state is being reformed from below by the tugs of subnationalism and from above by the pull of economic globalization (see, for example, Chapter 6 below).

To accommodate the new pluralism, the state must allow for demands for political reforms. With the revolution in Eastern Europe, the release of Nelson Mandela and the assertiveness of the human rights movement, the drive toward democratization has won legitimacy. Equally important, pro-democracy forces have gained confidence. But what type of democracy is appropriate for the late twentieth century? The answer is of course historically contingent. While democracy is a universal concept, there are different versions of democratic theory.

From a liberal perspective, democracy centres on the principle of accountability: in some manner the right to rule should be based on the consent of the governed. Liberal democracy calls for public influence on government through such institutions as political parties, regular elections and an alternation in power. However critics point out, that in practice, liberal democracies exclude some groups from both meaningful participation in politics and the distribution of economic benefits. In the Third World, it is often recognized that democracy is necessary for development, if democracy is understood to imply increasing social equality – an ingredient missing from ethnocentric and Western conceptions of democratization. Hence critics distinguish between democracy as an ideology of domination and as an ideology of resistance and struggle (Alves, 1988, pp. 9–13; Shivji, 1991, p. 82). Democracy as an ideology of domination and of resistance is simultaneously evident in the late twentieth century.

A restricted type of democracy has emerged in Latin America, most notably in Brazil and Argentina, which have experienced authoritarian and democratic phases of development. Authoritarian democracy – other qualifying adjectives ('limited', 'guided' and 'protected') are sometimes attached to the term 'democracy' – is an expression of the state's efforts to expand its links to civil society. In view of a regime's lack of legitimacy and weak economic performance, proponents of authoritarian democracy advocate a more flexible system of political representation and gradual liberalization. Class alliances are broadened, and the state makes concessions to pressure groups. However such attempts to modernize the state leave unchanged the basic structures of power and domination. Programmes for slow democratization typically include measures to restrain calls for social equality so that they can be accommodated by the political system. Armed with the power to enforce order, the state wields the means of coercion to safeguard the nation against 'chaos'. The transparency of this domination and its social ramifications engender mounting resistance: demands for the protection of human rights and pursuit of substantive justice (Alves, 1988, pp. 9–13; Mittelman, 1990, p. 67).

A challenge to democracy as an ideology of domination emerges from the mobilization of social movements seeking to assert popular control. The self-aggrandizing individualism and lack of accountability in the economic sphere characteristic of liberal and authoritarian democracy are rejected in favour of a belief that the individual depends on society for development. The liberal-democratic tolerance for social inequality is regarded as inconsistent with democracy, understood as the provision for maximum opportunity for all people to develop their potential (Macpherson, 1977; Mittelman, 1990, p. 67). In terms of performance, the ultimate test is whether the party will relinquish its preeminent role in political life, disengage from the state and permit real dissent. Popular democracy, while noble in theory, has yet to be proven viable at the national level, surely because of a combination of internal and external pressures. These pressures coagulate into one seemingly supreme challenge: how to both manage the social costs of economic reform and democratize. Put differently, the major problem is how to make economic revitalization compatible with democratization.

In the drive for rapid economic growth, the East Asian NICs have placed severe restraints on democratic rights. These states retain authoritarian controls to try to prevent the eruption of social tensions. Little dissent is tolerated, and the strong state is regarded as a prerequisite for good government and modernization (see, for example, Chapter 11 below).

Citing the examples of Taiwan, Singapore and South Korea, Deng Xiaoping and his cohorts sought to justify their contention that restraining democratic rights is essential for successful economic development. In crushing the prodemocracy movement in 1989, the Dengists held that too much freedom promotes disruption and impedes economic reform. Silent on the matter of political reform, the leaders voiced concern that given the chaos and turmoil experienced by China in this century, disorder is the gravest threat to development. In the absence of effective links between the state and civil society, the regime could only rely on guns and terror. In fact the economic reform programme required more flexible political structures to deal with increasingly autonomous groups in civil society – families detached from cooperatives by decollectivization, private entrepreneurs and industrialists, international traders, and students and intellectuals attracted by novel ideas entering China's open door (Mittelman, 1990, citing MacFarquhar, 1989, p. 8).

Just as autonomous groups are emerging in Chinese society, so too are new social movements bringing pressures to bear in global civil society. The globalization process encompasses not only the economy and the state but also civil society (see Chapter 14 below). Yet the globalization of civil society precipitates resistance from disadvantaged strata in a changing international division of labor.

The losers in global restructuring seek to redefine their role in the emerging order. In the face of the declining power of organized labor and revolutionary groups, the powerless must devise novel strategies of social struggle (cf. Chapters 8, 9, 14 and 15 of this volume). They aim to augment popular participation and assert local control over the seemingly remote forces of globalization. New social movements – women's groups, environmentalists, human rights organizations and so on – are themselves a global phenomenon, a worldwide response to the deleterious effects of economic globalization. With the globalization of social struggle, observers have been quick to celebrate the formation of autonomous movements within civil society. Relatively little attention has been given to the coalescence of these movements. Coordination is a crucial matter precisely because the proliferation of new social movements can splinter civil society, perhaps culminating in the Lebanonization of political life. The push for regional autonomy in areas such as Kurdistan has the potential to open a global Pandora's box. Another reason for caution is that new social movements can have a repressive side – for example the resurgence of anti-Semitism in the Soviet Union and Eastern Europe. Before the disintegration of socialist regimes in 1989, the Soviet Union and its Eastern European allies adopted anti-Zionist and anti-Israeli policies. Although the state did not sanction popular expressions of anti-Semitism, Jews were subject to discrimination in the bureaucracy. With the demise of socialism, however, anti-Semitism is flagrantly exhibited at many levels, with little sign of restraint, the impetus coming from autonomous groups in civil society.

FUTURE DIRECTIONS

Global restructuring entails a new correlation of economic forces, political power and social structure. This mosaic reflects a transformation from mass production to flexible (or niche) production, from a bipolar and state-centred to a multipolar and decentred system of international relations (see Boardman in Chapter 3), and from a pattern of global poverty in which three regions were most adversely affected to the marginalization of a single world region along with enclaves in other areas (see the Africa case studies below).

According to projections by the World Bank, in Asia the number in poverty will fall from 805 million in 1985 to 435 million by the end of this century; and in Latin America and the Caribbean from 75 million to 60 million in the same period. In Sub-Saharan Africa the number of poor will rise by 85 million, to 265 million in the year 2000. Thus Asia's share of the world's poor will decline to 53 per cent from 72 per cent in 1985; Latin America and the Caribbean's will drop to 11.4 per cent from 19.1 per cent; and Sub-Saharan Africa's will double from 16 per cent to 32 per cent (World Bank, 1990, p. 139). In other words there are holes in the global mosaic. Partial globalization leaves out the bulk of the continent of Africa. For the countries of Africa, the foremost challenge is to demarginalize when national options are severely constrained by the forces of globalization.

In projecting a new order, three scenarios are on the horizon. One is an alternative order led by disadvantaged groups. Notwithstanding the tenacity of such leftist organizations as Peru's Shining Path and the Philippines' National Democratic Front and Moro National Liberation Front, globalization has helped deprive revolutionary forces of their strength. Remaining traces of socialism – Vietnam, North Korea and Cuba – are isolated and under intense pressure to join the globalization trend. Plugged into modern communications with their faxlike speed, the masses in postrevolutionary societies want the material benefits of globalization. In Cuba this desire is felt keenly among youth, who are the majority – 70 per cent of the Cuban population was born after the revolution and 50 per cent of the population is 15 years of age or younger. Facing critical shortages of staples and other consumer goods, Fidel's Cuba now encourages tourism and is negotiating joint ventures.

At the end of this millennium liberation movements are a fading phenomenon, a relic of another era. Mozambique's one-party state, the Mozambique Liberation Movement (FRELIMO), which has dominated the country's political life since independence in 1975, opened the way for the creation of three parties in 1991. The Liberal Democratic Party of Mozambique, the Mozambique National Union and the Mozambique Independent Congress will compete with FRELIMO in legislative and presidential elections. Meanwhile South Africa's main liberation movement, the African National Congress, is converting to a legal political party. Having exposed the failings of oppressive states, and having posed questions about a transition to a just world, these revolutionary forces have placed indelible marks on the historical record, which, by definition, is cumulative and cannot be erased. However, at the close of the twentieth century, there is scant evidence that revolutionary movements will constitute the nuclei of a new order, rendering the first scenario the least plausible of the three forecasts.

Next is the emergence of a reestablished or new hegemon. By all indications, former Soviet republics, singly or together, are unlikely candidates for this role. For sources of power, Moscow can draw on its nuclear arsenal, the country's sizable population, a large land mass and a rich resource endowment. Yet the Russians are hobbled by a sagging economy, insufficient foreign exchange to maintain many of their overseas commitments, yesterday's technology (save military hardware and outer-space exploration), acute ethnic tensions and conflicts with neighbouring republics.

Whether the United States is also a declining power is the subject of much debate. Perhaps the United States will share the fate of the Soviet Union: a country with superpower military strength but without an economic base that can match Western Europe's and Japan's. The US share of total world output has slipped from one third in 1950 to less than one quarter today. This drop is partly attributable to the expanding economies of reconstructed Germany and Japan. The United States has been spending between 5 and 6 per cent of gross national product on military programmes compared with Japan's 1 per cent ('The "New Order" Is a Tall Order', 1991).

The United States has turned from the world's major creditor to the largest debtor nation, but surely economic problems cannot be forever deferred. A new world order based on military superpower cannot be sustained by outside financing. For the United States, the problems of growing budget deficits and debts are accompanied by lagging productivity, deteriorating infrastructure, high unemployment and an inferior educational system. To solve these problems the federal government could only offer a paradox, a stillborn plan of escape: states and cities have been asked to provide remedies for afflictions that are national or global in scope and for which localities lack the fiscal capacity. Washington has tried to shuck the macro problems of the nation-state, but they are not amenable to local solutions.

The only other contender for hegemonic status is Japan, a country often regarded as an economic superpower because of its spectacular technological achievements. Tokyo ranks very high in military spending (contrary to the popular impression) and is increasingly active in world affairs, as demonstrated by its support for the US-led initiative in the Gulf, its role in multilateral diplomacy at the United Nations and its growing aid programme. But what distinguishes the United States as a hegemon from Japan as a contender may be discerned in the realm of ideology. Whereas the United States diffused liberal values as universal norms, Japanese culture has not yet generated values for export. Business practices aside, Japanese values have not been embraced worldwide. Inasmuch as these values and, more generally, the intricacies of industrial organization are embedded in a traditional social system, it is difficult to identify aspects of that system that could be detached and universalized (Cox, 1989, p. 843). In the final analysis it is unlikely that a unipolar world order – whether centred on the United States or Japan – will emerge (see Chapters 3 and 15 below).

More likely to evolve is a strengthening of regional groupings based on three axes: the Pacific Rim, Europe with the possible participation of erstwhile socialist countries, and North America joined by Mexico and the Caribbean. The effects of regional integration as a means to enhance globalization are not yet known. But it is clear that many Asian countries and firms look to improve regional cooperation for access to a burgeoning regional market and as a sound base for sharing in globalization. This pattern is exemplified by the Japanese-led 'flying-geese' model of regional integration, spearheaded by private capital and involving countries at very different levels of development (Organisation for Economic Cooperation and Development, 1989, pp. 10, 26; Hirata and Nohara, 1989, pp. 434–62).

The emergence of competing regional blocs could lead to increased global conflict, probably originating with instability in the Third World. Poverty and non-democratic rule are the main sources of this instability. A host of proximate issues could ignite regional and global conflict – among others, ethnic and regional rivalries, a crisis of legitimacy and the proliferation of advanced weaponry. With the winding down of the Cold War, power is dispersed among more actors, and interregional competition is heightened. Paradoxically, globalization engenders the regionalization of conflict.

For large numbers of people in the Third World there is no hint of a new world order. Rather, life is marked by a deep divide between rich and poor. A global phenomenon, this divide is not limited to any single region. Nonetheless the greatest challenge is to reverse the marginalization of Sub-Saharan Africa, the consignment, at the end of this millennium, of 265 million people to poverty, with no hope for escape in sight.

Marginalization is a foolproof formula for world disorder. Conversely demarginalization is a necessary but insufficient condition for world order. In response to the non-accountable forces of globalization, a transition to a new world order must be grounded in the values of social justice and equity. How are these values to be realized? A generic prescription would be hazardous, for one must allow for diverse cases and historical contexts. Nonetheless the essential elements of a strategy of demarginalization are its multilevel, popular and democratic features.

No wonder heads of state endorse governmental solutions of a unilateral character, albeit legitimized by multilateralism, and identify the growth of world order with building state capacity. However it is questionable whether the state can function as an instrument of order and justice. In contrast with the non-accountability of globalization, social justice implies accountability, the cornerstone of democratic rule. It is also questionable whether the state system is capable of performing adequately in relation to the value of equity. Statism poses inordinate risks of authoritarianism, economic imbalance and environmental degradation (Falk, 1983, pp. 40–6). When leaders merely mark time because they cannot lead, when governments are stymied because they cannot govern, and when international organizations are hamstrung because they are intergovernmental forums, a millennial and critical perspective of a new world order can be an important mobilizing force.

Note

1.   Some of the ideas in this paper, first presented at the Dalhousie University Workshop on 'Political Economy and Foreign Policy in the Third World in the 1990s', Halifax, Nova Scotia, 26–8 September 1991, are elaborated upon in my 'Global Restructuring of Production and Migration', in Yoshikazu Sakamoto (ed.), *Global Structural Change* (Tokyo: United Nations University Press, 1993).

3 Triangles, Wrecked Angles and Beyond: The Post-Cold War Division of Power

Robert Boardman

INTRODUCTION

The existence of multiple centres of power is not a phenomenon restricted to the post-Cold War state system. This condition has historically been a more normal feature of post-Westphalia international politics than the bipolar organization of states into contending alliance formations. Because of their reverberations throughout the international system, the Northern events of the late 1980s and early 1990s – the transformation of the political map of Eastern Europe, the collapse of the Soviet Union and its successor states' rejection of socialism, and the termination of the Cold War – nonetheless sharpen the need for continuing assessments of the character of the late-century, and late-millennium, conjuncture.

The labels attached to the 1990s will no doubt change with the temporal standpoint of the observer. The 1920s and 1930s became an 'interwar' period only with the onset of the Second World War. Will the 1990s and early 2000s also be seen in retrospect as an 'inter-' or 'pre-' era of some kind? Or are we situated in a Toynbeean 'time of troubles' (Spence, 1993, p. 90), the complexity and turbulence of which defies conventional image-making or periodization? For the present, at any rate, we appear to be stuck in some form of 'post-' age: post-liberal and post-American (Wallerstein, 1993, pp. 3–4), post-hegemonic, post-socialist, or post-Cold War.

These developments have profound implications for the security of countries in the South. This chapter will adopt a primarily state-centric approach to discuss the shifts of power associated with the end of the Cold War. It looks first at structural changes in the relations among major poles, and then at differing conceptions of order and security that have figured in recent debates on their significance.

POLARITY STRUCTURES: MAGNITUDES AND DIMENSIONS

Among the conceptual attempts of Western analysts to model key features of the post-1945 international system, polarity models provide a convenient starting point. The notion of bipolarity incorporated many core elements of the structures of the international system from the late 1940s to the end of the 1980s. It pointed, for example, to the mixtures of cooperative and conflictual elements present at different phases of the rise and fall of the Cold War, the resultant structuring of international relations in the alliances formed by each of the superpowers, and their competitive postures in relation to Third World countries. Relations between Moscow and Washington were central to wider structures of world order, particularly in light of the emergence of the perceived condition of mutual nuclear deterrence and the learning generated by engagement in crisis decision-making from the early 1960s. Each had an interest in the negotiation of long-term arms control arrangements, containing and terminating wars in regional conflicts, and, within limits, in recognizing the autonomy of Third World states (Smith, 1991, p. 71; Miller, 1992, p.15).

The collaborative element in this relationship was significant. It was occasionally raised in the 1960s and 1970s as a means of building on detente and providing still further protection for mutual superpower deterrence relations by stabilizing Southern environments. In approaches to regional politics, there was de facto recognition by each of the superpowers of the appropriate jurisdictions, or spheres of relatively unchallenged influence, of the other. In practice, however, the competitive underpinning of US–Soviet relations meant that these kinds of understandings remained tacit (Keal, 1983, p. 45). Denial was also a product of the perceptions of other states. Other Western powers remained opposed to some form of duopolistic control of intergovernmental organization (IGO) structures. China's resistance to superpower hegemony led it to criticize UN peacekeeping efforts in the 1960s and 1970s as a device that would serve to enhance the combined power of Moscow and Washington in relation to international conflicts.

Several tendencies were evident in the 1970s and 1980s, and even earlier, however, that marked the erosion of important features of the various kinds of bipolar system models that were valid for much of the Cold War period. These included the persistence of nationalisms in both Eastern and Western Europe, recurrent tensions in US–European relations, the early disappearance of Sino–Soviet ideological and interstate solidarity, and the economic resurgence of Japan and the EC (Clark, 1989, pp. 173–4). Further, even at the height of their maturation, the bipolar structures and processes of the Cold War period had a limited spread within the international system. They excluded, for example, both traditional (European) neutral and new (Third World) non-aligned states, even though they exerted significant effects on the latter and were probably an important circumstance reinforcing the viability of the former. Regional systems, in the Middle East and elsewhere, were affected, often significantly, by the larger currents of US–Soviet and East–West relations, but they also possessed their own distinctive dynamics increasingly beyond the capacity of either superpower to influence. Finally, the bipolar relationship was not symmetrical. The United States retained a far greater capacity both to project power and to create and sustain patterns of world institutional order compatible with its interests.

A gradual shift to a condition of multipolarity became a more pronounced feature of the 1970s. After its break with the Soviet Union, China had fitted uneasily into prevailing bipolar models. This distinctiveness grew more evident as a result of its modernization plans of the late 1970s and Beijing's redefinition of its independent foreign policy stance in the early 1980s. Its subsequent economic growth was fuelled by strategies of international financial institution (IFI) membership, closer bilateral relations with Western economies, the creation of special economic zones, and domestic economic decentralization. Other characteristic developments included trade and other tensions between the United States and the integrating group of EC economies, and the apparently inexorable rise of Japan on key economic indicators.

The idea of multipolarity was also, though in a different vocabulary, compatible with both traditional and late 1980s Soviet thinking on world order. Even in analyses that emphasised the central roles of the two superpowers, the identification of different types and intensities of contradictions among Western states remained an important feature of ideologically grounded analyses (Gorbachev, 1987, p. 472). The complexity of the interdependent post-bipolar world has also been emphasised by Chinese analysts (Ma, 1991, pp. 1–2).

Multipolarity, however, does not fall on a smooth theoretical continuum connecting it in unilinear fashion to bipolarity. It usually implies a multifaceted definition of power, assumptions about the issue-contingent nature of many political (and interstate) interactions, and emphasis on the significance of a variety of subnational and transnational phenomena. It also acknowledges the post-1945 historical developments that have in effect taken the threat or use of force out of many issue areas in international politics, such as trade negotiations or debt (Holsti, 1985, p. 682). Thus it was obviously realistic to incorporate both the EC (or Germany) and Japan in discussions of multipolarity, even though the possession of military capability may be absent (in the case of the EC) or its use subject to powerful domestic and external political constraints.

Aspects of this kind of complexity have long been evident. Henry Kissinger noted in early 1971 that while, militarily, there were only two superpowers, economically there were at least five major powers or groups of states; and 'politically, many more centres of influence have emerged' (Keal, 1983, p. 215).

This condition further implied the erosion of the traditional patterns of authority, power and influence characteristic of various stages of post-1945 international relations. The economic rise of Japan, for example, brought with it a greatly expanded agenda of international economic policy issues for other OECD governments (Meeks, 1993, pp. 45–7). Western attempts to influence Japanese policies on trade restraints or the opening of regulated sectors of the Japanese market, however, have historically had only limited success (George, 1991, p. 14). Multipolarity also offered some opportunities to *demandeur* states, such as the Soviet Union in the late 1980s, missing in the more constricted world of bipolarity (Hough, 1988, p. 93).

In contrast, models of tripolarity were more closely associated in their basic assumptions with earlier bipolar formulations. Although in the 1960s and 1970s bipolar models retained much of their usefulness – as guides to such phenomena as alliance cohesion and hierarchy, and superpower competition and attempted coalition-building in the South – it was already apparent that alternative conceptions, or at least extensions of the basic image, were becoming necessary.

The crucial event here was the consolidation of the Sino–Soviet split from the early 1960s. By the end of that decade, Moscow and Beijing had each come to view the other as its chief adversary. Chinese hostility to superpower hegemonic politics became more pronounced (Legault, 1970). Shortly afterwards, fuelled by the beginnings of Washington's opening to China and its readiness to consider Chinese overtures, Soviet suspicions of the possibility of a new anti-Soviet coalition based on the evolving US–Chinese alignment grew (Nixon, Ordeshook and Rose, 1989, pp. 326–7). Each simultaneously maintained a stance of ideological and political opposition to the United States. Even as Sino–American trade and cooperative relations grew during the 1980s, for example, Chinese analyses emphasised the crisis of capitalism and drew attention to features of the US economy, political system and race relations that supported the general thesis of eventual structural collapse (Shambaugh, 1991; Martin, 1990). These conditions reflected and facilitated US strategies of cultivating enhanced security relations with the Soviet Union, particularly in arms control negotiations, while simultaneously promoting economic and diplomatic relations with Beijing. Conflicting features of historical US attitudes towards both the USSR (Nye, 1984, pp. 1–2) and China resurfaced: perception of threat on the one hand, enthusiasm for collaborative ventures grounded in an assumption of common interests on the other.

Analytically, this situation prompted the exploration of tripolar models of the changing international system. The resulting images were seen by some analysts as having continuing relevance into the late 1980s (Tatu, 1989; Goldstein and Freeman, 1990, p. 2; Rajmaira and Ward, 1990). However the assumptions that underpinned strategic triangle models were open to criticism on a number of grounds. Like other hierarchical and pyramidal models, these ignored or played down important features of world society (Cerny, 1993, p. 27). Such approaches often exaggerated the degree of influence exercised by the three states over the course of regional conflicts and the structuring of international relations in the South. Like other traditional perspectives, they assumed a traditional hierarchy of issues, with conventional security questions taking priority over other types; there was sometimes insufficient appreciation of the power of regional states and middle powers; and analyses paid insufficient attention to economic factors underlying important tendencies in interstate relations.

Further, this genre of analysis tended to be restricted to the West. Soviet academic observers in the 1980s were skeptical of the promise of triangle models on the ground that China was argued to be a different kind of state – less predictable and responsible – than either the United States or the USSR (Lukin and Nogorny, 1988). Chinese analyses also, though from a different theoretical perspective, supported different models of the key structures underlying world order. Among other things these emphasised the importance of the Third World, the inadequacy of Western models when these were viewed against class analysis criteria, and the normative utility of peaceful coexistence theory as a guide to the construction of a functioning post-hegemonic system. These also posited a fundamental distinction between China on the one hand – as a large developing country with no great power aspirations – and the two superpowers on the other. Thus, as Clark argued at the end of the 1980s, a 'self-conscious tripolarity ... failed to sustain itself' (Clark, 1989, p. 175).

In the late 1980s and early 1990s two central features of security relations became increasingly embedded in international structures and the attendant attitudes of governments and observers. These were, first, the retention by the United States of a dominant, if relatively declining, role in economic and security relations among Northern states. This trend, which became evident in the early 1970s, had profound, if delayed, implications for US relations with other Western states (Calleo, 1987). The main factors underlying the change have been summarized by Bell (1991): (i) the changing share of the United States in world GNP, which fell from around 45 per cent in the 1940s and early 1950s to less than 25 per cent; (ii) its declining share in world manufacturing output, in view of the reemergence of the European and Japanese economies and the rise of new industrial centres in the South, from as much as 50 per cent in 1945 to less than 30 per cent in the early 1980s; (iii) the process of foreign economic penetration of the US economy by Japan, Germany and Britain; (iv) the growing challenge to US technological prowess mounted by other OECD states, particularly Japan; and (v) the domestic political and external implications of the problems of the US economy in the 1980s, particularly as regards the trade and budget deficits.

The second feature was the progressive weakening of Soviet power, culminating in the disintegration of the state and the outlawing of its prevailing ideology and traditional political structures. The change was anticipated in various developments of the 1980s. Soviet trade with Western countries, for example, expanded dramatically during both the 1960s and 1970s, but then stagnated from the early 1980s. Exports to OECD countries in 1988 were about the same level as they had been at the start of the decade. Domestic economic growth in the Soviet economy averaged 1.9 per cent during the first half of the 1980s, and slipped significantly in the late 1980s; by the turn of the decade, key industrial production indicators were revealing significant shrinkage in the Russian economy (Boardman, 1994, Ch. 3). The traditional economic division of labour in Eastern Europe disappeared, and with it the formal collapse of the Council for Mutual Economic Cooperation. In response to these and other pressures, the Soviet leadership in the late 1980s sought both domestic economic change and, externally, integration in the Western world economy through membership of the World Bank, the IMF and GATT, and elimination of the remaining Cold War-related barriers to trade, capital and technology flows with Western countries.

Taken together, these changes meant that their respective relations with Washington emerged as a newly central element of the foreign policies of the EC and its member-states, Japan, China and the Russian Federation. Beijing, for example, had from the early 1980s made cooperation with the leading IFIs, and the expansion of bilateral economic relations with the United States and other leading Western states, crucial features of its economic planning for the decade (Jacobson and Oksenberg, 1990; Kleinberg, 1990). After the Tiananmen repression of the prodemocracy movement in 1989, the application by Washington of human-rights criteria to progress in key aspects of the relationship – particularly the annual confirmation of China's most-favoured-nation (MFN) status, and the approach to China's membership of GATT – set back temporarily the pace of these expanding relationships in the early 1990s.

Similarly, the continuing security and economic problems besetting Russia and the Soviet successor-states made this cluster of issues a central foreign-policy problem for each of the other poles. The disintegration of the USSR, for example, expanded the number of the world's nuclear powers. Nuclear weapons in Ukraine became part of that country's post-Soviet bargaining with Russia, along with the future of the former Soviet Black Sea fleet, the handling of the USSR's foreign debts and other issues. The magnitude of the economic construction requirements of the economies of the successor states compelled a degree of political attention from Western governments that reinforced the shift of North–South issues to the peripheries of agendas. Debates in the United States in the late 1980s on future economic relations with the Soviet Union led to the discounting of the option of massive Marshall Aid-type injections of development assistance and capital, but there was persisting concern about the US interest in averting the destabilizing impacts of spreading disorder, economic decline, ethnic conflicts and nuclear uncertainties (Layne, 1991).

In light of these various combinations of threats and opportunities, US thinking about world order questions tended to revert to the older polar alternatives of isolationism or leadership. Its domestic economic and social policy needs, combined with a restructured international system, gave impetus to the former, as it had in the aftermath of war in both 1919 and 1945 (Goldberg, 1991, p. 52). Removal of the central enemy of the post-Second World War period, and the failure of other potential candidates for this status to emerge unequivocally, is likely to continue to have repercussions for domestic US politics and the structuring of its economy in the 1990s. The situations in Yugoslavia and Somalia hinted at a future complex and turbulent world in which the requirements of conflict resolution and peacekeeping would take second place to the imperative of quagmire avoidance.

On the other hand it was clear during the termination phases of the Cold War that equality between the United States and Russia in managing the postwar world was not a preferred option on the part of Washington. The importance of US domination of the UN Security Council and other forums was acknowledged in US debates on these questions (Pfaff, 1991, p. 44). Nor was a handover of significant powers to the UN as a collectivity a realistic possibility, though this option continued to be debated among members of the academic foreign policy community in the United States in the early 1990s.

This aspiration was not challenged in practice by either Russia or China. The initial formulation of the foreign policy of the Russian Federation in 1992–3 pronounced it in effect a firm ally of the United States, committed to closer economic ties and constructive foreign policy and security policy cooperation. This strategy required domestic defence against nationalist sniping and the charge that Russian interests and responsibilities, for example in relation to Serbia and Bosnia, were being neglected. Russian behaviour in the Security Council was only occasionally marked by hesitation over Iraq or ex-Yugoslavia questions. Until a relatively minor vote in May 1993 over the financing of the UN force in Cyprus, Moscow also shunned resort to the veto. With its own conceptions of world order distinct from those of either the Western powers or Russia, China reverted to an older strategy of abstaining or refraining from participating in controversial Security Council resolutions, for example on the use of force against Iraq in 1990–1.

The emerging world of the 1990s, then, appeared to be increasingly marked by a mood of Northern introspection. Preoccupation with the regional and local security problems of Europe and the former Soviet Union was reinforced by the reemergence of ethnicity and subnationalisms as a major force in world politics, and by the new vulnerability of state boundaries to change in the wake of armed conflict. Debates about the threat of war dropped through levels of analysis from great powers to local factions. The complexity as well as the turbulence of world society was evident in the continuing variety of issues on international agendas, and by the continued vitality of non-state actors as political players in relaticn to armaments, environmental and other issue-areas (Ekins, 1992, pp. 58–63). This situation produced a number of official formulations of approaches to future world order and security questions.

FROM 'COMMON SECURITY' TO 'NEW WORLD ORDER': NORTHERN PERSPECTIVES ON A CHANGING INTERNATIONAL SYSTEM

Anticipation of the end of the Cold War prompted a search for alternative conceptions of world order to guide diplomacy in the 1990s. Some had well-established predecessors in the previous decade and earlier. Two in particular produced intensive discussion: the US concept of a new world order, and that of common security associated with the dying years of the Soviet Union.

Others, such as the Chinese conception of peaceful coexistence, failed to generate wider international debate. Japan tended to remain traditionally reluctant to articulate for international audiences its own ideology of international relations and view of political commitments (Taira, 1993, p. 255).

Of the two, elaborations in the United States of the notion of a 'new world order' were relatively short-lived instances of this exercise at the beginning of the decade. In part, the search for galvanizing images of the post-Cold War world was fed by a kind of yearning for the regularities and predictabilities of a bygone bipolar era. One of the conventional virtues assigned to bipolar structures during the 1960s and 1970s had been their enhanced degree of stability, as opposed to more inherently uncontrollable systems with multiple centres of power such as those of late nineteenth-century Europe or the 1930s.

US debates at the beginning of the 1990s on desirable future world orders often reflected traditional concepts and approaches. They were consistent with a realist cluster of assumptions about the character of international order, the origins of war, the roles of great powers and the primacy of security questions in the hierarchy of issues. World order perspectives often echoed older US conceptions of that country's unique position and self-defined responsibilities in a complex and dangerous world (Mead, 1991, p. 377). Formulations of the US role in a post-Cold War world also served the objective of defending the continuation of an active international role, whatever specific form it might take – the norm since the late 1940s – against threats from proponents of isolationist strategies of the kind that had alarmed Western European political leaders in the immediate post-1945 years (Cole, 1993, pp. 33–5).

New world order thinking was also a product of the immediate circumstances of the ending of the Cold War. If history is supposed to be written by the winners, it should not be surprising that post-Cold War concepts of order in the United States were frequently grounded in Western analyses of the causes of victory. According to one important perspective, domestic and external change in the USSR was prompted in large measure by US deterrence postures and determined external pressure on Moscow, for example through the high cost imposed on Soviet interventionism by the Reagan Doctrine or the cost to the Soviet economy of maintaining a high state of military preparedness (Campbell and Weiss, 1991, p. 92; Chernoff, 1991, p. 111).

While inadequate as an explanation of the roots of change in the USSR during the 1980s, variants of these belief systems nonetheless had objective political significance by the fact of their being held by key players in Western states in the early 1990s. For example, by virtue of its human rights record, the growing international impact of its economy and its position as a pivotal regional power in East Asia, China might again become a future target of the little understood psychological processes of enemy creation that characterized both Soviet and US perspectives on the Cold War.

The formulations of the early 1990s tended to differ from those of the height of the Cold War, however, in placing greater policy emphasis on international organizations, particularly the UN. The issue of security investment in UN institution-building in the 1990s became a pivotal issue in US foreign policy debates of the early 1990s. In a sense this focus harked back to a still earlier period: that of the mid-1940s debates on collective security through conventionally designed IGOs, before the con-solidation of Cold War relationships and the extensive use of the veto by Moscow in the UN Security Council.

In practice, however, the approach of the end of the Cold War and the col-lapse of the USSR gave these concerns more of a unipolar than a collective appearance. In this restructured concept of US hegemony, the qualification was not so much the bipolar requirement of US–Soviet cooperation as the emergence of a US-led system of nineteenth-century-like Concert deliberations (Miller, 1992, pp. 9–10; Craig and George, 1983, pp. 45–6) among Western powers. Russia was admitted to these as a member of the outer circle. In this alternative model, then, Russia shifted from an adversarial to a peripherally supportive position. It retained a measure of power by virtue of Western acknowledgment of a shared stake in its economic and internal political and ethnic future. However it was unable, or unwilling, to voice effective opposi-tion even when, as in the case of Iraq in 1990–1, the core interests of formerly close friends and clients were involved. As in the second Gulf War, moreover, the beginnings of post-Cold War politics held out the potential for greater US leverage over its Western allies, particularly Japan and Germany (Halliday, 1991, p. 225). China for its part appeared cautiously content to accept the reali-ties of US power in the UN Security Council.

Further, Western and Russian commentaries in the late 1980s and early 1990s on the renaissance of the UN as a genuinely collective world body tended to focus overwhelmingly on that body's classic security functions, and on the Security Council as the driving force of UN political dynamics. This perspective risked marginalizing global problems other than war, partly perhaps because of the capacity of this phenomenon more than others to galvanize human political activity (Rogers, 1981, p. 94). While the UN system has continued to tackle a diverse range of other issues, Western governments have in practice concentrated on those that appear to be most directly linked to the traditional security problematique.

In contrast, attention to such questions figured more prominently in common security approaches. Redefinitions of security to incorporate a wide range of

economic, ecological and social questions became increasingly prominent in
Western debates during the 1980s, partly as a result of security developments
in Europe connected with the CSCE process, and partly as a result of the
mounting priority attached to trade, environment and other issues (SIPRI,
1985; Matthews, 1989). Revised concepts of security implicitly underlay
approaches to the law of the sea, for example, particularly in the 1982 UNC-
LOS III Convention (Larson, 1985). This perspective acquired greater salience
and a sharper focus in Soviet formulations from 1986–7. The concept of international economic security, for example, was described by one Soviet analyst
as 'one of the pillars in the comprehensive system of world security based on
the interdependence of the modern world' (Andreev, 1989, p. 224).

Two sets of issues underlay this conceptual questioning of traditional perspectives on security. The first centred on the interdependence proposition: the
pursuit of security, if it is not to be self-defeating, is bound up with a search for
conditions assuring also the security of adversaries. If not, the actions and reactions of states and other actors may come to be tied in a 'vicious circle of security and power accumulation' (Herz, 1950, p. 157). Secondly, identification of
the issues considered to be security related greatly expanded to incorporate
such questions as the vulnerability of the national economies of developing
countries to shifts in world commodity prices, or the economic effects of the
transnational spread of air- or water-borne pollutants. Like Western critics of
the dominant realist paradigm of international relations (for example, Falk,
1983, pp. 13–15), common security theorists also tended to assume both that
global problems other than war were important, and also that states and other
actors were capable of engaging in sustained cooperation to handle them.

Various combinations of these elements are possible (Boardman, 1989, pp.
2–7). For example the traditional extension of the concept of security to
incorporate such factors as food production capabilities, or vulnerability to
interruptions in the supply of key imports, does not necessarily entail attention to problems of security interdependence among adversaries. Likewise
the wisdom of avoiding provocative acts and of engaging in security cooperation was intrinsic to the nuclear relationship of the superpowers, but such
calculations did not automatically or consistently involve the incorporation of
a spreading range of non-military items on to bilateral US–Soviet agendas.

THE NORTH–SOUTH SECURITY NEXUS: A PRELUDE TO DISCUSSION

These developments have many, and inherently uncertain, implications for
security in the South arising from the continuing repercussions of the

removal of adversarial East–West competition (for example Thomas, 1987; Ayoob, 1991; Campbell and Weiss, 1991, p. 92; and the country case studies in this volume).

This condition in one sense represents a continuation of the cooperative elements in Cold War superpower relations based on norms of behaviour aimed at the prudent avoidance of actions likely to intensify tensions in the central strategic relationship. It also reflected changing Soviet approaches to regional conflicts. Changes in Soviet behaviour in southern Africa (Nel, 1990) and in the Middle East (Boardman, 1993) were evident at least from the early 1980s. These were given a clearer ideological rationale in Gorbachev's 'new thinking', particularly as regards the emphasis on non-confrontational relations of interdependence in a 'deideologized' international security environment. By the early 1990s this perspective gave way to deeper policy change on the part of the Russian Federation, which proclaimed both political and ideological affinity with Western nations and acknowledged a constructive role for the main IFIs and for foreign capital in developing countries.

More specifically, many countries in the South have been affected directly or indirectly by the disappearance of both the Soviet model as a guide to economic development, and of the Soviet Union itself as an ally for governments or other actors, or as a card to play in dealings with Western powers. This factor, too, can be exaggerated. Moscow's relations with Arab states during the Cold War, for example, were often characterized by tensions, disruptions and a variety of unwelcome constraints. As in the case of the Horn of Africa, the circumstances of East–West confrontation often led to an exaggerated emphasis in analyses of the external as opposed to the domestic causes of political instability and conflict (Olsen, 1991, pp. 21–2). Similarly, Soviet critiques of Western neoliberalism and IFI strategies, including structural adjustment programmes in Southern economies, in practice had little impact on their course during the 1980s.

Even so, removal of the Soviet presence, direct or indirect, diminished the constraints on the exercise of Western economic and security policy preferences in relation to developing countries. One possibility is a greater future readiness on the part of US-led Western states to engage in intervention, whether unilaterally, in coalitions or in the form of official UN forces. In such exercises, key roles would be played by important Western actors and by interested Southern regional partners. The conflicts in the former Yugoslavia led to the creation of a more explicit EC peacekeeping, conflict-monitoring and mediation role. On the other hand, there are significant domestic political constraints on activism of this kind, for example in the United States, Japan and Germany. The UN Charter also has limited authority with respect to domestic matters. There are major constraints inherent in Western states' bilateral relations with important regional states in the South. Greater pressure on developing countries to proceed with the neoliberal agenda, including multiparty democratization and human rights protection, is, however, likely to be intensified.

A related factor is greater post-Yugoslavia (and post-Somalia) recognition on the part of Western governments of the need for quagmire avoidance. Much of the renewed optimism about the UN's security role displayed first by the Soviet Union in the late 1980s and then by many Western governments, especially in the immediate aftermath of the second Gulf War, was based on traditional conceptions of the nature of armed conflict in the international system. Iraq's seizure of Kuwait in 1990 fitted within conventional definitions of aggression and the established criteria for activating the provisions of Chapter VII of the UN Charter. This pattern of state-to-state military action may recur – for example among the countries of the former Soviet Union, or as a result of the projected emergence of more 'mid-level powers' in the Asian Pacific over the next several decades (Bobrow and Kudrle, 1991, pp. 237–8) – but it cannot be assumed to be typical of the situations likely to be faced by the international community in the early twenty-first century.

More probable are ambiguous and complex situations, perhaps involving the absence of central or local governmental authority, which involve a variety of state and non-state actors, and which spring from and have implications for social, ecological, ethnic and other processes. In the Albanian refugee crisis of 1991, for example, the Italian government sought an agreement with Tirana whereby it would train Albanian security forces and naval patrols in that country's waters. In many situations, moreover, the impact of IFI-sanctioned policies, for example by exacerbating gender inequalities (Nzomo, 1993, pp. 69–71), is also a relevant factor in assessments of the likelihood of the incidence and course of future conflicts.

In the short term, then, one of the main Western responses to the collapse of Soviet power was a concentration on European issues and a parallel disengagement from pressing questions of the South. This trend towards the marginalization of Southern issues on Northern agendas had begun earlier as a result of the beginnings of political change in Eastern Europe. It was reinforced by the overburdening of Western agendas produced by the various external and domestic economic and political forces evident in the 1980s (Campanella, 1993, pp. 190–1). However, the longer-term consequences of the removal of the Soviet Union's role as one of the integrating forces of Western interstate cohesion remain to be seen.

4 The New World Disorder: Towards Managed Trade and Economic Partnership for the Next Century

John F. Devlin

INTRODUCTION

The hope that the fragmentation of the Soviet subsystem would lead to the emergence of a 'new world order' appears increasingly remote. The high-consumption countries continue to face problems of weak growth, increasing unemployment, mounting public deficits and public debt, environmental decay, large trade imbalances and a continuing stand-off over the rules that will govern international trading relationships. For the low-consumption countries, the fragmentation of the old bipolar world has done nothing to resolve the debt crisis, the pressure for structural adjustment and the general stagnation of their economies. Ethnic tensions are rising not only within the old Soviet subsystem and in several low-consumption countries but also in the high-consumption countries with racist attacks on Turkish guest workers and immigrants in Germany, and on North African immigrants in France (see Chapter 5 below), and a new growth of racism in North America. The peace dividend is nowhere to be seen.

These conditions suggest not the emergence of a new world order but rather an increasing world disorder. This chapter argues that indeed the current conjuncture is one of increasing disorder, one that has its roots in the breakdown of the post-war international regime beginning in the 1960s. I offer an 'underconsumptionist' interpretation of this breakdown and consider some options available to both high- and low-consumption countries in trying to navigate their way toward a new international regime for the next century (cf. regional case studies below).

ACCUMULATION, CONSUMPTION, AND LONG WAVES

The post-war international order institutionalized in the United Nations system and the Bretton Woods organizations was a response to the economic and military crises of the 1930s. Two interpretations of that crisis set the debate. Liberals saw restricted trade as a central cause of depression. Through restricted access to crucially important raw materials, restricted trade was also a primary source of war. By resolving this access problem new economic and military crises could be averted. No country would have to fight for what it could easily buy. The goal of the liberals, led by the United States, was the breakdown of the imperial systems and the creation of a free-trade regime. Keynesians on the other hand saw trade as a secondary problem. For them the slump of the 1920s and 1930s was the result of domestic demand crises. The prevention of future crises required that countries have the capacity and the initiative to manage their domestic economies in order to sustain growth. Their concern was to create an international system in which no country would be forced to constrain its domestic growth in order to sustain its balance of trade. Beggar-thy-neighbour competition had to be avoided (Brett, 1985).

The compromise was the creation of a system of fixed exchange rates and an International Monetary Fund that would provide immediate short-term assistance to countries with balance-of-payments problems. To manage the transition to an open trading regime, existing systems of domestic management (particularly in agriculture) would be allowed to continue while a process of negotiated movement toward free trade was instituted. The General Agreement on Tariffs and Trade (GATT) would be a convenor for multilateral negotiations at which staged reductions in quotas and tariffs would be negotiated.

The post-war success of this combination of a managed monetary system and embedded liberalism (Ruggie, 1982) was sufficient to give both liberals and Keynesians ample confidence in the correctness of their theoretical positions. Expanding trade and domestic demand management were both correlated with the remarkable period of growth, the postwar boom. However both positions relied upon strong assumptions about the fundamental stability of market economies. When the postwar arrangements began to unravel with the breakdown of the monetary system in the late 1960s and the economic rollercoaster of inflation set in, there was little consensus over what was occurring. The imbalance appeared as an anomaly. Some blamed spendthrift governments, others the greedy oil producers, still others the protectionist proclivities of rent-seekers.

Underconsumptionists, however, had consistently argued that there was a structural problem in keeping market economies in balance. Accumulation and consumption do not automatically expand in a mutually support-ing and reciprocal manner. If this balance is not struck, the economy jerks from periods of investment-led growth to periods of recession.[1] Inter-national economic linkages increase the potential for large imbalances sustained over long periods, giving rise to long economic waves.[2]

The long wave of expansion that occurred over the late nineteenth cen-tury was made possible by the significant expansion of both investment and consumption stimulated by the opening up of the colonial territories, par-ticularly through the penetration of the railroads into previously uncol-onized hinterlands in North America, Latin America, Africa and Asia. The long slump of the 1920s and 1930s was a consequence of the exhaustion of this expansionary period. The problem was not a lack of financial capital or technological innovations. The problem was the constraint on expanding consumption that was caused by the exhaustion of the land frontier. Until some new source of demand could be found the 'will to accumulate' would remain in eclipse.

The escape from the long European slump was led not by the discovery of a new frontier but by state spending and state-supported expansion of consumption. Japan and Germany unravelled the knot of stagnation through military spending, stockpiling of arms, infrastructure development, military mobilization and imperial expansion. This process of expanding military consumption stimulated a partial reciprocation by the other Euro-pean nations but, until war was upon them, their militarization was not suf-ficient to shake off the consumption crisis. The United States, which partially avoided the long slump due to its heady period of debt-driven expansion during the 1920s, was cast into an even deeper crisis once the bubble burst in 1929. It eventually began to unravel the knot of stagnation through the New Deal, which combined state spending with job creation and redistributive programs. The New Deal expansion was overtaken by wartime mobilization, which put all the major economies into higher gear. Looking to the post-war period, analysts and politicians feared that peace would bring renewed depression, political turmoil, and perhaps more war. But post-war reconstruction and the expansion of the welfare state contributed to a boom that lasted into the 1960s.

Many argued that the institutional changes that encouraged the post-war expansion of consumption (asset redistributions, effective minimum wage laws, collective bargaining, public spending on social services) would destroy economic prosperity by deflecting economic resources away from investment. However, the postwar consumption boom did not destroy prosperity. The spreading of incomes and a generalizing improvement of living standards unlocked productive capacity. Post-war growth was dependent upon the balanced expansion of consumption and growing investment in infrastructure, manufacturing capacity, research and development, education and so on. The welfare economy never completely displaced the warfare economy. The Cold War, Korea, Vietnam and other revolutionary anti-colonial movements, and the emergence of internal civil strife maintained the demand for military goods and services. However, the joint expansion of private investment and mass consumption was the institutional engine of post-war growth.

THE NEW DISORDER

But embedded liberalism had built-in destabilizers. Open trade allowed countries to invest in productive capacity at a scale not justified by domestic demand but which could be sold into global markets. Overcapacity emerged incrementally in one sector after another. By the mid-1960s the high-consumption countries were entering a period of much higher levels of direct competition across a large number of product sectors. Liberal economic theory suggested that the result of this more intensive competition would be a global rationalization of production based on the operation of comparative advantage. However, the consequences of such rationalization were difficult to manage within the framework of liberal-democratic political systems. As the liberalization process advanced from the Kennedy to the Tokyo Round of GATT, the most straightforward protectionist policy tools, tariffs and quotas, increasingly were bargained away. With a declining capacity to protect domestic producers, governments began to compete with each other by offering incentives for business, tax cuts, export subsidies and a plethora of production-enhancing programmes. The result was a lowering of the revenue base, a shift of the tax burden from corporate to personal income taxes, an increase in consumption taxes, increased deficits, increased borrowing to cover deficits, higher interest rates as a result of increased borrowing, and inflation. These alternative strategies of competition were the beggar-thy-neighbour instrumentalities of the 1970s and 1980s. As this process gathered momentum the pressure on the welfare state programmes and on real wages increased and the rates at which consumption expanded began to decelerate. What had begun as head-to-head competition in the production system began to erode the institutional conditions supporting the sustained expansion of consumption. The balance between accumulation and consumption was lost and the institutional engine of growth was disabled. Recessions from the late 1960s to the early 1990s have had the same fundamental root, overcapacity and overcompetition linked to deceleration of private and public consumption (Peet, 1987).

While liberals and neoliberals continued to argue that increasingly free trade stimulated global expansion, the evidence pointed in the opposite direction. As trade increased and liberalization progressed, the post-war boom collapsed. Increased trade contributed to global recession. Bankruptcies and rising unemployment added to the stresses on income-support programmes. Potential investors began to shift their financial resources into short-term paper investments and existing assets (Bienefeld, 1989).

This general malaise was partially obscured by the success of a few countries – Japan, Germany and the newly industrializing countries (NICs) who were able to generate trade surpluses as the deceleration spread. It was also obscured by the oil-price increases and the exceptional boom of the 1980s. But the oil-price increases of the 1970s and the Reagan administration's deficit-created boom in the mid-1980s simply inflated the global economy and increased global debt loads. Neither created nor resolved the fundamental imbalances between the expansion of productive capacity and the expansion of consumption entitlements. As the chronic imbalance between the US economy and the main surplus economies became apparent, the Reagan, Bush and Clinton administrations have encouraged the surplus countries to increase their levels of domestic consumption and imports. But surplus countries such as Japan and Taiwan have been reluctant to bargain away their competitive advantages (van Wolferen, 1990). Like their European and American precursors, they have shown a preference for foreign investment as the primary mechanism for the recycling of surpluses, thus maintaining the rules established by the postwar settlement.

As continued liberalization via GATT became an increasingly unrealistic option, regionalization has been attempted. However, regionalization within the EC, North America and Asia faces the same structural difficulty. Free trade within regions will create competitive deflation just as it has done globally. The slowdown drew the German economy into recession in the 1980s and it has even begun to draw the dynamic Japanese economy into recession in the 1990s. The political costs of further liberalization are unlikely to be manageable. Unstable political regimes is one indicator of this instability. Long-standing governments have fallen or are tottering – the liberal-democrats in Japan, the republicans in the United States, socialists in France, the Christian democrats in Italy, the conservatives in England. Progress toward European unity grows increasingly tenuous in the face of temporizing over ratification and implementation of the Maastricht Treaty, including one lost (then won) referendum, the close French vote and the temporary rejection of the social chapter in the British parliament.

The economics of European unity appear threatened by the run on the pound, the lira and the franc resulting from German borrowing to finance reunification. In North America the Clinton administration's insistence on side agreements to the NAFTA, plus a new liberal government in Ottawa, leave the future of the Free Trade Agreement and the North American Free Trade Agreement in some doubt (see Chapter 13 below). Although the OECD in November 1992 called for a general expansionary policy in the high-consumption economies [3] and President Clinton went into the recent Group of Seven (G7) discussions with a concern to manage trade relations with Japan,[4] the impasse of embedded liberalism has not yet been formally recognized. The hold of liberal ideology over national governments and international relations remains. Competitive disorder remains the order of the day.

DISORDER IN THE LOW-CONSUMPTION COUNTRIES

Low-consumption countries never entered the heady days of growth created by consumption-led investment. Thus the post-war arrangements did not fundamentally alter the international division of economic activity established during the imperialist era. Low-consumption countries were expected to continue as resource-export economies. Structuralists argued that import-substitution based on protectionist tariffs would generate industrialization, but their entrepreneurial classes were weak and remained primarily engaged in rentier and mercantile activities. Many politicians and entrepreneurs were happy to join external agents in the continued extraction of natural resources. Despite import-substitution policies, investment levels remained low, much of their complex organizations, technologies, skills and financial capital continued to be drawn from external sources, multinational corporations, aid, international bank loans and so on. Where stronger forms of economic nationalism arose they were roundly attacked as at best a break with the post-war logic of the open-trading system, and thus economically irrational, and at worst as communism and thus crushed as a move on the chessboard of post-war geopolitics (Blum, 1986).

Weak industrialization was encouraged by the internationalization of financial markets, which allowed rentiers to export their financial assets into more secure foreign accounts and investments. Efforts to control capital flows were consistently criticised by international financial institutions, who saw free capital movement as one of the foundations of the postwar settlement. The inability of Southern governments to effectively implement progressive taxation systems meant that the incomes and assets of the high-income groups are not under political control and are available for investment and redistribution. This forced most low-consumption governments to inflate the money supply and assume growing debt loads, debt loads that were primarily floated domestically and which thus kept the state under the control of the domestic rentier. Most importantly the potential for expanding consumption was foreclosed by patterns of distributive exclusion that kept tenants, small farmers, urban workers and petty entrepreneurs locked into low-income cycles. Domestic pressures for redistribution were crushed by domestic elites with the active assistance of high-consumption countries. The import-substitution process was blocked by both investment and consumption constraints. Without a sustained expansion of consumption, whatever domestic industrialization was achieved in low-consumption countries quickly reached the limits of the internal market.

The tensions generated by inflation and stagnation in living standards generated political instability and authoritarian pacts of debilitation that saw transnational corporations, military aid and authoritarian governments in the South work in partnership to maintain and often increase the gap between elite and mass-consumption levels. Basic human rights are regularly contravened and periodically suspended. Such patterns of resource-dependent exports, weak domestic production systems and stagnant domestic markets left the low-consumption countries bobbing in the economic waves of the high-consumption countries rather than establishing their own independent growth dynamics.

During the 1970s the overproduction crisis in the high-consumption countries led to the debt crisis. Excessive financial assets (particularly after 1973–4), finding few investment opportunities in the high-consumption countries, were pushed upon governments in the low-consumption countries. International interest rates were often much lower than domestic rates. It appeared that current development could be financed out of future exports. But this was a false hope. The overproduction crisis precluded any major expansion of the global market. The foreign debt could never be repaid on the basis of resource and labour-intensive exports.[5] At the same time the decade of easy money allowed governments in the low-consumption countries to put off the changes in their domestic fiscal capacity required to put them on a firmer developmental footing. Weak states and weak domestic economies were thus reproduced through the inflow of foreign debt. The state increasingly was blamed for the dismal performance of domestic elites.[6]

FROM COMPETITION TO PARTNERSHIP

The implications of underconsumptionist analysis reverse most of the current neoliberal prescriptions for international restructuring and domestic growth. The neoliberal answer to the economic stagnation and the debt crisis was to invite in multinationals to set up export-oriented manufacturing operations as supplements to resource-intensive exports (see Chapters 12 and 13 below). But this shift from a resource-based to a labour-based export sector did nothing to resolve the fundamental incapacity of the domestic economy to establish an autonomous growth cycle. Export-led growth has always been over estimated by liberals.

In the miracle economies of the post-war era – Japan, Taiwan and South Korea – nationalist, state-managed investment programmes combined with improved asset distributions and growing real wages generated dynamic growth (cf. Chapter 11 below). The process involved the creation of domestic organizations with domestic entrepreneurs and domestic managers of production. While technology and skills were learned, borrowed or bought from foreign sources, the planning and pacing of investment was based on national priorities and the creation of a domestic industrial capacity. This national investment programme was supported by the expansion of the mass-consumption entitlements through support programmes for small farmers and small business and rising real wages. The emergence of effective economic nationalism in Japan, Taiwan and South Korea is largely explained by their position on the Cold War perimeter, their lack of any strategic resources, the elimination of their rentier–landlord classes through land reform immediately after the Second World War and the particular ideological conjunction of statism and anticommunism that won them unrestrained support from US foreign policy-makers.

The global recession plus the intense competition between potential export platforms has made the labour-based export strategy increasingly less viable as an engine of growth (cf. Chapter 12 below). Markets for labour-intensive manufacturing are of limited scope given the consumption ceiling in the high-consumption countries. Exports to the high-consumption countries do not offer a general engine for growth. Collectively, the low-consumption countries will continue to face weak markets and will be forced into competitive recession as they outbid each other to be the export enclaves of choice and entice foreign investment through the usual array of low-wage, labour-repressive, low-tax, high-service provisions and so on. The levels of accumulated debt simply exaggerate the pressure on low-consumption countries to export at all costs. This simply increases deflationary pressure globally and reduces the potential for renewed global expansion (Payer, 1991). International markets are certainly incapable of absorbing the levels of output that would be required to pay off the debt of the South and put the majority of the unemployed and the underemployed to work in export-oriented activities unless there is a massive expansion of domestic consumption across the low-consumption countries.

Structural adjustment programmes and rigorously enforced debt repayments are the exact opposite of what is required for renewed growth (see Chapters 8, 12, 14 and 15 below). Getting the state out of the way opens the path for transnationals to organize production on a global scale. While this may indeed increase efficiency through a massive rationalization of the production process, it does nothing to address the problem of inadequate aggregate private and public consumption. Structural adjustment strategy does little to encourage the expansion of the domestic market, which provides a potentially much larger source of economic dynamism for the low-consumption economies. The domestic economy, not trade, is the key to economic development (cf. the regional cases below).

In low-consumption countries the pressing need is for growth of the domestic market using domestically mobilized resources to supply goods and services to domestic consumers. To alter the patterns of weak investment that constrain their industrialization processes, income will have to be shifted from politically influential rentiers to industrial investment. Import substitution can be reintroduced. But efforts to support the domestic private sector will require a more active state and a progressive taxation system. Resource- and labour-intensive exports will continue to play a role but the deepening of the domestic manufacturing and service sectors will be the crucial factor. A state-guided industrialization strategy that offers ample opportunities for market competition within the domestic economy but does not abandon the responsibility for guiding the development process and managing trade relations is needed. Such arguments are currently being put forward by Latin American analysts under such labels as 'neo-structuralism' or 'endogenous industrialization' (Sunkel and Zuleta, 1990; Anglade and Fortin, 1987; Browder and Borello, 1987; cf. Chapter 13 below).

None of these efforts will be successful unless there is a parallel shift in income from elite to mass consumers and thus an expansion of domestic demand. This must be managed by the state. A new domestic partnership between domestic producers and consumers will require new distributive policies. The bureaucratic mechanisms of progressive taxation, wage and labour law, tenancy and land reform, and expanded welfare services are well understood.

It is clearly the problem of political power that constitutes the major obstacle (see, especially, Chapters 8 and 9 below). Redemocratization has been one dimension of the general effort by neoliberal policy-makers to reduce the power of the state and increase the potential for external interests to penetrate national communities. The shift from authoritarian rule to competitive politics does not assure an increase in the political influence of industrialists or redistributive social movements over policy. The transfer of power to traditional elites with strong rentier and mercantile ties to resource exports and multinational corporations and the alignment of new governments with the agenda of structural adjustment implies a decline in autonomous domestic industrial investment and in mass living standards.

However, without significant improvements in domestic industrial capacity and structures of distribution, low-consumption economies cannot advance no matter how democratic their political systems. It is precisely the linkage of democratic institutions to emergent groups of private and public industrialists and to the institutionalization of distributive inclusion that constitutes the central steps in the economic development of the liberal-democratic high-consumption countries. Democratic institutions under the control of rentier and mercantile interests willing to align themselves with neoliberal structural adjustment policies, guarantees that the long-term economic growth of the low-consumption economies will continue to be compromised. And the inevitable return to suspension of electoral systems is virtually assured.

Such programmes of distributive inclusion do not require provision of aid, they require support for the distributive constituency that can be found in every low-consumption country among farmers, workers, domestically-oriented businesses and intellectuals. One dimension of a new North–South partnership would be the increased moral and material support for redistributive movements in the name of development (see Chapters 7, 9 and 14 below).

Shifting all economic transfers from debt to grants would be an additional step in the right direction. The myth that the current levels of debt can be repaid must be abandoned. Both the low-consumption debt and the US debt are simply never going to be repaid. That debt should be written off, as most banks are doing through non-performing-asset adjustments and special funds. But the write-off need not come without conditionalities. The value of payments cancelled should be based upon the value of taxation raised from internal sources and applied to the expansion of domestically financed infrastructural investment and expansion of social services, health, education, community and family support, and programmes of income transfers to the needy and the elderly. If governments knew that their foreign currency outflows would be reduced in step with their internal revenue mobilization and redistributive expenditures, the motivational structure for state efficiency and good government would be significantly enhanced.

The potential for a rapid turnaround in most low-consumption countries is high. It is the preoccupation with foreign earnings and balance-of-payments problems that is the major stumbling block. However, so long as aid programmes support governments that seek to maintain patterns of low investment, distributive exclusion and external dependence they are not contributing to development.

The pretence that the cartel of high-consumption countries is not engaged in political interference in the low-consumption countries should be put aside. The promotion of structural adjustment as a development strategy has exposed the hypocrisy of the donors and the international financial agencies. Structural adjustment demands constraints on state expenditure on health, education and other social services. It demands major shifts in trade policy, privatization of public assets, and a large number of other policy changes. Structural adjustment thus constitutes a significant interruption in the internal affairs of low-consumption countries. Demands for an adequate enforcement of minimum wage laws, or the easing of restrictions on labour union organization, or the implementation of effective land reform programmes would be no more interventionist. What is required is a shift in the logic of clientalism from one that encourages dependence to one that supports partnership.

Most low-consumption countries are resource rich but poor in all facets of industrial production. They produce similar products and existing patterns of economic exchange link low-consumption countries to high-consumption countries rather than to each other. The potential for economic linkages is thus low. At the same time the economic interests of many of the most powerful economic and political actors continue to draw them toward an engagement in the international economy under its current configuration rather than toward an effort to alter the international configurations through alternative regional initiatives. However the economies of scale possible from pooling investment programmes in research and development, the creation of 'regional' firms in heavy industry, efforts at integration of transportation systems, and sharing of markets, all offer some hope of developmental partnerships. Such partnerships must be based on the agreed objective of moving away from resource-based economies toward industrial- and service-based economies and upon the shared objective of raising mass-consumption levels thus avoiding tendencies toward competitive deflation. Debtors' consortia continue to be the most pressing need and, hence, constitute another form of South–South linkage.

Before the global economy can once again reestablish a general trajectory of expansion, the high-consumption countries must recognize that the current practises of competitive deflation are counterproductive and that what is required is a general reflation of their own economies and the creation in low-consumption countries of the institutional configuration of national domestic investment plus distributive inclusion that supported the postwar boom.

Reflation in the high-consumption countries can take a variety of forms. Rebuilding and expansion of infrastructure, expanded social services, new income-distribution programmes, new employment generation and improved environmental management, including the mothballing of environmentally destructive plant, equipment and technologies.[7] All such effort will require greater social control by public authorities, greater cooperation between nations, and a decline in the freedom of private organizations to threaten jobs and fiscal stability through capital mobility. Thus the shift from liberalization to managed trade is an essential condition of any reflation effort. The freedom of international financial institutions and transnational corporations to move financial capital and production activity in and out of countries must be sharply reduced. The state must once again become the gatekeeper for the national economy and the major voice of the national interest. Managed trade implies a continuous negotiation over trading balances based on the principle that trade outcomes are central objects of economic policy and cannot be left as the accidental consequence of market competition.

The end of head-to-head competition could not only remove the attraction of low wages, environmental exploitation and inadequate public services as dimensions of export strategies but also increase the scope for international debate over living standards and quality-of-life issues. With managed trade it would be possible to move toward minimum global labour standards, the long-run goal of the International Labour Organization, minimum global environmental standards, the objective of the United Nations Environment Program and the Rio Summit. It would be possible to advance human rights and even bring social welfare systems into closer proximity.

Economic partnership between North and South implies less foreign development lending, a preference for grants over loans, and most importantly the transfer of skills and technologies on a non-commercial basis. The high-consumption countries must allow the low-consumption countries room to develop. This does not mean increased access to markets and increased prices for resources, the major demands of low-consumption countries within the regime of embedded liberalism, but rather free access to technology, support for nationalist development plans, an end to the overturning of nationalist governments pursuing independent economic development, an end to the support for repressive governments keeping mass-based redistributive movements at bay through repression, and an end to pressure for increased liberalization and structural adjustment (however see Segal's discussion in Chapter 13 of the 'rationale' driving the move toward a North American Free Trade Area).

Such policies can be pursued in the knowledge that encouragement of the distributive expansion of the low-consumption countries is one of the major potential sources of future growth for high-consumption countries. An international regime of managed trade, national industrialization and domestic distributive inclusion would represent a significant advance on the road from the imperialism of the nineteenth century to the community of nations that was the promise but has not been the reality of the United Nations system. In this transition the era of embedded liberalism will appear as a passing phase. A phase during which competition continued to dominate cooperation as the foundation for international relationships and economy continued to be understood as the optimization of individual utility and corporate profit. But out of this disorder may emerge an era in which cooperation dominates competition and economy comes to be understood as the application of knowledge and labour to the problems of social provisioning on a global scale.

CONCLUSION

Underconsumptionist theory suggests that international institutional reform is required for both the high- and the low-consumption countries to establish or reestablish satisfactory trajectories of economic development. The reemergence of the nation-state as a primary economic space, reduced international economic competition, managed trade and renewed private and public consumption must be the cornerstones for constructing an economic partnership that will allow both high- and low-consumption countries to take advantage of the remarkable technological capacities that are now in hand for improving global living standards.

Notes

1. There is an extensive underconsumptionist debate beginning with Malthus (1936) and continuing through Marx and Keynes up to the present. Some useful references include Kenway (1980); Burris (1984); de Janvrey and Sadolet (1983); Miller (1988); and Wilkinson (1988).
2. Locating the current recessionary phase within the patterns of longwaves is generating a growing literature. For a general introduction to longwave models see Berry (1991). For an introduction to the Marxist tradition see

54   *The New World Disorder*

Burris (1984); Kotz (1987); Lembcke (1991). For the French regulation
school see Lipietz (1987a; 1987b). For the American social structures of
accumulation school see Weisskopf, Bowles and Gordon (1985) and Bowles
and Gintis (1986). The tension between the more structuralist approach of the
French regulationists and collective behavioural approaches of the Americans
is explored in Kotz (1990). The world-systems theorists also place major
stress on such large-scale movements: Hopkins, Wallerstein and associates
(1982).

3.   'OECD recommends spending to speed up economic recovery', *Toronto
Star*, 11 November 1992. But the approach is very cautious. 'To maintain the
confidence of business and financial markets, governments would have to
promise to reverse any easing of their tax and spending policies once growth
picked up.' This would, of course, assure that the pick-up in growth would
be immediately cut off and the global economy thrown back once again into
recession.

4.   The US trade deficit with Japan is currently some $50 billion a year. Clinton
entered the G7 meetings with the intention to negotiate 'quantifiable results-
oriented' trade in sectors such as cars and components, and in foreign investment and government procurement policies. This tilt toward managing the
trading relationship is being strongly resisted by the Japanese, who are quite
happy with the current arrangements (see 'America and Japan. Result: out-
rage', *The Economist*, 19 June 1993). However when he emerged from
discussions he was at pains to point out that the framework agreement was
not an agreement to manage trade (see 'Japan, U.S. reach deal of trade
framework', *Globe and Mail*, 10 July 1993).

5.   Payer (1991) notes that this structural repayment problem was recognized by
development analysts in the 1940s and 1950s and was the basis of their
recommendations for grants in aid rather than lending programmes to help
low-consumption countries. However, giving away excess capital appeared
irrational while investing or lending it appeared rational. Thus the stage was
set for the debt crisis of the 1980s.

6.   It should be noted that this is not simply a matter of corruption, one of the
favourite whipping boys of neoliberals. Corruption in Japan is surely
astronomical and has brought down several prominent liberal-democratic
leaders and now the Liberal-Democratic Party itself, but Japan is one of the
leading industrial economies, if not the leading industrial economy at this
time. Thus corruption is not the source of economic stagnation. Corruption
simply moves financial resources through alternative channels. If a large
bribe was turned into real capital through investment in a manufacturing
plant, it would make the same structural contribution to economic development as a grant made to the same plant. What makes corruption reprehensible
is that it often redirects resources intended to expand real capital or the consumption of lower-income groups and channels those resources into paper
investments that make no real contribution to the economy.

7.   Increased militarization is another option, but one that hopefully will be
avoided.

Part III

Present Trends and General Responses: Structural Change, New Regionalisms, Civil Society

5 Europe and the South in the 1990s: Disengagement to the South and Integration to the North of the Sahara

Christopher Stevens

INTRODUCTION

This chapter aims to paint a picture, using a broad brush, of the changes that appear to be underway in EC attitudes and policies towards the South. Its purpose is to explain one of the elements in the external environment facing countries of the South. It is hoped that it will help commentators from the South the better to identify an appropriate development path, avoiding strategies that are based on an unrealistic expectation of the degree and nature of European involvement. But it makes no effort to iden- tify of what such strategies might consist – that is the task of other chapters in this book. The argument of this chapter is that:

- external relations are founded in a mix of political and economic interests;
- the existing pattern of Europe's relations with the South no longer reflects its economic interests as a result of the changing international division of labour;
- although the old pattern might have continued under the weight of government inertia, the single European market (SEM), Eastern Europe and the GATT talks will provoke changes;
- the new pattern will be created by two sets of forces: the changes associated with the SEM and so on are likely to 'downgrade' some LDCs, including many of the poorest; but the higher profile given to issues such as public health, migration and the environment will act in the opposite direction in some cases;

- one result may be a growing politicization of EC relations with Sub-Saharan Africa, illustrated by the inclusion in Lomé IV of structural adjustment;
- these changes will alter the environment in which states of the South have to operate and, inter alia, alter the balance of the argument for and against intra-South (and intra-African) cooperation.

THE PATTERN OF EURO–SOUTH RELATIONS

The Foundations

The present pattern of Europe's relations with the countries of the South has been woven from twelve bilateral sets of policies and a thirteenth, partly cross-cutting, EC-level set. In all cases development aid is only one vehicle for Europe's influence, and usually not the most important. The balance between the bilateral and EC levels is set by the distribution between them of those powers that are most relevant to LDCs.

The extent of EC-level relations is limited by the characteristic of the EC Commission that it does not possess the full array of attributes of a nation state. It cannot conduct a normal foreign or defence policy; even its responsibilities on debt are limited. Among this limited range of instruments there are three principal foundations for EC-level policies affecting the Third World. They are the common commercial policy (CCP), the common agricultural policy (CAP) and the partially common aid policy.

Bilateral interests, such as those of France in Africa, are indulged using both the instruments that have not yet been transferred to EC level and the national element of partially common policies, notably on trade and aid. Although the foundations of Europe's foreign-trade regime are established at EC level, the CCP's purity is reduced in practice as member states adopt to a greater or lesser extent national policies that influence trade flows. Most important are the growing number of non-tariff barriers (NTBs) to imports, such as bilateral voluntary export restraints (VERs) and national quotas within EC NTBs. The precise number of effective national NTBs is unknown, but an indication of their extent may be gauged by analysing member states' recourse to Article 115 of the Treaty of Rome.

During 1988 and the first seven months of 1989, there were sixteen cases of LDC exports being excluded from an EC national market through the use of Article 115, and a similar number of cases in which there was surveillance of imports (Davenport and Page, 1991, p. 43). The import exclusions were imposed in the French, Italian and Spanish markets; the

LDCs affected were Brazil, China, Hong Kong, Singapore and Taiwan; and
the products involved were footwear, umbrellas, toys, car radios, televi-
sions, silk, handtools, sewing machines, slide fasteners, videos, imitation
jewelry and cars.

Only a small part of the aid provided by the EC member states is channelled through EC institutions. The greater part is disbursed either through
the bilateral programmes of each member state or through other intermediaries, such as the multilateral institutions. The proportion of aid that is
channelled through EC institutions varies widely between the member
states (Table 5.1). Of the larger EC states, the UK has the highest proportion of its aid going through the EC (at 26 per cent) and France has the
smallest (at 10 per cent).

Some of the bilateral aid programmes tend to reinforce the geographical
and political bias of EC efforts, but with others the reverse is true. EC aid
has tended to focus on Sub-Saharan Africa, which has accounted for
around 60 per cent of the total over the past fifteen years, and, to a lesser
extent, the Mediterranean and South Asia (see Table 5.2). The principal

Table 5.1   Sources of EC aid,[†] 1990

Member state	Contribution to EC aid	Total aid	Contribution to EC as % of total aid	Share of EC aid %
Belgium	121	732	17	4
Denmark	68	959	7	2
France	764	7778	10	26
Germany	784	5246	15	26
Ireland	23	47	49	1
Italy	435	2768	16	15
Netherlands	192	2156	9	7
United Kingdom	587	2304	26	20

Notes:
[†]ODA net disbursements, $ million at 1989 prices and exchange rates.
Columns may not add up due to rounding.
This table includes only those EC states that are members of the OECD DAC. It
excludes, therefore, Greece, Luxembourg, Portugal and Spain. Except in the case
of Spain, these are relatively small donors; their 1988 ODA was equivalent to
under
2 per cent of disbursement by the other member states.

Source: OECD, *Development Cooperation*, 1991.

Table 5.2 Geographical distribution of EC aid (percentage of gross disbursements)

Countries	Sub-Saharan Africa			South Asia			Other Asia & Oceania			Middle East & North Africa†			Latin America & Caribbean		
	75–6	80–1	89–90	75–6	80–1	89–90	75–6	80–1	89–90	75–6	80–1	89–90	75–6	80–1	89–90
Belgium	66.6	66.0	75.0	5.8	5.0	3.6	8.9	11.9	6.0	12.5	12.2	5.8	6.2	4.9	9.6
Denmark	52.7	51.6	61.3	17.9	31.2	22.5	16.4	8.9	5.2	9.8	6.2	7.1	3.3	2.1	3.9
France	46.5	48.0	54.3	4.2	2.8	2.7	11.1	12.9	14.0	14.6	12.5	9.7	23.6	23.8	19.2
Germany	20.8	29.5	36.4	27.2	20.6	12.3	9.2	9.4	13.6	30.4	28.8	26.2	12.5	11.7	11.4
Ireland	79.8	96.7	95.2	12.5	1.0	1.7	–	0.6	0.3	2.9	0.3	2.1	4.8	1.3	1.0
Italy	24.3	56.1	55.9	18.2	1.7	4.4	6.8	6.6	6.0	45.6	28.1	13.5	5.1	7.5	19.9
Netherlands	19.7	31.2	36.2	24.2	24.9	18.5	14.9	10.6	17.5	4.3	5.4	5.7	36.9	27.9	22.2
United Kingdom	28.4	37.0	50.5	41.0	40.0	26.7	11.6	8.5	10.5	6.5	8.3	4.5	12.5	6.2	7.8
EC	59.6	60.3	64.8	20.8	16.9	10.6	1.9	4.9	5.2	12.4	11.8	7.6	5.4	6.0	11.8

Notes:
†Includes small amounts to Southern Europe.
Percentages in lines add up to 100 per cent for regional distribution in each two-year period for each individual country/institution.

Source: OECD, Development Cooperation, 1991.

differences in current geographical orientation between the EC and the bilateral programmes of the large member states are that the latter tend to give less weight to Africa. Even France has a less dramatic concentration on Sub-Saharan Africa, even though this remains the most important region, and provides a higher proportion of aid to Asia and Latin America/Caribbean. In the case of Germany, the focus on Sub-Saharan Africa is much less marked whilst a higher proportion of aid is directed to South Asia, other Asian countries and the Mediterranean. The most important difference with the UK is that its aid programme gives more prominence to South Asia than does that of the EC.

THE 'PYRAMID OF PRIVILEGE'

The EC has a complex set of over twenty agreements with different LDCs and regional groupings that build upon these foundations to provide a combination of trade preferences, sometimes of CAP products, and of aid. This wide variety of treatment, however, is more apparent than real. In terms of practical provisions the agreements divide into three broad bands that form a hierarchy.

–   At the apex in formal terms are the 69 ACP signatories of the Lomé Conventions.
–   In the middle are the non-EC Mediterranean states, almost all of which have a bilateral agreement with the EC. The formal provisions of the agreements are less favourable than those of the ACP but, because of their location and higher economic base, these countries are often better placed to take advantage of such concessions as exist.
–   At the base are all other LDCs, including South Asia, ASEAN and Latin America, which, despite a rich variety of agreements, all receive the same modest preferences.

They form a hierarchy in the sense that the value of the provisions to those states at the top depends upon their being treated more favourably than those at the base. Hence the Lomé preference on duty-free entry for coffee is of value to Côte d'Ivoire only because its competitor, Brazil, pays 4.5 per cent duty under the Generalized System of Preferences. The extreme case is provided by ACP bananas, which until 1992 enjoyed an absolute preference in the UK, French and Italian markets over non-ACP supplies (and are now subject to controversial new regulations intended to safeguard this position).

In consequence, changes to the treatment of some states affect the value of the preferences accorded to others: improved preferences on clothing for Eastern Europe, for example, would devalue existing preferences to Turkey and Morocco. Whereas generalized liberalization may well be a positive-sum game, a partial extension of preferences that effectively redistributes the rent arising from an artificial restriction of supply is more likely to be a zero-sum game.

The Pattern of Trade

The share of all third parties in total EC imports and exports has fallen since 1960 as the creation of the Common Market has encouraged members to trade with each other (see Figures 5.1 and 5.2). However, whilst non-EC developed countries (DCs) were more severely affected by this decline than were LDCs in the period 1960–75, since then the reverse has been true. The LDC share of EC imports has continued to fall (from almost one quarter in 1975 to only about one eigth by 1990) whilst the DC share has stabilized (and was slightly higher in 1990 than its 1975 level). In the case of EC exports, the DC share has tended to hold up better than that of

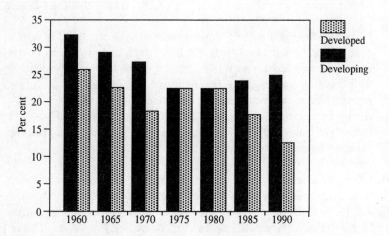

Source: Calculated from data supplied by Eurostat.

Figure 5.1   EC imports from developed and developing countries as a share of total imports (intra and extra), 1960–90

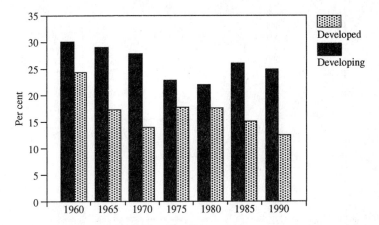

Source: Calculated from data supplied by Eurostat.

Figure 5.2   EC exports to developed and developing countries as a share of total imports (intra and extra), 1960–90

the LDCs throughout the period, although once again the differentially poor LDC performance was more marked during the second part.

The sharpest fall in trade share has been experienced by the ACP. Their share of EC imports from outside the EC fell from 10 per cent in 1960 to 4 per cent by 1990 (Figure 5.3), and a similar picture applies to EC exports (Figure 5.4). The share of Latin America in both imports and exports also fell sharply, whilst that of the Mediterranean and ASEAN held broadly stable. The only states to have experienced a steady rise in trade share are the East Asian NICs of Korea, Taiwan and Hong Kong. Their share of extra-EC imports rose from 1 per cent in 1970 to 5 per cent by 1990, while for exports the rise was somewhat slower: from 1 to 4 per cent.

These changes are related to the commodity composition of trade (Figure 5.5). Over the period there has been a change in the relative importance of various sources for European growth, with non-traded services and intra-developed country trade increasing in relative significance. The distortions caused by the CAP have simply accentuated a trend away from the traditional colonial trade pattern of importing raw materials from the South and exporting manufactures to it. In its place, a trade has developed with parts of the South that emphasises a two-way flow of manufactures and services. The leaders of the new pattern of trade have been, on the European side, the states with relatively weak colonial ties (notably Germany) and, in

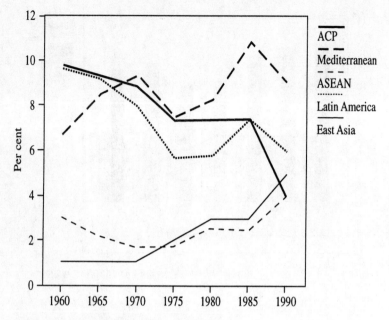

Note: East Asia = Korea, Taiwan, Hong Kong.
Source: Calculated from data supplied by Eurostat.

Figure 5.3   EC imports from developing countries by region as a share of extra-EC imports, 1960–90

the South, the countries of East and Southeast Asia. In contrast, formal development policy has been fashioned largely by the major ex-colonial states (France and the UK) and has focused on the recent colonies.

THE NEW FORCES

Sources of Tension

A striking feature of recent trade patterns is that they are the inverse of the pyramid of privilege: trade has grown fastest with some states at the base of the pyramid and slowest with those at the apex. The principal constraint on further deepening of relations with East and Southeast Asia is not a lack of European interest but its lack of competitiveness vis-à-vis Japan and the United States. In the case of the ACP there has been a substantial decline

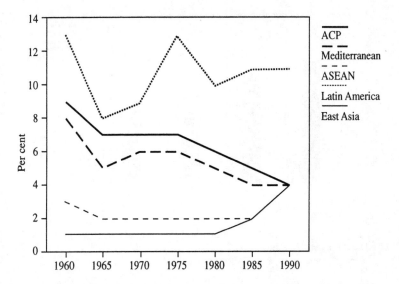

Note: East Asia = Korea, Taiwan, Hong Kong.
Source: Calculated from data supplied by Eurostat.

Figure 5.4   EC exports to developing countries by region as a share of extra-EC imports, 1960–90

first in economic and now, increasingly, in political relations largely as a result of European withdrawal. In contrast, relations with the Mediterranean and the Middle East have remained strong, reflecting substantial European economic and political interests in the region. South Asia and Latin America have retained fairly close links with some member states but have remained on the periphery for the EC as a whole.

A tension has developed, therefore, between the orientation of Europe's economic interests and the orientation of its formal policies towards the South, especially those framed at EC level. The tension has been defused partially up to now because each EC member state has retained control over many of the most potent commercial policy instruments. Germany, for example, may use export credits, investment promotion or debt rescheduling to promote its interests in South-East Asia, regardless of the EC focus on the ACP. Indeed it may prefer the EC to concentrate on the ACP so as not to queer its pitch in Asia. But if further powers are transferred from national to EC level this capacity to run an independent shadow policy will wither; the emphasis of EC level policy acquires a direct importance for national interests.

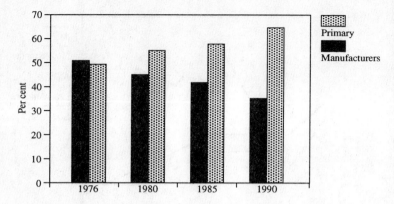

Note: † The value of primary commodities and manufactures in total extra-EC non-oil imports by value.
Source: Calculated from data supplied by Eurostat.

Figure 5.5   The relative importance of primary products and manufactures†

A similar tension has developed on the political front. It can be argued strongly that the region of the South with greatest political and security importance for Europe is the Mediterranean. It is of clear geopolitical importance, not least given the substantial increase in migration and the well-publicized problems of satisfying some Islamic aspirations in European society. Moreover it has borne the brunt of the adverse external consequences of the Iberian enlargement and may do the same for a future extension of the European economic space to the East.

At the same time the potency of other forces that moulded the old pattern has been declining. The panoply of policies that fostered relations with Africa, for example, may be regarded partly as a psychological device to ease the process of decolonization and disengagement for the Europeans. As with the Commonwealth, so francophone and the Lomé Conventions created the appearance that the break between metropole and colony following decolonization was less than total. This was comforting not only to the Europeans but also to the europhile elites in the new states. As time has passed, however, the European need for such psychological support has diminished.

A related point is that post-colonial agreements gave the appearance and, to some extent, the reality of safeguarding traditional markets for both sides. On the European side, however, this was of interest primarily to

France and the UK as the most recent colonial powers. These states have become relatively less powerful influences on Euro–South policy and, in addition, have begun to regard traditional commercial links with Africa as an irrelevance or, worse, a distraction.

As formal policy and effective practice have diverged, the framework of policies established after independence has become increasingly a hollow shell. Despite this the old ways might have continued for some time under the weight of government inertia and the difficulty of devising new policies. The existing policy instruments available to the EC are designed primarily to assist poor, not-very-competitive states; they are not well-suited to the task of reinforcing relations with highly competitive, middle-income states. Attempts to implement more appropriate policies have hit two hurdles: most are dependent upon private- rather than public-sector action, and those that are in the public domain (for example on trade policy) often face strong opposing lobbies.

Recent events, however, have begun to fracture the shell, a process that is likely to intensify in the medium term. The principal agent of change is trade liberalization, externally within the GATT talks and internally with the completion of the single European market (SEM). It is not that the interests of the ACP will be deliberately downgraded in the EC. This suggests a more positive posture than governments are wont to take. Reaction rather than action is the norm. Rather, other problems will force themselves to the top of the pile leaving less time for those that relate to areas of declining economic importance for the EC.

The Effects of External Trade Liberalization

The value of trade preferences to the beneficiary is related inversely to the level of protectionism (at least if the matter is viewed only in a short-term, static perspective). If protection is high the competitive advantage afforded by preferences may be substantial. By the same token, if protection is low the opposite is true. Despite the setbacks on GATT, there is a reasonable chance that the 1990s will be a decade of liberalization. Hence the whole edifice built up over the years by the EC is likely to subside gently as its foundations are weakened by liberalization.

The declining share of the ACP countries in EC trade may appear to cast doubt on the utility of trade preferences and, hence, on the cost of their erosion to the beneficiaries. In fact the case against trade preferences has been overstated. The ACP countries' poor overall performance primarily reflects the fact that their exports are more heavily concentrated than are those of other LDCs on commodities for which world demand is growing slowly and which have suffered serious price falls since 1980. Because of this heavy concentration on traditional primaries, the ACP countries in practice benefit from rather few preferences, despite the apparent liberality of the Lomé texts. The Convention provides them with either zero or very limited preference over their major competitors for the vast majority (around 90 per cent) of their exports.

To receive deep preferences the ACP countries need to diversify their export products. And indeed some states – a minority but not an insignificant one – are beginning to break out of the traditional commodity range and to diversify into precisely those goods for which Lomé preferences are most marked, notably clothing and horticulture (McQueen and Stevens, 1989). Whilst the preferences are only one of many factors affecting exports, there exists circumstantial evidence to suggest that they have had a positive influence (Stevens, 1990; Riddell, 1990; McQueen, 1990). Hence their loss through liberalization could slow down or even suffocate diversification into what are extremely competitive markets. As the two most preferred regions, the ACP and the Mediterranean will face the greatest adjustment to any such generalized liberalization.

The Effects of the Single European Market (SEM)

Since the declining vitality of preference-based policies comes at a time when the pace of European integration is quickening, we may expect that a new edifice will be thrown up to replace the old. The EC institutions will acquire a wider range of powers. Among them, no doubt, will be instruments that are of value to the South and may be used to construct a new relationship.

Why should the new ways not be just as favourable as the old to those states at the apex of the pyramid of privilege? The answer is that to an extent they may, but that full replacement of the old by the new is unlikely for two reasons. The first is that current EC policy reflects the interests of the past; the new policies and practices are more likely to reflect current interests in which the ACP countries, at least, are less prominent. The second is that parts of the ACP region appear to be ill-prepared to take advantage of Europe's new methods and instruments.

The impact of the SEM on LDCs may be profound, simply because it brings into play a host of other issues on which an EC decision will be required to deal with the new circumstances. It is these consequential decisions that may have the most potent effects on Euro–South relations. The removal of border controls as part of the SEM, for example, is removing the power of member states to limit imports from their neighbours, and hence their opportunity to police any national NTBs that may be in place. The very serious problems being faced by Caribbean banana exporters owing to the wind of change blowing through their heavily protected traditional markets in the UK and France represent only an extreme example of a broader issue. The countries that have made most use of national NTBs are France, Ireland and Italy. Those with the fewest restrictions over and above EC-level quotas are Germany and Denmark. Hence states that export primarily to France, Ireland and Italy have more reason to be worried about possible increased competition from the NICs and other third-party exporters than do countries exporting primarily to Germany/Denmark or having a broad geographical spread. France tends to be the largest market for the manufactured exports of both ACP and Mediterranean countries.

Aid provides another example of the indirect effects of the SEM. There are no direct references to development aid in the plan to complete the single European market, but as in many other cases there may be an indirect link. It is not likely that there will be any major changes in the near future but there could be subtle changes in the medium to long term resulting from both the SEM and other facets of European integration. There are four principal reasons why the SEM might have effects on both the absolute level of aid and its distribution.

Procurement

The most straightforward effect on EC aid will occur if the logic of open procurement for internal government contracts is extended to aid. The EC Commission's programme of directives designed to create the SEM includes measures that would require each EC member state to accept tenders from companies based in other member states when awarding contracts for public works. There are no plans at present to extend this open procurement policy to aid contracts, but it is clearly within the 'spirit of 1992' that this should happen in due course. The Netherlands government has indicated a readiness to open procurement, but only if other members increase their aid/GNP ratios to the high Dutch level! If in due course procurement is widened it would tend to improve the value for money of the member states' bilateral aid by allowing recipients to source goods and services from the cheapest EC supplier.

Aid volume

A second, less desirable, effect may follow from this. If the member states are able no longer to use their programmes to support domestic industries they may become less willing to provide aid. The quality of the aid cake may improve but its size may diminish. The impact of both the open-procurement and the aid-volume effects will vary between LDCs. Both will tend to be greater in respect of those states (donors and recipients) to which aid is currently tied.

Aid channels

There may be a third effect on the channels through which aid is provided. At present only around one eighth of the aid provided by the twelve EC states is channelled through EC institutions. The remainder is disbursed bilaterally, through the multilateral institutions or via non-governmental organizations. Open procurement may reduce the member-states' interest in running their own bilateral programmes. It could lead, therefore, to a diversion of aid to the EC level and/or to one of the other delivery vehicles.

Diversion

The remaining potential effects concern the possible diversion of aid away from some existing beneficiaries. This may have both intra- and extra-EC facets. The creation of the SEM will cause serious adjustment problems for some parts of the EC. There will be pressure to increase budget spending in support of depressed parts of the EC. If there is also a tight budget constraint this increase in intra-EC aid may occur at the expense of extra-EC aid.

At the same time, some LDCs will be more adversely affected by the SEM than others. The Caribbean, for example, may eventually lose its banana exports to the UK. The Mediterranean states may face stiffer competition from a more efficient post-1992 Europe or may suffer from increased EC protectionism. There will be a tendency to offer increased aid to states most seriously affected, particularly if they have a strong political or security importance for Europe (as does the Mediterranean). And, again, if budget constraints are tight this may be at the expense of the LDCs that are not so obviously affected.

The Impact of Eastern Europe

A further source of shock to the shell of formal Euro–South relations is to be found in the EC's need to redefine its policies towards its Eastern neighbours, although this time the ACP (but not the Mediterranean) should be spared negative effects. A successful shift to a free-market economy in Eastern Europe is likely to be accompanied by an increased demand for external capital and greater exports of basic manufactures and temperate agricultural products. Failure to make the adjustment successfully could result in an increase in outward migration.

In either case the tendency would be to increase competition for some LDCs in the short term (although in the longer term the boost to world output and demand could benefit all). Eastern Europe will be competitive with the Mediterranean in particular as a host for foreign direct investment and a borrower of commercial and semi-commercial funds; as a supplier of manufactured exports to the Community; and as a source of migrant workers.

In contrast the ACP could benefit if rising incomes in Eastern Europe result in an increase in world demand for tropical products. Eastern Europe is one of the few areas of the world in which substantial increases in per capita consumption of tropical products could occur in the medium term.

The Jokers in the Pack

Extrapolation from the past suggests a European withdrawal from the ACP, continued efforts in Asia and neglect in Latin America, plus political fire-fighting in the Mediterranean; but, as everyone knows, extrapolation from the past is frequently misleading. Are there any new features of Euro–South relations that might counsel caution in predicting such changes? Among the factors that loom on the horizon are migration, the environment and public health.

Whilst the broad nature of these issues may be stated simply, it is far from clear how they may affect EC policies. In all three cases LDCs are perceived by EC governments as a source of danger which they may seek to remove by direct involvement. But probably the degree of involvement that is politically acceptable will fall far short of what is needed to remove the danger.[1]

The problem may be observed most clearly in relation to migration. The perceived danger is that markedly unequal rates of population and economic growth on the northern and southern shores of the Mediterranean are creating pressures for migration flows into the EC that exceed politically tolerable levels. Commission officials talk of the Straits of Gibraltar as being 'Europe's Rio Grande'.

The Mediterranean periphery is already the main source of legally registered aliens (and probably of illegals as well). Of the 12.9 million aliens residing legally in the EC in 1987, 7.9 million originated outside the EC and some 75 per cent of these came from the Mediterranean periphery (Tovias, 1991). Over four million of the non-EC aliens are in the economically active social groups. They still form a very small share of the total EC population of 324 million, but they are not evenly spread among member states. The two principal hosts are Germany (with 41 per cent of the 1987 stock) and France (with 27 per cent). These two countries also have the highest proportions of non-EC foreign workers in relation to their labour force: 3.6 per cent in the case of Germany and 2.3 per cent for France (with Luxembourg, the UK, the Netherlands, Belgium and Denmark having shares of over 1 per cent but less than 2 per cent). Estimates of illegal migrants reach up to one million in France, 600 000 in Italy and 90 000 to 170 000 in Spain; in May 1991, 5000 illegal Moroccan workers were expelled from Spain in a single week (Tovias, 1991).

The numbers wishing to migrate can only increase. Current demographic projections put the population of Turkey at 65 million in the year 2000 and that of the three Maghreb states at 72 million (an increase of 28 million over 1988). It is improbable that their economies will expand sufficiently rapidly to absorb all of this increase in the labour force. One ILO forecast is that there will be some four million people of working age unable to find suitable work in these four countries by the end of the decade (Tovias, 1991).

This increased supply of potential migrants will face competition from other sources. After a decade in which the flow of new legal immigrants fell to very low levels (less than 0.1 per cent of the EC population), there has been an upsurge in the past three years. This has been due largely to inflows from Eastern Europe into Germany. Although this flow may have fallen off following the revolutions, the experience of population movements between the eastern and western parts of Germany suggests that there remains strong potential for economic migration from the east. If growth is slow (as is quite likely in the short term) the movement of people will continue. Moreover, one effect of post-1992 industrial rationalization could be an increase of unemployment in the EC periphery and, with the free movement of labour, greater intra-EC migration.

Even without the undoubted racist pressures to exclude non-white migrants, this increase in potential supply is a source of concern. The response of the EC so far has been to try to improve conditions in the supplying states in order to reduce the desire to emigrate. One of the explicit aims of the renewed Mediterranean policy of the EC is to give aid to the Mediterranean periphery for labour-absorbing activities. But it is most unlikely that this will make any significant difference; it smacks of the need to be seen to be doing something. Studies on rural–urban migration inside LDCs indicate that conditions in the source area have to be improved very considerably (or those in the host area worsened greatly) before there is any major effect. People take the decision to migrate if they have the possibility of a job in the urban area; for them to decide to stay at home there has to be an actual job for them.

If this is the case, what can the EC do? It might put pressure on its neighbours to enforce 'voluntary export restraint' in the case of labour. But VERs on goods work for two reasons: they offer the exporter a share of the rent that arises from the artificial restriction in supply, and they are backed by the threat of recourse to other restrictions that have no offsetting benefit for the exporter. In other words there is both a carrot and a stick. Moreover both the exporting and importing states are normally sufficiently in control to enforce any deal that they make; smuggling into DCs reaches serious proportions only in respect of very high-unit-value goods such as drugs.

None of these preconditions applies to migration. Unless the EC and source states enter into the kind of agreements that have applied to workers in the South African mines, whereby a part of migrants' earnings is remitted direct to their government, there is no 'carrot' for the countries of surplus population in restricting supply. Indeed if the choice for them is between chronic unemployment leading to social strife in the EC or at home they may well prefer the former. Nor are the potential sticks very effective: the EC may restrict legal immigration or threaten reprisals in other areas if its neighbours do not impose emigration controls, but the effectiveness of such actions will be limited by illegal migration.

Precisely the same conundrum applies in the cases of the environment and public health. The threat is clear enough but the same cannot be said for the defensive actions that the EC might take. The extent (and expense) of effective action is likely to be politically unacceptable; what is politically feasible will be ineffective.

In one case the concern is that actions such as deforestation are being taken in LDCs, with or without the connivance of governments, that are damaging the environment not only in the country concerned but, directly or indirectly, in the EC as well (for an appropriate example of environmental 'spillover', see Chapter 10 below). In the other case the concern is that, with the explosion of global travel, diseases originating or endemic in LDCs are being transmitted to Europe.

The EC could attempt to use bribes (such as aid or debt relief) or threats (for example trade barriers) to persuade LDC governments to clean up their acts, but there are many circumstances in which these would be ineffective. In most cases the bribes would have to be very large – either to eradicate the source of the problem, as in the case of public health, or to provide a financially viable alternative to the unacceptable practices. Even if they were sufficiently large, and almost certainly if they were not, LDC government promises of good behaviour would have to be treated with scepticism. Promises of action may fail to be translated into deeds either because the government is insincere in its commitment or because it lacks the necessary implementation capacity.

The experience of the 'policy-based lending' of the IMF and the World Bank during the 1980s provides a salutary lesson on the limits of financial leverage. As the international financial institutions (IFIs) have increased their support for combined stabilization and structural adjustment programmes (SAPs) so the number of loan conditions related to politically sensitive macroeconomic policies has grown. Recipient governments have agreed to all manner of conditions, ranging from changes to budget and taxation policy to privatization, as the price of obtaining desperately needed foreign exchange. Except in cases of a clear 'ideological conversion', with the government committed to the same agenda as the IFIs, few of these conditions have been fully adhered to (Mosley *et al.*, 1991). Yet, compared with the requirements for environmental and health improvement, the conditions attached to SAPs are relatively easy for governments to adopt and for donors to monitor.

Structural Adjustment in Lomé IV

Experience from the application of policy-based conditionality now has a more than academic interest for the EC as structural adjustment has been incorporated into the Lomé framework. This raises the possibility that the Convention, first hailed as a partnership of equals on the road to a new international economic order, will become increasingly a patron–client relationship as ACP countries' dependence on EC handouts increases and European interest in African markets declines.

The EC has become involved in structural adjustment because it could not avoid it. Although no formal provisions for structural adjustment lending were made in Lomé III (1985–90), during the course of implementation it became clear that supplementary facilities were required. In 1987 the EC launched a 'special Community programme to aid certain highly indebted low-income countries in Sub-Saharan Africa'. This was a package of money administered outside the formal Lomé framework, although it had been cobbled together from bits and pieces saved or transferred from Lomés I–III plus a small amount of additional money. Its aim was to provide quasi balance-of-payments support to low-income African states.

The new programme arose because the difficulty confronting the EC and ACP countries was that, in a country facing acute 'import strangulation', traditional methods of spending aid were simply unviable. The conventional approach of financing a discrete project risked being, at best, an irrelevance and, at worst, a distraction (of human skills and recurrent resources). During the Lomé IV negotiations, therefore, the question of formally incorporating structural adjustment in the package was confronted head on. The two key questions were: what proportion of the Lomé IV resources should be available for structural adjustment and what proportion for traditional activities such as projects, Stabex and so on. And, within the structural adjustment component, what stance should Lomé take on policy-based lending. Under the traditional Lomé arrangement the EC has imposed relatively few controls on the use of aid. But, given that the IMF/World Bank were gaily imposing pages of policy conditions, a decision by the EC not to become involved would result simply in Washington-based institutions' requirements going unchecked. On the other hand, if the EC did become involved it had to decide what its 'conditions' would be.

The compromise to result from the Lomé negotiations is that there are several channels under the present Convention through which the EC can provide quasi balance-of-payments support to the ACP countries. One part, the largest, is a special structural adjustment facility. This totals Ecu 1.15 billion, equivalent to 14 per cent of the total 'programmable grants' of Lomé (that is, excluding Stabex, Sysmin and risk capital). This will be made available to those ACP countries that apply and are deemed to be worthy. As in past Conventions, the rest of the programmable grants will be preallocated to each member of the ACP group and used for purposes decided upon jointly during the course of the Convention. There are various facilities for using part of these national allocations for quasi balance-of-payments support. The extent to which the ACP countries will request that this be done, and the extent to which the EC will approve such requests, remains to be seen. However it has been suggested that the volume of quasi balance-of-payments support through these national programmes may reach broadly the same level as the special structural adjustment facility. In which case, of course, the total provided for structural adjustment would approach 30 per cent of the package. In addition it is possible for the EC to provide food aid, which is outside the Lomé framework, to those countries engaged in structural adjustment, thus increasing still further the volume of resources in support of the programme.

The judgement to be made on these compromises depends very much upon the observer's views about structural adjustment. If one believes that some form of structural adjustment is necessary and that past efforts have been undermined by inadequate funding, then the involvement of Lomé can be welcomed as potentially a move in the right direction. The addition of Lomé resources may help the structural adjustment exercise to reach 'critical mass' and the involvement of the EC as a third party (between the

ACP and the IMF/World Bank) may lead to an improvement in the policy conditionality being applied to all structural adjustment funds. If, on the other hand, one believes that structural adjustment is an inherently flawed mechanism and that other uses of aid are better (as is suggested by Ihonvbere, McBain and others in later chapters of this book), then the Lomé IV compromise must be deemed to be, at best, a disappointment.

What evidence do we have that the EC is using its influence to promote better policy conditionality? The answer is that, so far, there is very little evidence either way. The EC Commission has tended to characterize the difference between its own style and that of the IMF/World Bank in terms of pragmatism versus textbook theory. It argues that although some of the policies advanced by the IMF/World Bank may be correct according to the current conventional theoretical wisdom they may not work in practice, either because LDC governments do not give them wholehearted support or because of fundamental design flaws owing to the different circumstances found in LDCs. With its lengthy experience of the ACP countries and the fundamentally different political relationship that exists between the Lomé partners compared with the IMF/World Bank and their debtors, the Commission claims that it can bring to structural adjustment a missing element of political and economic realism.

But it is far from clear how such an involvement in structural adjustment would operate in practice. The Commission has acknowledged the need not to present the ACP states with two conflicting sets of policy recommendations. But this implies that those agencies involved in structural adjustment must either agree ex ante a compromise package of conditionality or agree ex post to operate their separate programmes in such a way that they do not interfere with each other. It is inherent in the idea of compromise that there is give and take on both sides. Hence coordination implies that to a certain degree the Commission will alter its approach to fit in with the requirements of the IMF/World Bank as well as the reverse.

The Commission's response to such arguments is that it does not envisage having its own 'policy package' to impose upon the ACP countries. Rather it would tend to support ACP countries governments when they seek to amend the proposals of the IMF/World Bank to make them more politically acceptable and development oriented. The question mark that must hang over this position concerns the extent to which ACP states are able to articulate a coherent rejoinder to the conditionality proposed by the IMF/World Bank. Without such an autonomous policy package to relate to, the Commission will be left with a choice between accepting the IMF/World Bank approach or devising its own. Not the least of the obstacles in the way of the latter alternative is the acute lack of the appropriate skills in

Brussels; the Commission has created only a small unit to handle structural adjustment.

Whatever happens, it seems likely that the EC's entry into structural adjustment will increase the 'politicization' of Lomé. There exists already evidence of increased politicization of IFI decisions on country programmes, which undermines the legitimacy and effectiveness of the adjustment movement. The resulting lack of uniformity of treatment across countries has been near-scandalous in some cases and, in particular, has led to the diversion of major amounts of scarce resources to governments with little serious intention of implementing rigorous adjustment policies.

Consider the procedure likely to be adopted to deal with structural-adjustment requests to the EC by ACP states that are in policy disagreement with the IFIs. Like traditional aid projects, they will be assessed by a committee representing the EC member states. Some EC states (notably the UK and the Netherlands) are much keener to impose IFI-type conditions than are others (notably France and Italy). It is likely that requests from ACP states with close political relations with France, Italy or like-minded states will receive an easier passage than those with closer ties to the UK. In other words, Senegal will get the money but Zambia will not.

CONCLUSION

Whilst the direction of economic and political relationships may diverge for a period it is usually the case that in the longer term they move in the same direction. Hence Europe's relations with the poorest countries will tend to atrophy while those with states that are richer and growing faster will be reinforced. This analysis does not imply that Europe's relationship with Sub-Saharan Africa will collapse tomorrow. But it is reasonable to infer that, as shocks arise over time, they will be dealt with more effectively when they concern Asia and the Mediterranean than when Black Africa and Latin America are involved. The first test was the response of France and its partners to the growing stresses in the franc zone (ODI, 1990); there was a dramatic devaluation in early 1994.

Even so it is probably not realistic to expect a total withdrawal from an entire region. Even in the relatively neglected areas there will continue to be pockets of interest defined in relation to commercial, political or environmental/health/migration concerns. Moreover humanitarian concerns may continue to sustain some relations in the areas that lack economic or political interest, but at a lower level than in the past.

Whether the aim is to return the LDC to a path of sustainable development, or to restore a collapsing civil order, or to head off emigration/
environmental destruction, the EC or the member states will be forced into
a more interventionist posture than most have been wont to take in the past.
The shift within the Lomé Convention away from traditional aid projects
(available to the ACP countries as of right) towards structural adjustment
grants (to be approved on a case-by-case basis) is a straw in the wind.
Humanitarian aid to the states outside the inner circle will not necessarily
be spared such politicization. The non-governmental organizations that
have been given an increased role as delivery vehicles for such aid over the
past decade often have very pronounced views on the political agenda in
recipient states which they seek to enforce via their local counterparts (see
Chapter 7 below).

Since such conditionality is unlikely to remove the 'new dangers' even
in the circle of favoured states, let alone those outside, it is not unreason-
able to expect that in addition the EC will reinforce its external barriers.
The fear of a 'fortress Europe' has been expressed primarily in relation to
goods; perhaps it is more realistic to expect it to emerge in relation to
people: tighter border controls; more stringent health checks on aliens. In
any event, the free movement of labour after 1992 will require changes to
member-state policies.

Note

1.   This section will not enter into a debate on the validity of the perception, or
     of its morality given that on several scores Europe is, or has been, among the
     guilty parties. It simply identifies issues that EC governments may consider –
     rightly or wrongly – to pose threats, and the responses that they may wish to
     make.

6 Regional Approaches to Security in the Third World: Lessons and Prospects

Amitav Acharya

INTRODUCTION

This chapter is an historical and conceptual analysis of regional approaches to security in the Third World. Such an exercise is important and timely for two reasons. First, the study of regionalism in the literature of international relations has suffered undue neglect in recent years; the academic disillusionment with the subject in the mid-1970s obscures the proliferation of regional institutions in both the developed and developing worlds (see, for example, Taylor, 1990, pp. 151–71). Secondly, the end of the Cold War has brought about fundamental shifts in global and regional alignments, calling for new approaches to peace and security. As Third World countries explore new security strategies to deal with the dangers and uncertainties of a multipolar world, the relevance of regional approaches has become an important policy concern, meriting a fresh appraisal of the historical record of existing regional groups and exploring the possibilities of new approaches opened up by the end of superpower rivalry.

This chapter has two main aims. The first is to analyse the various frameworks of regionalism in the international system of the postwar era and to assess their performance in the Third World context. The second is to examine the changing role of regional organizations, especially in the aftermath of the Cold War. Emerging patterns of regionalism in the Third World are assessed in order to derive some broad conclusions about the continued relevance of regionalism as an approach to order and stability in the Third World.

THREE FRAMEWORKS FOR REGIONAL SECURITY COOPERATION

In the postwar era three conceptions of regionalism provided influential frameworks for addressing the security concerns of developing countries. Each of these frameworks, though not mutually exclusive, found expression through a particular type of regional organization. An examination of these frameworks provides the necessary background to consideration of more recent attempts at regionalism in the Third World.

Hegemonic Regional Systems

Regionalism as an approach to security received little attention in the Eurocentric international system of the prewar period (Hinsley, 1963, pp. 242–55). The idealist thinking that emerged triumphant after the First World War emphasised the need for a universal collective security system, while regional arrangements were equated with 'old-fashioned' military alliances of the nineteenth-century balance-of-power system. But the failure of the League of Nations revived interest in regionalism as an alternative to idealist universalist principles (cf. Banks, 1969, and MacDonald, 1965). Regional arrangements at this time meant the geostrategic spheres of influence of existing or prospective great powers.

Against this backdrop the first framework of regionalism was articulated by realist thinkers and policy-makers in the interwar period, especially E.H. Carr, Walter Lippmann and Winston Churchill. Walter Lippmann, for example, identified four such regional systems: an Atlantic system managed by the United States and the USSR; a Russian system; a Chinese system; and eventually an Indian system. Within such hegemonic regional systems 'the preponderance of a great power was to be recognised; each small power was to accept the protection of the great power in whose region it found itself, and was to forego the right to form alliances with any extra-regional power' (Bull, 1977, pp. 222–3).

But this notion of 'hegemonic regionalism' did not gain immediate acceptance. With the outbreak of the Second World War the idea of a universal collective-security organization once again exerted a powerful appeal among nations. The momentum towards the formation of the UN saw a debate between the so-called 'universalists' and the 'regionalists' regarding which constituted the better approach to conflict resolution. Although multipurpose regional organizations such as the Organization of American States (OAS) and the Arab League were accepted as legitimate players in the proposed universal collective-security system, they were made subordinate to the authority of the newly established United Nations.

But with the advent of the Cold War hegemonic regionalism made a forceful comeback. Two factors accounted for this. The first was the failure of the UN to fulfill its promise. The second was the failure of non-hegemonic Third World regional groups, especially the Arab League, in developing effective alliance roles. Power aggregation in the case of non-aligned Third World regional alliances, as Liska (1968, pp. 50–4) put it, was 'an aggregation ... of weakness' while the participants 'continue[d] to derive their real security, both internal and external, from markedly unintegrated and even merely de facto alliances with extraregional great powers'. Realist conceptions of regionalism at this stage stressed the need for alliances within 'great-power orbits' as a viable approach to Third World security. The escalating superpower rivalry in the Third World provided ideal conditions for the realization of such frameworks. The United States, after the creation of NATO, turned its attention to the Third World, sponsoring alliances with newly independent states as part of its policy of containing the communist threat. This quest led to the formation of the Southeast Asia Treaty Organization (SEATO) and the Central Treaty Organization (CENTO). The Soviet Union's attempt to match the US effort in the Third World was considerably less successful, as is evident from the stillborn idea of an Asian Collective Security System mooted by the Brezhnev regime.

But transplanting European-style regional-security alliances in the Third World proved to be an elusive goal for the United States as well. The weaknesses of these groupings stemmed largely from the tremendous disparities of power between the Western and Third World partners and the consequent sense of being manipulated experienced by the latter (Liska, 1968, p. 36; Yalem, 1973, p. 225). In addition the decline and eventual demise of these alliances can be attributed to three factors: the problems of 'credibility', 'relevance' and 'compatibility'. The credibility of these groups suffered from weak commitments on the part of the great-power patrons. While in the case of NATO the US response to Soviet aggression was assumed to be automatic, the Asian allies in CENTO and SEATO were disappointed by the lower level of assurances and security guarantees offered by the United States. The question of relevance or utility arose because security objectives diverged between the great-power partners on the one hand and their Third World clients. The global nature of US security interests and its ability to concentrate its resources within one theatre was seen to conflict with the regional security environments in which security challenges to its allies were largely indigenous in origin. Many of the Third

World partners saw internal challenges to regime survival as the main threat to security, rather than the overt communist aggression or subversion that had been advanced by the United States as the major rationale for creating these groupings. Neither did the Cold War alliances provide for any mechanism for conflict resolution. Given that intraregional conflicts were more serious challenges to Third World alliance partners than external communist aggression, the relevance and utility of these groups were questionable (Miller, 1973, p. 62).

The Cold War alliances also suffered from what may be called global and regional incompatibility. They were at odds with the political aspirations and visions of the great majority of the Third World states who preferred non-alignment over the great-power security umbrella. In this sense Cold War alliances in the Third World generated greater instability by inciting great-power rivalry in the regional theatres since alliance with one superpower was sure to invite response and competitive coalition building by the other superpower.

The final blow to Cold War-oriented regional-security alliances was the superpower détente of the early 1970s, which severely undermined the credibility of the US commitment to anti-Soviet regional coalitions in the Third World. Détente also raised the unsavory prospect of a superpower condominium that might compromise or ignore the security interests of the Third World states in general. Faced with these prospects, the Third World clients in Cold War alliances chose to change tack and distance themselves from superpower spheres of influence, thereby rendering them rapidly obsolete. The disbanding of SEATO in 1975 and CENTO in 1979 are cases in point.

Regionalism as Conflict Control

While the idealists successfully resisted the idea of hegemonic regional groups at the birth of the UN, they were to concede some ground to a somewhat different 'regionalist' coalition that opposed unbridled universalism without necessarily advocating the principle of 'great-power orbit'. This coalition comprised representatives of the Latin American states, who saw an all-powerful UN as a threat to the autonomy of the OAS, and some of the newly independent or soon to be independent countries (especially in the Arab world) that espoused the dual principles of equality and autonomy within regional groupings, neither being available from the hegemonic frameworks or from the UN.

In arguing their case with the 'universalists', the 'regionalists' advanced a number of arguments (see, for example, Padelford, 1954, and Wilcox, 1965):

- Geographic neighbours have a better understanding of local disputes than distant actors operating through a global body; and the former are better able to provide assistance to victims of aggression than the latter.
- Regional groups, by undertaking peaceful settlement of local disputes, would act as 'stepping stones' to global order by promoting the 'habit' of cooperation.
- The mediation role of regional groups would deny outside powers, especially the superpowers, the opportunity to intervene and escalate the conflict from its local level.

These arguments constituted what may be called a second framework of regionalism in the international political system. While the realist vision was represented in Cold War alliances, the second framework was best represented in the three 'original' macroregional political groups, the OAS, the Arab League and the Organization of African Unity (OAU) (created in 1963). Apart from the emphasis on peaceful settlement of disputes among their members, in the case of the Arab League and the OAU this framework of regionalism was committed to the process of regional autonomy, including decolonisation and resistance to external interventions within the region.

Yet this framework also faced major limitations and failures in the Third World. It was the OAS which proved to be the most successful initially at the task of conflict-resolution, a fact attributed to the special position of the organization having a superpower, the United States, as its dominant member (Haas, 1986, p. 31). The OAU and the Arab League, more representative of the needs and aspirations of the newly independent nations, presented a contrasting picture. Instead of developing long-term and stable institutions to facilitate conflict resolution, the League and the OAU degenerated into highly personalized and politicized processes of diplomacy that achieved little success in settling the myriad interstate conflicts unleashed by the decolonisation process. Furthermore both groups proved to be more or less incapable of handling intrastate conflicts such as civil wars, which accounted for a large percentage of conflict in the Third World.

Perhaps the major irony, and the most serious challenge to the effectiveness of these groupings, was the fact that the major conflicts in their respective regions were directly concerned with the role of a non-member country or countries. Thus the Arab League was faced with Israel, the OAU with South Africa and Rhodesia, and the OAS with Cuba. This led to the distortion of their originally intended roles: instead of controlling conflict, they assumed alliance postures vis-à-vis the regional pariahs that were not subject to their jurisdiction or norms (Wilcox, 1965).

The credibility and effectiveness of the original regional organizations suffered serious erosion in the 1970s and 1980s. Moreover, throughout this period and into the 1990s the UN and the regional groups competed with each other; hence the decline of regional groups can at least be partly explained by the success of the UN. Haas's conclusion, that 'there is no global division of labour among conflict management agencies now, and there probably never was', is significant for the contemporary period, in which the UN's useful role in several regional conflicts (Afghanistan, the Gulf War, Angola, Namibia, Cambodia and to a lesser extent Central America) contrasts sharply with the failure of the original regional organizations in handling such disputes (Haas, 1986, p. 29–34). Particularly noteworthy is the virtual irrelevance of the OAS in the Nicaragua–El Salvador conflict, the total failure of the Arab League to deal with the Lebanese crisis, the Iran–Iraq War and the Iraqi invasion of Kuwait, and the OAU's lack of effectiveness in the Morocco–Polsario and Chad conflicts.

Regional Security Communities

With the demise of the Cold War alliances and the decline of the original groups, another conception of regionalism became prominent towards the late 1950s and early 1960s. This was rooted firmly within the liberal tradition. Its most sophisticated expression was regional integration theory.[1] Integration theorists were not directly concerned with security in its traditional 'high-politics' sense. Hegemonic regionalism found expression through Cold War regional alliances and the conflict-control framework through macroregional political groups. The third framework was realised through microregional economic organizations, of which the original model was provided by the European Economic Community. From the vast conceptual terrain of integration theorists, two central ideas established a crucial link between regional integration and regional security. The neofunctionalist school, following the lead of classical functionalist David Mitrany, emphasised the notion of spillover. This theory postulated that issue-based regional cooperation in areas of 'lesser salience' could eventually move national actors towards a path of cooperation in areas of higher salience, including political and security cooperation. According to this logic, if functional regional groups could successfully foster economic integration, regional security would ensure that the actors would, over a period of time, learn to resolve their conflicts peacefully and come to cooperate on common security issues. The transactionalist or communication approach pioneered by Karl Deutsch and his associates (1957, p. 2) contributed the influential concept of 'security community' as the end product of such integration. A security community comes into existence when a regional group develops 'institutions and practices strong enough and stable enough to assure, for a "long" time, stable expectations of "peaceful change" within its population'. Security communities could either be 'amalgamated' through formal political merger of the participating units, or remain 'pluralistic', in which case the members would remain formally independent. In either case security communities are characterised by 'mutual interdependence of diverse political units; mutual responsiveness of political units; and simple pacification or the abandonment of the use of force among political units' (Yalem, 1979, p. 217).

Several regional-security communities now exist in the developed West, the most prominent example being the EC. In contrast, such communities are virtually non-existent in the Third World. Although in the Third World several microregional groups over the past three decades have sought to emulate the EC, none has succeeded in achieving a level of integration that would create the conditions for a security community, whether of the amalgamated or the pluralistic variety. Neither has economic regionalism based on the EC model – involving market centralization and generation of welfare gains – produced the desired 'spillover' effect leading to cooperation over security issues. Microregional integration groups, which proliferated in Africa and Latin America, have 'founder[ed] on the reefs of distrust, non-cooperation and parochial nationalism', thereby raising basic questions regarding the applicability of a functionalist approach to the Third World (Duffy and Feld, 1980, p. 497).

The limits of the regional integration experience in the Third World are most evident in Latin America, once thought to have the best potential for such experiments. The Central American Common Market, initially regarded as the very model of the neofunctionalist approach, suffered a long paralysis. The Latin American Free Trade Area was abolished in 1980; its members, experiencing different levels of development and conflicts over the distribution of benefits among them, realised the futility of developing a free-trade area and a common market. African regional integration efforts have foundered with the eclipse of the East African Community and the UDEAC. Only the more recently formed Economic Community of West African States (ECOWAS), set up in 1975, has shown some potential for integration, but ECOWAS is a long way from realising its promise of 'an economic Union that coordinates domestic policies at the regional level' (see Okolo, 1985, pp. 121–53). The problems experienced by microregional economic groupings also casts serious doubts on the likelihood of the creation of an African Economic Community by the year

2000 (see Chapters 8 and 9 below) or the success of newly (re)formed economic groups in the Caribbean (see Chapters 12 and 13) and Central Asia (see Chapter 10).

The foregoing analysis shows that all the three principal regional approaches to security, conceived in the West, did not find durable institutional expressions in the Third World. Yet, regional approaches have continued to emerge, albeit with new institutional forms and different, sometimes wider, sets of security objectives (see the country and regional case studies below).

REGIONALISM IN TRANSITION: THE RISE AND DECLINE OF SUBREGIONALISM

The decline of the OAU, the OAS and the Arab League coincided with the emergence of subregional frameworks for conflict mediation and management in the Third World (see, for example, Tow, 1990). Several of these groupings became prominent in the late 1970s and early 1980s, such as the Association of Southeast Asian Nations (ASEAN), the Gulf Cooperation Council (GCC), the Contadora group, the South Pacific Forum, the Economic Community of West African States (ECOWAS), the Front Line States of Southern Africa (FLS), the Organization of Eastern Caribbean States (OECS), the South Asian Association for Regional Cooperation (SAARC), the Arab Cooperation Council and the Greater Maghreb Union.

To some degree their goals were similar to those of the original regional groupings, especially in the area of conflict resolution. Yet a closer look reveals some important of differences, especially when one looks at the role of the three most important of such groupings: the Association of Southeast Asian Nations (ASEAN), the Gulf Cooperation Council (GCC) and the Contadora framework.

ASEAN and the GCC shared an important feature not found in the original regional groupings. Both were subregional political groups that emerged in response to a commonly perceived security threat linked to a revolutionary insurrection within their respective neighbourhoods (see Acharya, 1992, pp. 143–62). Thus ASEAN's security role was a direct response to the communist victories in Indochina and the subsequent Vietnamese invasion of Cambodia. The GCC, set up in 1981, was similarly a response by the conservative Gulf states to the threats posed by the Islamic revolution in Iran and the outbreak of the Iran–Iraq War. Although these groupings performed conflict regulation at the subregional level, that is, conflicts among their members, they were agents of conflict creation. By limiting their membership to ideologically compatible regional states they aggravated the Cold War divisions existing within their respective regions. This in turn was a major factor undermining the credibility and effectiveness of their conflict-mediation role (ASEAN in the Cambodia conflict and the GCC in the Iran–Iraq War).

The role of the Contadora group in the Central American conflict spurred by the revolution in Nicaragua was in marked contrast to the role of ASEAN and GCC. Like the member regimes of ASEAN and GCC, the neighbouring states of Nicaragua felt vulnerable to a revolutionary upheaval in the neighbourhood that brought to power a regime intent on exporting its radicalism throughout the region. As Kenneth Roberts (1990, p. 69) points out, 'Nicaragua's mix of Marxism and revolutionary national-ism clashed with the moderate-to-conservative regimes in surrounding states, most of which were close political allies of the United States and wary of the destabilising effects of a revolutionary neighbor'. But unlike ASEAN and GCC, which in effect used their subregional frameworks to legitimize their external (US) security linkages, regional peace efforts by the Contadora group actually 'constrained US policy options and shielded Nicaragua from US coercion'. At the same time, partly in exchange of their effort, they succeeded in exerting 'pressure on the Sandinista government to make political concessions in order to facilitate a settlement' which led to the end of the Contra War and to Nicaraguan acceptance of the democratic elections that produced the downfall of the Sandinista regime.

Another trend in regional approaches to security in the Third World in the 1970s and 1980s was the emergence of subregional defence coopera-tion. Attempts by the original regional organizations to develop such arrangements have had not been successful, as is evident in the failure of the OAU in developing an African High Command (Imobighe, 1980) or the Arab League's failure to mobilize its collective defence provisions against Israel (MacDonald, 1965). The relative compactness and homogeneity of subregional groups was more suited for defence cooperation. Among the subregional groups, the GCC (Acharya, 1989; Guazanne, 1988), the Regional Security System (RSS) comprising members of the OECS and Barbados (Lewis, 1986), and the collective security and defence provisions of ECOWAS developed such arrangements (Okolo, 1985).

Unlike alliances in the conventional mould, which usually focus on external threats, these groupings are geared against both external and inter-nal threats. In case of GCC, RSS and ASEAN, internal security cooperation (including intelligence sharing) received greater emphasis than external defence. The ECOWAS framework allowed collective intervention in domestic strife, as demonstrated in its recent intervention in Liberia

(Inegbedion, 1992a). In general, subregional groups proved more effective in the area of internal security than in ensuring external defence. Although military cooperation initially developed as a means to reduce the dependence of the regional actors on outside security guarantees, the collective ability of regional actors was not adequate to meet the perceived threats. The subregional groups are incapable of achieving self-reliance in defence and security. For many, regionalism was not a substitute for reliance on external security guarantees. As a result little progress was achieved in the realization of more ambitious forms of defence cooperation geared to external threats such as a joint intervention force (GCC, ECOWAS), joint military exercises (ASEAN, GCC), weapon standardization (GCC, ASEAN) and the development of a joint defence industry (ASEAN, GCC). The only possible exception is ECOWAS, which in 1990 carried out a large-scale, partially successful intervention in Liberia to contain a bloody civil war among tribal factions (Inegbedion, 1992b).

REGIONAL SECURITY ARRANGEMENTS IN THE POST-COLD WAR ERA

Against this backdrop, the end of the Cold War has a number of implications for regional approaches to security in the Third World. Firstly, regional frameworks have found a new appeal partly in response to the perceived limitations of the UN's peace and security role in a 'unipolar' international system. Despite its recent successes in a number of regional conflicts, the UN is seen by many Third World countries as being dominated by a handful of Western powers. The Third World nations have demanded a democratization of the UN decision-making system, including the expansion of the Security Council to include some Third World countries. But this appears to be a remote possibility. As such, regional groupings are seen as the kind of fora in which Third World actors may be able to exert a greater share of decision-making power in relation to peace and security issues. Such regional-security arrangements need not be viewed as competitors to the UN, but rather as frameworks whose role might complement the function of an overburdened UN.

A second impact of the end of the Cold War is the transformation of subregional security arrangements towards a more 'inclusionary' outlook. The Cold War was responsible for intraregional ideological polarization in many parts of the globe; its demise opens up opportunities for regional reconciliation. Thus subregional arrangements that thrived on external backing and Cold War-inspired solidarity are under pressure to widen their security focus.

Against this backdrop the Conference on Security and Cooperation in Europe (CSCE) is considered to be an appropriate model. The CSCE process was launched in Helsinki in 1975 and expanded substantially in Stockholm in 1986. The most important aspect of the CSCE is its goal of 'constraining the option of military force in conflict management'. At the centre of the CSCE process was a set of confidence- and security-building measures (CSBMs) which aimed at reducing the threat of surprise attack, if not reducing the military capabilities of the parties involved in waging a war (Rittberger *et al.*, 1990, p. 56). The CSCE is potentially the fourth major type of regional security arrangement following the hegemonic, conflict-control and integrative (security community) models. It differs from the Cold War regional-security arrangements in important ways. It is neither an outer-directed alliance nor an inward-looking formal organization in the mould of the 'original' groupings (which combined the twin functions of the pacific settlement of regional disputes and collective security). Nor does it represent a security community evolved through a process of economic and political integration. The CSCE can best be called a regional-security regime.[2]

A security regime is a formal or informal arrangement whose main objective is to significantly reduce, if not eliminate, the likelihood of war by securing adherence to a set of norms and rules that constrain the conflictual behaviour of the regional actors in relation to one another. The notion of security regime, despite some scepticism regarding its usefulness, is important to the study of regional-security arrangements because it directs attention to the possibility of security cooperation in the absence of a common external enemy, as well as in situations where regional actors share neither a vision of integration nor a commitment to regional collective security and conflict resolution within a strong organizational framework. Security regimes are thus relevant to a regional context in which the interests of the national actors 'are neither wholly compatible nor wholly competitive' (Gross Stein, 1985, p. 600) and where it might be possible to secure compliance with 'principles, rules and norms that permit nations to be restrained in their behaviour in the belief that others will reciprocate' (Jervis, 1982, p. 357).

But caution should be expressed in evaluating the prospects for duplicating European-based models of regional security cooperation in Third World theatres (see Dewitt, 1987, and Findley, 1989). Nonetheless CSBMs provide a potentially effective way of dealing with the challenge of regional reconciliation that has become urgent in several regional theatres with the end or prospective end to several regional conflicts shaped by Cold War dynamics.

A third and related impact of the end of the Cold War is the growing preference of Third World countries for regional arms-control and disarmament measures. While the main security function of the original regional groups was to manage and control interstate disputes, regional arms-control measures could help prevent latent disputes from escalating into armed confrontation. Such regional arms-control measures have assumed importance not only because of concerns about the growing militarisation of the Third World, including the proliferation of nuclear, biological and chemical weapons and ballistic missiles (Klare, 1991). It is also due to the limited utility and discriminatory nature of global non-proliferation measures, such as the Nuclear Non-Proliferation Treaty (NPT), the Missile Technology Control Regime (MTCR) and the Australia group on chemical weapons. These regimes are essentially supplier clubs that seek to control proliferation through restrictions on export of military or dual-use technology. But a major limitation of these regimes is their failure to address the underlying local/regional factors that give rise to conflict in the first place. It is in this context that regional arms-control measures could be useful.

A fourth impact of the end of the Cold War is the weakening of regional military arrangements among Third World countries. The end of regional conflicts in many parts of the Third World removes the rationale for such arrangements. Moreover such arrangements have not helped Third World states to achieve self-reliance beyond low-level internal security threats. The GCC's response, or the lack of it, to the Iraqi invasion of Kuwait is illustrative. Against such major threats the role of external guarantors continue to be vital. At most regional military alliances can create the basis for partial self-reliance through a 'division of labour' with their great-power allies, in which the former are able to deal with low-level threats while the latter are relied upon to provide ultimate protection against aggression from powerful enemies.

A fifth implication of the end of the Cold War is the growing salience of economic security as a regional concern. Despite the poor record of regional economic integration in the Third World, economic issues remain a major motive force of Third World regional groups. But classical models of economic cooperation through 'integrative regionalism' have lost their appeal in favour of 'developmental regionalism' and 'regional economic security' (see the regional cases below).

Axline (1977) has argued that Third World regional integration schemes of the 1960s and 1970s were in reality conceived largely as a strategy of economic development. In this sense critics of integrative regionalism have contended that regional economic cooperation aimed at promoting growth and self-reliance through specific programmes of cooperation is more appropriate for Third World countries than the comprehensive market-integration approach advocated by liberal theory.[3] This preference for developmental regionalism has been a marked feature of contemporary African regionalism. Shaw (1989) argues that Africa has witnessed both a revival as well as 'redefinition of regionalism as self-reliance', and this shift is most clearly represented by two of the most prominent African sub-regional groups, ECOWAS and the Southern African Development Community (SADC). In addition, regional groups in the Third World have undertaken programmes to achieve food and energy security as part of their drive towards self-reliance. ASEAN, SAARC and SADC have created food security reserves, while energy security through sharing of petroleum in emergencies has been developed by ASEAN and SADC.

In sum, while liberal theory viewed economic regionalism as an approach to an integrated security community, recent Third World regional economic structures have largely avoided integrative concepts and measures. Instead their contribution to security is seen to lie in promoting cooperation aimed at 'enhancing economic development through collective self-reliance' (Mutharika, 1981, p. 92).

At the same time regionalism among developing countries is increasingly sensitive to threats emanating from the global economic environment, such as protectionism, low export-commodity prices, essential-raw-material supply disruptions and debt burden (see, especially, Chapters 8 and 12 below). Indeed, shared vulnerabilities to the global economic pressures have redefined the economic goals of regional groups.

A look at contemporary regional groups in the Third World reveals that many have emphasised the goal of economic security through collective bargaining, policy coordination and other cooperative initiatives at international multilateral fora. In Asia, the role of ASEAN exemplifies this kind of economic regionalism, especially collective bargaining with Western countries for better market access, and a collective effort to stabilize the market prices of the main primary commodities exported by members. The quest for greater bargaining leverage has led ASEAN states to expand the scope of their cooperation with developed economies of the Pacific region, especially Japan and the United States, within the framework of a macro-regional economic group, called Asia Pacific Economic Cooperation (APEC).

The prospective role of Third World regional groups in relation to global economic security would seem to bear on two alternative scenarios. First, regional groups can mediate between the bilateral level and global bargaining formulating negotiating positions of the developing countries and articulating their common interests on issues such as debt and protection-ism. This role could be undertaken within the political–economic frame-work of North–South relations, with regional groups being segments of the South. It is arguable that in the post-Cold War era, Third World states may be better able collectively to bargain over these issues through regional forums than larger groups such as the Group of 77 (see Chapter 15 below).

An alternative scenario, increasingly mentioned in academic and policy-making circles, is the proliferation of regional trading blocs (see Chapters 2 and 3 above). A Latin American trade bloc dominated by the United States and Canada and an East Asia trade bloc dominated by Japan are possible examples of such hegemonic trade blocs. Participation in such arrangements would theo-retically expand market opportunities for Third World states and provide them with a counter to protectionism in world markets. But such regional trade struc-tures would also pose a new danger by legitimizing the economic domination of the regional economic hegemon, and thus usher in a new form of depen-dency and exploitation of Third World states. Barry Buzan's warning about the position of Third World states in regional trading blocs dominated by an eco-nomic superpower is pertinent here. According to Buzan, participation in such blocs might be counter-productive for Third World states unless it was accom-panied by a sense of genuine regionalism binding the hegemon and the less developed members within its economic sphere of influence. Such a regional-ism, Buzan believes, would help 'to moderate exploitation of the periphery by the centre' (1983, p. 141).

It should be noted that the opportunity to participate in regional trading blocs is open to only a handful of Third World countries that have achieved relatively higher levels of economic success. While developing countries in Asia and Latin America can enjoy the benefits of closer integration with developed countries, Africa would risk being ignored (see Chapters 2 and 15). Efforts by African states to respond through their own regional trading arrangements are unlikely to be an adequate counter to trading blocs dominated by industrial powers. The problems facing Malaysia's proposal to create a trade bloc in East-ern Asia, the so-called East Asia Economic Grouping (EAEG) now renamed as East Asian Regional Caucus, under Japan's leadership testifies to the limita-tions of Third World regional trading blocs geared to countering the threat of regionalism in North America and Europe (see Low, 1991).

CONCLUSION

In the first two decades after the Second World War the major expression of Third World regionalism was through three 'original' regional organizations: the Organization of American States (OAS), the Arab League and the Organization of African Unity (OAU). With the spread of the Cold War in the Third World, a relatively small number of Third World countries chose to join superpower-sponsored regional-security alliances, although these experiments were largely ineffective and short-lived. In the 1970s and 1980s the trend in the Third World was clearly toward subregional groups.

Trends are evident towards new regional arrangements to address the emerging security problems of a multipolar world. Of particular significance is the appeal of regional-security regimes based on the CSCE model, although there is yet to be a viable example of this in the Third World.

The decline of postwar regional organizations and the changing dynamics of superpower relationships have already led to a redefinition of the perceptual boundaries of regions in the Third World. In the 1970s and 1980s the emergence of a number of subregional groups, such as the GCC, Contadora and ECOWAS, indicated that regional boundaries coinciding with the macroregional groups, such as the Arab League, the OAS and the OAU, were too wide to satisfy the specific security concerns of Third World states. The end of the Cold War, in contrast, has led to a demand for the widening of regional boundaries established by subregional frameworks, whose very emergence reflected the polarization of the region due to superpower-influenced regional conflicts and intraregional competition. In Southeast Asia, anticommunist ASEAN is deemed too narrow a framework for the task of regional reconciliation that would be essential for regional security in view of the prospective settlement of the Cambodia conflict. Moves are already afoot to bring into its fold the communist Indochinese countries. The GCC is similarly considered inadequate for addressing the security problems of the Gulf area in the aftermath of the Iraqi invasion of Kuwait; moves towards a new regional security arrangement in the area are based on participation by Iran as well as other Arab states.

Regions are also being redefined in response to global economic developments that reflect an increasing divergence between political and economic bases of regional identity. While its member countries continue to see ASEAN (possibly including Indochina) as a suitable political forum, in the economic sphere, in order to fight protectionist trends in the international economy, they find the need to participate within an East Asia Economic Grouping centred on Japan's economic might. The changing regional boundaries bring a new relevance to regional cooperation that could not be appreciated by looking only at the three models of regional cooperation mentioned earlier.

In the final analysis, regionalism as an approach to security continues to evoke a great deal of interest in the Third World, despite the fact that most of the past attempts at Third World regionalism have not been able to duplicate Eurocentric models. The changing global political and economic environments have brought to the fore many challenges that can be dealt with through regional cooperation. These challenges have also widened the range of tasks that existing regional groups and arrangements can perform. A new era in Third World regionalism is a possibility that should receive serious consideration in efforts to build a new international security order for the post-Cold War era.

Notes

1.   There is a vast body of literature on integration theory, especially on its most influential approach, neofunctionalism (see, for example, Haas, 1964; Puchala, 1984).

2.   The concept of 'security regime' grew out of the literature on international regimes, but remains underdeveloped as an explanation of a Third World regional-security arrangement (see Jervis, 1982, pp. 357–378; Nye, 1987, pp. 371–402).

3.   It should be noted that growth and development were also goals of market-integration approaches, but the record is a poor one (see, for example, Mazzeo, 1984; Shaw, 1989; Swatuk, 1994).

7 The World Bank and NGOs

Mark E. Denham

INTRODUCTION

The role of non-governmental organizations (NGOs) and civil society in global development seems to be commanding additional attention in the post-Cold War period. Perhaps this is a result of the realization that past practices, particularly state-centred and state-directed development, have failed to bring about sustainable growth in most parts of the South. Or perhaps, in the context of contemporary, deflationary economics (see Chapter 4 above), donor states are neither able nor willing to make sufficient capital available to the South, given the absence of political and economic returns they might receive. Or perhaps it is the emerging expectation that democratic politics should be closely associated with economic development. Most likely, of course, the increased interest in the role of civil society and non-governmental organizations in development is some combination of these kinds of reasons (see Chapters 9, 14 and 15).

In Africa in particular, the declining in-flow of investment and aid has helped to create an atmosphere of political instability. In this region, where capital flows are negative, the ability of the state to meet the demands of its society is even more limited (Shaw and Swatuk, 1993). Moreover African states in particular are increasingly portrayed as 'predatory' (Bayart, 1993; Frimpong-Ansah, 1991; also Chapters 8 and 9 of this volume). In contrast civil society is increasingly seen as somehow more noble, and less tainted, than persons and institutions that are more closely associated with the state.[1]

It is in this context that major international donors have turned to NGOs – both endogenous-based and those based in the North – as the hope for Africa's future. The associated increase in number and wealth of these organizations might be seen as one crucial effect of emerging global divisions of labour and power, which together make Africa's economic and strategic value more marginal and its authoritarian political systems less tolerable.

Given this increased attention paid to the role of NGOs, this chapter summarizes the extent and content of collaboration between them and a central actor in the international development regime, the World Bank. General characteristics of NGOs are described and NGO–World Bank project collaboration is characterized. Finally, attempts of NGOs to influence the policy and philosophy of the World Bank are explored.

Officially sponsored 'development decades' have come and gone. Significant amounts of development assistance, much of it concessional, have flowed from North to South. Private organizations have raised and distributed billions of dollars of aid in the form of food, labour, equipment, supplies and technical assistance. Development theories – import substitution industrialization, export-led growth, dependency or autarky – have been proposed by a variety of agencies, governments and academics. The United Nations system has created a proliferation of organizations and committees whose purpose is to address the problems of poverty and underdevelopment of the South. What has resulted from these efforts?

Although significant social and economic achievements have occurred in the last few decades, at least one billion people today live in conditions of absolute poverty. Although a large number of Southern countries have seen positive growth in aggregate income, the gap between rich and poor continues to grow. Clearly even the best-intentioned efforts of the international community have not resulted in substantially improved living standards of a large proportion of the earth's population.

By the late 1980s it had become obvious, even to the most economically orthodox, that development policies as practiced were having little of the desired effect on targeted populations. Although some observers came to believe that the problems of maldevelopment were so severe that they were intractable, many became increasingly willing to consider alternative perspectives or alternative procedures that might more effectively address the needs of the poor.

Even the World Bank, one of the most consistently orthodox of all major providers of development assistance, has occasionally questioned its liberal economic philosophy. Although its focus has always been on funding large-scale projects such as those aiding transportation or power generation, the problems of maldevelopment in most of the South has led to the search for other solutions. As a result of criticism from both within and without the Bank, there has been some shift away from the exclusive funding of infrastructure projects to those that more directly address the needs of the poor, such as education or health care programmes. Such social programmes, however, have not been the result of a wholesale reordering of Bank priorities. Although some questions have been raised about its economic philosophy, the Bank, and its sister institution the International Monetary Fund, have not swayed far from their ideological commitment to the promotion of the liberal development model that includes commitment to the integration of Southern economies into the global capitalist market as the long-term solution to the maldevelopment of Southern economies. Despite some modest recent efforts to engage in programme lending, they have come to insist ever more strongly on macroeconomic adjustments in Southern economies in the form of structural adjustment programmes.

The content and consequences of these adjustment programmes have been described widely in both the popular press and academic literature (see Chapters 4, 5, 8 and 12 below). Typical adjustment policies demanded by the multilateral financial institutions[2] include the removal of price controls, government financial subsidies and limiting total central government expenditures. The long-term goal of these policies is to more fully integrate the economies of targeted countries into the international market economy, which theoretically should also improve Southern countries' economic growth and development. However the short-term result of these 'shocks' of structural adjustment programmes has been the contraction of Southern economies, whose costs are born by domestic constituencies that are least able to pay them through higher prices for almost all consumer items, including food, and typically a major reduction in government services, often including health care and education.

While maintaining a belief in the importance of adjustment, the Bank has not been entirely oblivious to the costs that such programmes present to fragile domestic political systems. In particular the Bank is aware that the result of adjustment programmes whose cost is paid by the middle and lower classes (in the form of higher food prices, for example) can often be political instability. Demands from domestic constituencies are consistently made on Southern governments that leaders can not adequately address while at the same time responding to the external insistence of its major creditors and its only source of additional financing.

Throughout the 1980s there have been many sources of increasing pressure on the Bank to address these immediate short-term consequences of adjustment policies. The UNICEF study, *Adjustment with a Human Face* (Cornia, Jolly and Stewart, 1987), for example, detailed the consequences of the economic conditions in the South that have resulted from structural adjustment. The South Commission's report, while acknowledging the validity and need for adjustment, was especially concerned about 'the complete disregard of equity in prescriptions for structural adjustment consisting of cuts in public spending and changes in relative prices [that] had devastating effects on vital public services like health and education, with especially harmful consequences for the most vulnerable social groups' (South Commission, 1990, p. 78).

Thus in the mid-1980s both the World Bank and the IMF seemed to begin to rethink some of the policies and consequences of adjustment. The Bank issued a number of directives instructing Bank staff to consider the effects of adjustment policies on the poor. In 1986 the managing director of the IMF stated that 'the forms of adjustment that are conducive to growth and to protection of human needs will not emerge by accident. They have to be encouraged by an appropriate set of incentives and policies. They will also require political courage' (quoted in Jolly, 1988, p. 165).

By 1987 the Bank appeared to more explicitly discuss these issues, illustrated by the release of a document, *Protecting the Poor during the Process of Adjustment*.[3] In any case it appears that the Bank has become at least somewhat sensitive to these critical voices, and particularly to the short- and medium-term consequences, both economical and political, of structural adjustment. This is reflected in a 1991 statement by a senior vice-president of the Bank, Moeen A. Qureshi:

> It is crucial ... that we pay much more attention to how the international community can organize itself to accommodate the emerging empowerment of people, for example, how can global, regional and national economic institutions begin to address more effectively the fast growing demands of people in many countries for rapid transformation of their societies to market-oriented principles, for better governance and for poverty reduction?... The World Bank has learned from its experience of development that popular participation is important to the success of projects economically, environmentally and socially. Our most important lesson has been that participation and empowerment are questions of efficiency, as well as being desirable in their own right (Qureshi, 1991, p. 2).

Such statements seem to reflect a new rhetoric from the Bank. Statements such as Qureshi's recognize the importance of 'poverty reduction' as well as issues of 'participation and empowerment'. This suggests that the Bank is cognizant of the dangers of structural adjustment. Popular constituencies in Southern countries that may have been marginally satisfied by government programmes of food subsidies and government health and educational programmes may become vocal or violent when such government programmes are removed and replaced by externally imposed structural adjustment programmes. Demands for 'participation and empowerment' emerge from dissatisfaction and poverty and such demands threaten the political and economic stability upon which adjustment policies and associated lending is built. The price of adjustment (at least in the short term) is increased levels of poverty in large segments of Southern societies.

One of the ways the Bank has sought to soften the blow of adjustment has been the institution of a number of programmes that attempt to directly address the needs of the poor. These have, for example, included social programmes related to health care and education. In recent years, increasing amounts of Bank capital have been made available for such programmes. This differs from most conventional Bank loans that are collateralized on the immediate financial benefits of the project (electric generation, for example) that would allow the borrower to increase overall tax revenue or other forms of profit to repay the loan. Lending for social programmes seldom has the immediate financial payoffs that can allow borrowers to make repayments.

A second, but related, way the Bank has attempted to implement programmes designed for the poorer sectors of society has been through cooperating with non-governmental organizations. These groups often have better access to and work more effectively with the poor than do governments. In addition they tend to be better acquainted with providing social services than the Bank, whose expertise is much stronger in financing infrastructure development. This chapter now turns to a brief description of NGOs before more directly discussing their work with the World Bank.

NGOs AS AGENTS OF DEVELOPMENT

Non-governmental organization is a term that can refer to a wide variety of different entities. For our immediate purpose we are interested in those organizations that may collaborate with the World Bank in the planning or implementation of development projects. The Bank has defined NGOs in an operational directive (World Bank, 1989, para. 1):

The diversity of NGOs strains any simple definition or classification. NGOs include a wide variety of groups and institutions that are entirely or largely independent of government, and characterized primarily by humanitarian or cooperative, rather than commercial, objectives. The terminology varies: for example, in the United States they may be called 'private voluntary organizations' [PVOs] and most African NGOs prefer to be called 'voluntary development organizations.' Although organizations such as universities or research institutes may be non-governmental this directive refers principally to private organizations that pursue activities to relieve suffering, promote the interests of the poor, protect the environment, provide basic social services, or undertake community development.

Included are three general types of NGOs: international, national (or indigenous intermediate) and local (or grassroots). International NGOs are organizations based primarily in the North that finance and implement projects and programmes in Southern countries. These are usually charitable or religious associations and may be involved in a wide variety of projects such as family planning or agricultural development. National NGOs, often called 'indigenous intermediate organizations' by the Bank , are usually organized at the provincial or national level and may be federations of smaller or locally-based NGOs. Local NGOs, frequently referred to as grassroots organizations by the Bank, are usually community-based organizations, sometimes rather loosely organized, that may include such groups as water users' societies or consumer cooperatives.[4]

There are many of these organizations and their numbers are rapidly increasing. Determining the actual number, by category or in total, is impossible. A number of sources suggest that there are well over 4000 NGOs based in OECD member countries. David Korten reports one source as listing 13 000 international NGOs and internationally oriented national NGOs. The number of local NGOs concerned with development issues is undetermined, and the total number of local NGOs is assuredly astronomical (Korten, 1991, pp. 21–2).

As cogently described in Chapter 14 below, the resulting variety of orientation and activities of these groups is obviously extremely diverse with different purposes, serving different target populations and espousing different and sometimes conflicting development philosophies. David Korten (ibid., pp. 24–5) has identified four primary areas in which development-oriented NGOs are involved:

- *Relief and welfare*: this includes the administration of food aid programmes, and is typically the primary purpose of the largest international NGOs, such as CARE or Catholic Relief Services.
- *Human resource development*: these programmes are focused more on development than relief, often for small enterprise development, small-scale credit programmes and expanding the capabilities and skills of individuals.
- *Political activism and empowerment*: an important component of a significant amount of NGO work in Latin America and Asia and an especially important theme of liberation theology, these programmes

focus on 'self-reliance, responsibility, human dignity, and freedom from oppression'. Such organizations have drawn attention 'to extreme inequalities in the sharing of goods and power – identified as the underlying causes of persistent poverty' (ibid., p. 25).

– *Policy advocacy*: an important focus for a number of NGOs based in Canada and Europe is education and advocacy that seeks to challenge dominant global economic perspectives. Typically this advocacy is directed toward the policies of the NGO's home government or occasionally the organization directs its attention to the economic philosophy and programmes of multilateral institutions.[5]

These organizations in all of their variety have often been promoted as efficient and cost-effective ways of reaching the poor in Southern countries. Frequently they have been viewed as having attributes that make them preferred over multilateral or bilateral forms of assistance and have been increasingly utilized by Western governments.[6]

In general those promoting NGOs suggest that there are numerous advantages that these organizations provide that neither governments nor multilateral governmental organizations enjoy. These include:[7]

– NGOs tend to be efficient providers of assistance to recipients, especially with respect to overhead expenses. Gorman (1984, p. 71) states that 'overhead costs are generally quite low', reporting that many NGOs operate with less than 2 per cent of funds being allocated to overhead costs and most ranging from 8 to 15 per cent. In addition many NGOs use volunteers or very low-paid personnel both to raise funds at home and to staff projects in the field. Others (Bolling, 1982, p. 190) have reported an overhead figure of 3 per cent and compare that amount to an average of 20 to 30 per cent overhead for many bilateral government aid programmes, and even higher for some multilateral programmes.

– NGOs have been reported to be capable of mobilizing significant resources, both human and financial, especially at home in the donor country.

– NGOs frequently have fewer bureaucratic constraints than government agencies and multilateral institutions. Thus they may be able more effectively to initiate and sustain projects.

– NGOs have often been successful in promoting 'indigenous participatory institutions' in recipient countries, better helping recipients to help themselves.

– Since NGOs have a much lower profile than most governments, they are sometimes able to provide assistance in politically sensitive situations and thus are more able to gain the support of the recipient government -- local or national or both.[8]

- NGOs are accomplished in reaching the rural poor and operating in remote areas. Frequently their programmes are located in areas where government services and programmes are limited, ineffective or non-existent.
- Some observers also argue that collaborating with governments or major multilateral institutions enhances the quality of NGO efforts, since these contracts often 'require NGOs to make improvements in management and technical skills. The result is that they become more businesslike, more objectively critical about what they are doing, more deliberately involved in long-term development, and less influenced by a slap-dash emergency relief mentality' (Bolling, 1982, p. 193).

Whatever the supposed advantages, NGOs have not and are not always recognized as valid partners with governmental and multilateral aid agencies. In fact only recently have NGOs been more favourably viewed by governments and official aid practitioners. This is a less recent development for many European and Canadian donors than for the United States,[9] and the World Bank did not begin extensive cooperation with NGOs as readily as did governments. Some collaboration did take place in the 1970s, but it was not until the mid-1980s that NGO–World Bank collaboration was officially encouraged by the Bank itself. This is reflected in an increasing number of internal directives recommending the use of NGOs in Bank-sponsored projects. The defining statement from a Bank official was that made by Barber Conable when he was president of the Bank:

Government policies and public programmes play a critical role in poverty alleviation. But governments cannot do everything. Non-government organizations in many developing countries have enormous potential for flexible and effective action. I have encouraged Bank staff to initiate a broadened dialogue with NGOs.... I hope and fully expect that this collaboration will continue and flourish (quoted in Salmen and Eaves, 1989, p. 1).

Officially the Bank views NGOs as having a number of strengths that are congruent with those previously listed. Specifically the Bank seeks to cooperate with NGOs because they can (i) often *reach poor communities and remote areas* with few basic resources or little infrastructure and where government services are limited or ineffective; (ii) *promote local participation* in designing and implementing public programs by building self-confidence and strengthening organizational capability among low-income people; (iii) *operate at low cost* by using appropriate technologies, stream-lined services, and minimal overheads; and (iv) *identify local needs, build upon existing resources, and transfer technologies developed elsewhere.* Some approaches and ideas now prevalent among official development agencies began as NGO innovations' (World Bank, 1989, para. 6, emphasis in original).

At the same time the Bank recognizes a number of limitations that NGOs face. These, according to the Bank, include:

- *Limited replicability*: many NGO-sponsored activities are too small and localized to have important regional or national impact. In attempting to scale up their operations with public-sector support, some NGOs may lose their innovative quality and become top-down, non-participatory and dependent on external and governmental support.
- *Limited self-sustainability*: like many government programmes, NGO-sponsored projects may not be designed with sufficient concern for how activities will be sustained.
- *Limited managerial and technical capacity*: even some professionally staffed NGOs are poorly managed, have only rudimentary accounting systems and sometimes initiate infrastructure projects with inadequate technical analysis.
- *Lack of broad programming context*: although experience varies by region and sector, NGO development projects often are implemented individually, outside the framework of a broader programming strategy for a region or sector, and with little regard even to other NGOs' activities.
- *Politicization*: some NGOs combine development concerns with political or religious objectives that limit the extent to which the Bank can work with them while safeguarding its primary relationship with its member governments (World Bank, 1989, para. 7).

WORLD BANK–NGO COLLABORATION

Table 7.1 summarizes the number of Bank-supported projects that have utilized NGO participation. Most NGO–World Bank collaboration has occurred with projects in Africa; 50 per cent of them were located there from 1973–91. Most are agriculture and rural development projects, and most of the cooperation with NGOs has been at the project implementation stage rather than at the design or evaluation stage. These projects have usually been related to producer or user groups such as irrigation associations,

Table 7.1 Patterns in World Bank–NGO collaboration, fiscal years 1973–1991

	1973–88		1989		1990		1991[1]		Total 1973–91[1]	
	No.	%	No.	%	No.	%	No.	%	No.	%
By region (number of projects)										
Africa	111	51	27	59	22	44	39	48	199	50
Asia	51	24	8	17	14	28	23	28	96	24
Europe, Middle East and N. Africa	16	7	4	9	3	6	9	11	32	8
Latin America and Caribbean	40	18	7	15	11	22	11	13	69	18
Total	218	100	46	100	50	100	82	100	396	100
By sector (number of projects)										
Adjustment-related	2	1	4	9	8	16	9	11	23	6
Agriculture/rural development	102	47	15	33	18	36	21	26	156	39
Education/training	20	9	4	9	5	10	11	13	40	10
Environment	2	1	2	4	4	8	3	4	11	3
Industry/energy	22	10	4	9	1	2	7	9	34	9
Infrastructure/urban development	41	19	8	17	5	10	14	17	68	17
Population/health/nutrition	26	12	7	15	9	18	16	20	58	15
Relief	3	1	2	4	0	0	1	1	6	1
Total	218	100	46	100	50	100	82	100	396	100
By type of NGO (number of NGOs)										
Grassroots	75	30	29	41	30	42	56	30	190	33
Indigenous intermediary	75	30	28	40	26	36	104	56	233	40
International	104	40	13	19	16	22	25	14	158	27
Total	254	100	70	100	72	100	185	100	581	100
By function (number of NGOs)										
Advice	75	27	7	10	7	8	26	15	115	19
Cofinancing	10	3	5	7	8	10	21	12	44	7
Design	33	12	11	16	19	22	29	17	92	15
Implementation	162	58	42	59	46	54	78	45	328	54
Monitoring and evaluation	1	0	6	8	5	6	18	10	30	5
Total	281	100	71	100	85	100	172	100	609	100

Source: World Bank, 1991b, p. 97.
[1] Preliminary.

herders' organizations or cooperatives (Beckmann, 1991, p. 139). The most evident trend over time has been the increasing use of grassroots and indigenous intermediary NGOs as opposed to international NGOs. From 1973–88, 40 per cent of all NGO–World Bank projects were with inter-

Table 7.2   Operational collaboration between NGOs and the World Bank by type of
NGO, fiscal years 1973–87 and 1988–90

	1973–87	1988–90
Grass-roots	25	45
Indigenous intermediary	31	35
International	43	20

Source: Beckmann, 1991, p. 137.

national NGOs. By 1991 this proportion had fallen to 14 per cent (see
Table 7.2).

A second notable trend has been the increasing use of NGOs in adjustment-
related projects. In the fourteen-year period from 1973–88 only 1 per cent
of all projects were classified this way, whereas in 1990 it was 16 per cent
and in 1991 11 per cent. As we have suggested, this trend seems to represent an attempt by the Bank to address the social problems associated with
adjustment (Beckmann, 1991, p. 138).

Some of the most frequent uses of NGOs by the World Bank include:
(i) the implementation of population, health and nutrition projects, enlist-
ing the assistance of NGOs at the community level for project implementation (World Bank, 1990b, p. 9); (ii) assistance in dealing with the
involuntary resettlement of people affected by Bank-financed projects such
as flooding from the building of dams; and (iii) funding of development
education programmes, primarily by international NGOs in their work in
the North. NGOs are actors capable of influencing public opinion and public policy in the North, and as such can be important allies of the Bank.
'Bank–NGO cooperation in development education may help fund-raising
efforts both for NGOs and for the bank's concessionary lending through
the International Development Association (IDA) to the poorest borrowing
countries at below market rates' (Cernea, 1988, p. 37).

NGOs AS ADVOCATES FOR INSTITUTIONAL CHANGE

World Bank staff member Michael Cernea (1988) cites a number of
studies[10] that suggest that NGOs have been able to directly influence the
policies of the Bank. This influence has been most apparent in the area of
poverty issues as they relate to adjustment and to environmental issues.
According to Cernea it was partly in response to the vocal concerns of

NGOs that the bank 'has taken a number of steps to sharpen its focus on poverty and to lighten the social costs of adjustment especially by targeting better the support for social expenditures' (Cernea, 1988, p. 38).

The NGO critique of the World Bank's inattention to the environmental impact of its projects is neither new nor uniquely an NGO complaint. However Cernea reports that a number of NGOs convinced some Bank member governments to insist on increased environmental sensitivity and suggests that:

> The results have been significant, leading to considerable improvements in some specific projects, to changes in policies and in the international Bank organizational structure and staff allocation. Specifically, in the environmental field, the Bank has developed its dialogue and collaboration with organizations like the World Resources Institute (WRI), the Environmental Defense Fund (EDF), the International Union for the Conservation of Nature (IUCN), and others. Even though their criticism of certain Bank-assisted projects has sometimes been harsh, it was received with respect and professional consideration and it has helped the Bank and some of its borrowing agencies become more keenly aware of some projects' implications on vulnerable groups, on resettlement, on nonrenewable resources, etc. (ibid., pp. 38–9).

If the relationship between the Bank and NGOs is at times less than amiable, the relationship between NGOs and the governments of Southern countries is frequently even less cordial. In many cases NGOs have been vocal critics of governmental policies and programmes. Some NGOs have as their explicit purpose the 'political empowerment' of the poor. Such objectives are usually not met with support by governments. In some cases the Bank has urged, and sometimes required, governments to tolerate or even support the work of NGOs. An example is the Bank's action related to the implementation of a Bank-financed large-scale agricultural-water-management project in Pakistan. As a condition for Bank financing, the government of Pakistan was 'asked ... that special national and provincial legislation be issued to establish a legal framework for creating grassroots organizations of water users along each watercourse' (ibid., p. 40).[11]

One formal means of NGO–World Bank interaction has been institutionalized by the creation (in 1981) of the NGO–World Bank Committee. The group is composed of 26 NGO members (sixteen of these are based in the South) who meet with staff and other representatives of the Bank. (The NGO members of the Working Group are found in the Appendix.) NGO members of the committee serve fixed terms and are responsible for electing new representatives. The committee members include international NGOs as well as indigenous intermediate NGOs.

This committee has met annually and has been a forum for dialogue between the two parties. At times the Committee has been a source of vocal critiques of Bank policies and projects. Of particular importance is a recent Position Paper of the NGO Working Group[12] that severely criticizes the Bank, particularly for its inattention to the immediate social and economic effects of structural adjustment programmes on the poor. This working paper's preamble sets forth the NGOs' position:

> It is one thing ... to make speeches and even to institute new policies; it is quite another to secure institutional change. In [most] areas ... there have been, at best, marginal improvements at the Bank over the past few years, while NGOs around the world continue to witness widespread suffering too often caused by Bank-supported programmes and policies that reflect little of the new rhetoric.... All the speeches and all the dialogue within the Committee have not changed the harsh realities faced daily by the majority of the people in the South (NGO Working Group, 1989, pp. i–ii).

The Position Paper, both in content and in tone, is highly critical of adjustment policies promoted by the Bank and the IMF. In particular it states that:

- The group finds 'no evidence to justify the Bank's confidence that adjustment helps the poor in the long run.'
- Adjustment programs 'exacerbate the economic and social problems of the countries of the South ...' when they are focused on the generation of hard currency in order to service countries' debt.
- The Bank has focused too much on 'meeting macro-economic targets related to export performance and too little on dealing with domestic hunger considerations.'
- Gender has seldom been taken into account. The Bank has seldom recognized that poor women usually suffer most under adjustment.
- Many Bank-financed large-scale projects are designed without input from 'affected populations and without sufficient consideration of their long-term ecological and economic sustainability'.
- Although the Bank is utilizing increasing number of NGOs at the project implementation stage, it seldom seeks out local organizations at the identification and design stage. 'Without dramatic increases in local consultation and in access to information, local populations will remain unable to gain or maintain a measure of control over their own

environments or to assist the Bank in making development planning more effective and relevant' (NGO Working Group, 1989, pp. iv–v).[13]

These are not, of course, new criticisms of the Bank. Nor is it unusual that NGOs would level these complaints against the Bank. But it is notable that these criticisms are coming from a Bank-sponsored committee.

The Bank responded very quickly to the NGOs' position paper, publishing a response only three months later. The response, while acknowledging the fact that the committee has 'provided helpful advice and assistance in guiding the broader process of the World Bank's expanding engagement with NGOs', also expressed dismay at its content and tone, saying:

> [W]e appreciate the passion for justice that pervades the Position Paper, but find little tolerance for the frailties and complexities that characterize even the most well-intentioned human efforts. The Position Paper echoes old debates and stereotypes in a shrill tone, at a moment when many nations and institutions are breaking from the patterns of the past and forging new possibilities (World Bank, 1990c, para. 88).

Whereas the Bank appears to have been somewhat receptive to critiques concerning the environmental impact of its projects and to the early attention that needed to be given to issues of the poor, the effect of this criticism of adjustment is unclear. The basis of the NGOs' critique summarized above, cuts to the core of Bank philosophy: it questions the development ideology of most multilateral institutions (cf. Macdonald's discussion of radical NGOs in Central America in Chapter 14 below). Earlier critiques dealt with how specific programmes were implemented that could be dealt with by 'adding on' components to traditional projects. Critics of adjustment policies go much further in questioning more basic issues and assumptions, and how the Bank will respond is not certain.

This is just one illustration of NGO attempts to influence World Bank policy from within. It appears that these criticisms are becoming more organized and more vocal. At the 1990 annual meeting of the World Bank and the IMF, some 150 NGOs were admitted by their governments as visitors to the official meetings, whereas only 60 were admitted the year before. During the meeting a coalition of environmental and advocacy groups from both the North and the South met with Bank executive directors as well as finance ministers of individual governments (World Bank, 1990a, p. 12).

These activities are illustrative of a much more vocal and radical critique of World Bank policy and practices emerging from a group of organizations than the Bank seems to want to utilize in its own programmes. The future of this collaboration, the effectiveness of the criticism and the Bank's response is still to be determined.

CONCLUSIONS

In general our knowledge about non-governmental organizations is limited, as is the sophistication of our theory that might help us understand their impact on global political and economic phenomena. This is especially true of our understanding of relationship of non-governmental organizations with the World Bank and with multilateral governmental institutions in general. A good deal more must be discovered in order to more adequately assess a number of very important issues. Some of these include:

– To what extent are NGOs able to affect the agendas, decisions and programmes of multilateral institutions?
– How does collaboration with the Bank affect the independence and effectiveness of NGOs?
– Does collaboration on Bank-financed projects prevent NGOs from being as vocal and as critical of governmental policies?
– Do NGO-sponsored development education efforts in the North that are partially or wholly funded by the Bank implicitly or explicitly reflect uncritical, liberal development philosophies?

Whereas these questions focus specifically on research questions related to World Bank–NGO collaboration, the research is really a part of a much broader agenda. Specifically it raises questions about the role of NGOs in the new international division of labour as well as their relationship to Southern states and their regimes:

– Do NGOs step in and provide social services (such as education or health care) or technical assistance (such as agricultural advice) when state governments are prevented from doing so by conscious policy or externally imposed structural adjustment programmes?
– Are NGOs thus protecting Southern regimes from domestic criticism by substituting their programmes for those formally assumed by the government? Are they providing basic social services that assuage the anger or disappointment of the most severely affected sectors of Southern societies?
– Do NGOs provide mechanisms for political societies to organize for change in governmental policy or makeup? Can they effectively

aggregate and empower the poor and their interests so that change in macroeconomic policies can be instituted?

In the end the answers to these questions will invariably be dependent upon the subset of NGOs examined. In fact it may be very difficult to make generalizations about all NGOs, given the diverse types of organizations (which vary from Northern-based aid agencies to Southern-based farmer cooperatives) and the variety of interests these actors pursue (from support for liberal economic policies to a radical critique of existing economic paradigms). Some NGOs attempt to be more 'apolitical' than others, while some view their contribution as challenging oppressive power structures. Others seek to provide limited health care to isolated villages, while others want to advise governments on national health policy. Where some seek to educate Northern constituencies about the structural causes of poverty and maldevelopment in the South, others avoid such education so as not to threaten their most effective fund-raising techniques, which include the use of photographs of starving children. Whereas some NGOs justify their acquiescence to host-government policies and interests in order to pursue their objectives without interference, others seek to avoid being tainted by an alliance with corrupt and unjust regimes.

In light of this diversity and complexity, do NGOs deserve to be cast into a role of 'saviours' in development? Do they deserve to be seen as organizations that 'truly' and accurately represent the interests of civil society? Are they a more just and equitable means of aggregating political interests than those utilized by most state governments in the South? Or are NGOs simply means utilized by the multilateral agencies and Southern governments to impart the appearance of sensitivity? By providing resources in amounts that are equivalent to years of fundraising, do NGOs sacrifice their creativity, neutrality and effectiveness to become little more than extensions of the powerful and rich interests of the North? The findings in this volume, particularly those expressed in Chapters 8 and 14, suggest that the answer may, at least in part, be 'yes' to each of these questions. Whatever one's perspective, NGOs of all sorts are increasing in number, in the financial resources they command and in the attention they receive from diverse members of the 'development community'. In any case it is incumbent on practitioners and analysts to avoid sweeping generalizations and move toward a better understanding of the myriad forms and roles of NGOs in today's new international division of labour.

APPENDIX: NGO MEMBERS OF THE NGO–BANK COMMITTEE 1990–1

Listed is the organization's name, acronym (where appropriate) and country in which the organization's headquarters is located.

American Council for Voluntary International Action (InterAction), United States.
Amigos de Terra/Acao Democratica Feminina Gaucha, Brazil.
Association of Voluntary Agencies for Rural Development (AVARD), India.
Bangladesh Rural Advancement Committee (BRAC), Bangladesh.
Canadian Council for International Cooperation (CCIC), Canada.
Caribbean Conference of Churches (CCC), Barbados.
Caritas Internationalis, Holy See.
Danish Coalition for North/South Cooperation, Denmark.
Development Group for Alternative Policies (D-GAP), United States.
Federation des Associations du Fouta pour le Developpement (FAFD), Senegal.
Fundacion Dominicana de Desarollo, Dominican Republic.
Inter-Africa Group (IAG), Kenya.
International Institute for Rural Reconstruction, Philippines.
Islamic African Relief Agency, Sudan.
Japanese NGO Center for International Cooperation (JANIC), Japan.
MISEREOR, Germany.
National NGO Council of Sri Lanka, Sri Lanka.
NOVIB, The Netherlands.
OXFAM-Belgique, Belgium.
OXFAM, United Kingdom.
Programa de Economica del Trabajo (PET)/Academica de Humanismo Cristiano, Chile.
Reseau Africain pour le Developpement Integre (RADI), Senegal.
SOLIDARIOS, Dominican Republic.
Third World Network/Consumers Association of Penang, Malaysia.
World Council of Churches, Switzerland.
Zimbabwe Freedom from Hunger Campaign, Zimbabwe.

Notes

1. See, for example, the special issues of *Review of African Political Economy* (1992) entitled 'Democracy, Civil Society and NGOs' and *Theoria* (1992) entitled 'The State and Civil Society'.
2. Usually, recommendations or demands for the institution of structural adjustment programmes are made by the IMF. The Bank, as well as many other sources of capital, both public and private, have often followed a policy that makes their loans contingent on borrowing countries adequately following IMF-mandated policies.
3. See Jolly (1988) for a concise and more detailed chronology of the Bank's attention to the effects of adjustment policies on vulnerable groups.

4. See Salmen and Eaves (1991) for a more detailed discussion of these different types of NGOs, as well as a number of categorizations of the types of projects in which NGOs have participated.

5. For example, the magazine *The Ecologist* (1985) dedicated an entire issue to a criticism of the work of the World Bank, entitled 'The World Bank: Global Financing of Impoverishment and Famine'. A number of the articles were written by staff persons of Northern-based NGOs, including the lead piece by Anders Wijkman, secretary general of the Swedish Red Cross, and Lloyd Timberlake, editorial director of Earthscan, London.

6. For example the several commissions studying US foreign aid programmes (Draper, Clay and Peterson) recommended not only more use of multilateral channels for the distribution of aid, but also the use of non-governmental organizations as a means of distributing US official development assistance (ODA). This has also been the case for Canadian and other OECD donors.

7. The following advantages of NGOs are compiled primarily from de Silva (1984), Bolling (1982, pp. 189–91), Cernea (1988, pp. 17–18) and Bolling's citing of Schwartz (1978).

8. However in other instances NGOs may be seen as little different from other Western official aid agencies. They often cooperate with Western governmental agencies, receive funds or supplies from them, and have interchangeable staffs.

9. This is reflected in a recent USAID policy paper (USAID, 1982) which has been seen as the 'first unified and comprehensive AID policy toward' NGOs (Minear, 1984, p. 26).

10. These include Schuh (1987), World Bank (1987) and Aufderheide and Rich (1988).

11. For a discussion of government–NGO relations in Africa see Bratton (1989) and Fowler (1991).

12. When the NGO representatives on the NGO–World Bank Committee meet as a separate group, they are referred to as the NGO Working Group.

13. See also Clark's (1990, pp. 173–5) similar listing of more general criticisms made by NGOs of the effects of adjustment policies.

Part IV

Africa

8 Political Conditionality and Prospects for Recovery in Sub-Saharan Africa

Julius O. Ihonvbere

INTRODUCTION

In some African countries, the political consequences of ... adjustment measures have been severe and have met with popular resistance in the form of riots on account of, for instance, the rising cost of food. Indeed, the social consequences of these programmes are threatening the very foundation and stability of the African social and cultural structures.

OAU, 1988.

There is particular bitterness over the fact that the seeming disengagement from the continent comes while the majority of African countries are pursing politically risky economic policy reforms that were urged on them by donors as prerequisites for increased assistance and investment.

Salim Lone, 1990a.

It has become obvious that the choice for Africa in the 1990s is between reform and further decline. The state of the continent today is, to put it mildly, very alarming. On all indicators of growth and development, Africa lags behind all other continents. In fact the 1980s hardly showed any improvement as debt, drought, instability and famine diverted attention and scarce resources from well-intentioned reform policies. Today the continent is more unstable, marginal and crisis-ridden than it was three decades ago. On the basis of current location and role in the international division of labour, state of politics, power and production relations, the future of the continent would seem very bleak.

Yet there have been numerous responses to the African crisis from regional and continental organizations as well as donor agencies. Initial policies of indigenization, nationalization and other forms of state capitalism have recently given way to structural adjustment programmes requiring the rolling back of the state, deregulation of the economy, devaluation of overvalued national currencies, export drives and reduction in the number of public employees. These policies have been pressed forward despite massive internal opposition from popular forces, the increasing delegitimization of the state and the intensification of intra- and interclass contradictions and conflicts. In the midst of mounting foreign debts and debt-servicing obligations, declining foreign assistance, internal conflicts and other internal and external economic and political pressures, the major powers, international finance institutions and donor agencies are now making new demands on Africa: political reforms through the introduction of multiparty democracy and other forms of 'political restructuring'.

This new call has generated extensive debates and divisions within the continent and between the continent and other extra-African interests. My purpose in this chapter is to examine in brief, first, the nature of the African crisis; second, responses to the crisis through stabilization and structural adjustment; third, the political and social costs of adjustment; fourth, the call for political reforms; and fifth, the prospects for democracy, reform and recovery in the continent.

THE NATURE OF THE AFRICAN CRISIS

The origins of the African crisis must be located in the inheritance, at political independence, of very fragile and unstable political structures; deep-rooted contradictions between the power elite and the people; regional, ethnic and religious antagonisms within African states; weak unproductive economic structures and the domination of state structures by largely unproductive and highly factionalized dominant classes. Postcolonial politics witnessed the depoliticization of the people as the new leaders failed to meet the promises of the nationalist struggles. It also witnessed the use of state power for personal enrichment and repression; ideological containment through the dilution of the more militant and nationalistic ideological postures of the nationalist era and reliance on defensive radicalism and various forms of political and ideological experiments.

As well, African leaders began to experiment with all sorts of political structures, ideological forms, economic models and the strengthening of patron–client relations. The end result was that scarce resources were wasted on prestige projects while inefficiency, corruption and mismanagement ruined the best-laid economic plans. Accumulation through politics and unequal alliances with transnational interests furthered sectoral disarticulation, surplus transfer and the neglect of rural areas and rural producers. With limited progress in agriculture, industry and financial management, and the failure to establish viable political structures, the continent has remained marginalized and vulnerable to pressures in the global system.

The conditions described above were made worse by incessant coups and countercoups, political intolerance, corruption, elite manipulation of primordial loyalties and differences, rural neglect, urban decay, bureaucratic inefficiency and ineffectiveness, lack of regime continuity, the politicization of resource allocation, repression and widespread human-rights abuses. The chimera of freedom and independence quickly evaporated and contradictions between the state and the people, within and between social classes, between rural and urban areas, between foreign and local capitals and between the military and politicians combined in various forms to render the continent a weak actor in the international system, vulnerable to all sorts of internal and external pressures.

To the rather debilitating conditions described above we can add the oil-price increases of the 1970s, collapsed commodity prices, declining foreign investment and foreign assistance, higher interest rates, and political destabilization, especially in Southern Africa. The conditions above resulted in declines in per-capita incomes, mass poverty, an inability to service contractual obligations and foreign debts, erosion of previous achievements in the areas of health, education, foreign trade, agricultural investment, rural development, infrastructural development and the provision of basic human needs. By the end of the 1970s the Economic Commission for Africa (ECA) had reached the conclusion that:

> There is no gainsaying the fact that Africa cannot afford to continue to perform in the field of development during the next decade or two at the same rate as in the last 15 years or so. If it does, the African region will be a much poorer part of the rest of the world than it is now; the gap between it and the rest of the world will be wider and its economic and technological backwardness will be much more pronounced (Adedeji, 1977, pp. 3–4).

The ECA was correct. The situation of the continent in terms of internal structures and relations to external forces has generally deteriorated since the 1970s. As Adebayo Adedeji has noted, the continent 'experienced a vicious and unremitting socio-economic crisis' throughout the 1980s (Adedeji, 1990b, p. 11). Africa has 7.5 per cent of the world's population but accounts for only 1.2 per cent of global GNP, 1.6 per cent of global export earnings and only 1.1 per cent of global public expenditure on health. Average per-capita income declined from $752 in 1980 to $545 or lower in 1988. Investment as a proportion of GDP declined 25.2 per cent in the 1970s to 15.8 per cent in 1988. Export/import growth rates, which were 11.2 per cent and 1.9 per cent respectively in 1978, declined to 3.8 per cent and 0.3 per cent in 1988. In the same period balance-of-payments deficits increased from $3.9 billion to $20.3 billion, inflation rose from 15.1 per cent to 21.3 per cent, foreign debt increased from $4.3 billion to $257 billion and debt-servicing obligations amounted to between 40 per cent and 100 per cent of export earnings. In addition to the dismal picture painted so far, per-capita private consumption fell by a fifth, gainful employment declined by over 20 per cent, unemployment and underemployment figures increased to 30 million and 95 million respectively, the illiterate population rose to 162 million in 1985 (up from 124 million in 1960), the average share of health and education in public expenditure declined from about 26 per cent in the early 1980s to less than 19 per cent in 1988, and over 34 million Africans became directly affected by malnutrition and disease. The number of less-developed countries rose from 17 in 1978 to 28 in 1989, and once-prosperous countries such as Nigeria and Ghana have been reclassified by the World Bank as 'low-income countries'. Some 10 000 children die daily from avoidable diseases, and export volumes declined by 2.7 per cent between 1980 and 1989. Within the same period gross fixed capital formation fell by 1.9 per cent annually; import volumes by 3 per cent, commodity prices by 3.1 per cent, and the continent's share in the value of world trade fell from 4.7 per cent in 1980 to 2.2 per cent in 1989 (Adedeji, 1990b; ECA, 1990a; Ihonvbere, 1989; IFAA, 1989).

These deteriorating conditions forced the ECA to declare the 1980s as 'Africa's lost decade' and period of 'general economic and social retro-gression' (ECA, 1990a, p . vii). In a sober reflection on the African crisis, the Chief Minister of Zanzibar recently declared that 'thirty years of inde-pendence had not benefited the peoples of Africa . .... Leaders had become pawns of extra-continental powers, economies remained appendages of the metropole and cultural values and beliefs had been discarded' (Juma, 1989, p. 6). The World Bank, in its recent review of the situation in the continent, easily reached the conclusion that 'Overall Africans are almost as poor today as they were 30 years ago' (World Bank, 1989, p . 1).

To say the least, the crisis in the continent has reduced the relevance of the state to the living conditions of the people, heightened conflicts, antag-onisms and tensions and eroded the social fabric of African societies. There is widespread misery, cynicism and disillusionment. The lack of opportuni-ties has encouraged a massive brain-drain out of the continent and scared-off foreign investors. There has been increased political violence and political instability as well as human rights abuses by desperate regimes. Overall, marginalization and vulnerability of the continent in the global system has increased. The need for urgent and drastic responses to the deepening crisis was inevitable by the mid-1980s.

One such response was the introduction of stabilization and structural adjustment programmes inspired and supervised by the International Monetary Fund (IMF) and the World Bank.

THE CONTENT OF AFRICA'S STRUCTURAL ADJUSTMENT PROGRAMMES

African governments were forced to accept stabilization and adjustment programmes by a combination of factors. First, agreement with the IMF was required by credit clubs and donors as preconditions for further assistance and credits. Given the very restive nature of urban dwellers in the absence of 'essential commodities,' many of the regimes had few options but to accept the conditionalities of the IMF and the post-stabilization prescriptions of the World Bank. The second reason for adopting stabilization and adjustment was the belief that such policies would lead to a major increase in foreign assistance from the international finance agencies. While this has occurred in a handful of cases, it has not been the case in the majority of countries. Third, African leaders believed or at least expected a massive increase in foreign investment. This has hardly occurred. Finally, it was expected that economic recovery would result from the adjustment programmes. Again, it is difficult to find an actual case of recovery beyond some improvements in macroeconomic indicators.

The components of Africa's stabilization and adjustment programmes differ substantially from packages implemented in other Third World societies. Both types of programmes have generally involved, first, the attainment of macroeconomic balance by streamlining national expenditure and national income; second, efficient resource allocation by switching resources across economic sectors; and third, resource mobilization over a long period of economic growth and increased living standards. Specifically these broad programmes have involved the elimination of subsidies for basic food items and social services, mass retrenchment of workers to reduce the size of the public service and currency devaluation at the stabilization stage. This was followed at the restructuring stage by policies of institution building and reform such as the abolition of agricultural marketing boards and the privatization of government-owned businesses. Policies of desubsidization, trade liberalization, deregulation, privatization and devaluation are anticipated to promote economic recovery and put the economies on the path to growth and development.

The first phase of Africa's adjustment programme was between 1981 and 1984. This phase concentrated on the restoration of macroeconomic balances necessitated by 'earlier over-expansionary monetary and public finance policies, underwritten by levels of foreign borrowing well beyond the debt-servicing capacity of the countries' (UNDP and World Bank, 1990, p. 3). The second phase, between 1984 and 1986, focused on 'improving resource allocation and growth' while retaining the policy instruments of the first phase. This involved the restructuring of 'economic incentives through a comprehensive revision of trade and exchange rate policies as well as through institutional reforms, especially in marketing' (ibid., p. 4). The on-going third phase incorporates programmes aimed directly at 'poverty reduction as a *fundamental objective* of adjustment policy along with improved efficiency and economic growth' (ibid.).

Unfortunately the implementation of adjustment programmes in Africa has not been as straightforward and easy as it looks on paper. The seriousness, adherence to policies and results have differed markedly between countries. External support has equally differed, as has the extent of public support. Virtually all the adjustment packages in Africa are on the extreme end of the scale without due consideration of the depth of preadjustment economic crisis, the statecraft of the leaders, the strength and capacity of political institutions, the credibility of political leaders, available resources and room for manoeuvre in the global system, as well as the power of social forces to resist the imposition of harsh reform policies. These factors, combined with internal conditions of poverty, tension and corruption, mediate the impact of adjustment. While the political costs of adjustment have been very high, the social costs have tended to mobilize opposition to adjustment, thus forcing regimes to abandon the programme or review it in the interest of political stability and the survival of regimes.

THE SOCIAL COSTS OF ADJUSTMENT

There is considerable agreement among scholars and policy-makers that structural adjustment programmes have had a negative social impact on the poor and middle classes in Africa. Their political impact has been equally grave. Adjustment has led to riots, political violence, coups and counter-coups, political intolerance and the resort of people to ethnic, religious and other chauvinistic ways of self-reproduction. Increasingly the state has been unable to protect vulnerable groups and provide for their basic needs. As well, the policies of adjustment have promoted the curtailment of basic rights, the repression of popular organizations and the promotion of antagonism, cynicism and disillusionment in society. In fact Adebayo Adedeji, the former secretary-general of the ECA, has gone to the extent of arguing that 'orthodox structural adjustment or economic recovery programmes also promote political authoritarianism and the militarization of politics in Africa and elsewhere because they are so anti-people and unpopular that only authoritarian regimes can implement and sustain them' (Adedeji, 1990a, p. 37).

Such perceptions have arisen from the tendency for repression and human rights abuses to increase with the implementation of adjustment. As subsidies are removed from social services, workers are retrenched, and new fees, levies and taxes are introduced, people are compelled to organize and politically oppose adjustment. Hence in Zaire, Zambia and Nigeria, where the regimes had very limited credibility and where adjustment widened the gap between rich and poor, adjustment policies culminated in riots and repression. The state and its custodians, in their effort to hold on to power and keep their policies going, responded to such protests with massive repression and human rights abuses (Ihonvbere, 1993). The social costs have been equally heavy.

The *Dar es Salaam Declaration*, adopted at the end of the international conference organized by the London-based Institute for African Alternatives (IFAA) in December 1989, noted 'with alarm, the deteriorating conditions all over the continent'. Of particular concern to the conference was the 'sharp decline in living standards for the great majority of the people, economies are faltering, education standards are falling steeply and social services are collapsing' (IFAA, 1989, p. 7). Hundreds of thousands of able-bodied workers have been retrenched without any social-insurance protection. Food prices have gone up drastically, and inflation has been fuelled by the devaluation of currencies and the scarcity of essential goods. The imposition of new fees and levies, as well as the removal of subsidies from fuel and social services, have made life very difficult for vulnerable groups. True, cash-crop producers did make a few gains initially from the export-drive policies, but these gains evaporated with the collapse of commodity prices and internal inflation. Crime, prostitution, cynicism and anger have taken over from once robust cultures of harmony, hope and participation. Today 'over one thousand children are dying daily in Africa and some million ... are starving' (ibid., p. 3).

In its recent report the South Commission noted that adjustment programmes have had 'devastating effects on vital public services like health and education, with special consequences for the most vulnerable social groups ... at a time when the poor were suffering an already substantial drop in income, governments scrapped or sharply reduced, in the name of efficiency, food subsidies and other selective redistributional measures' (South Commission, 1990, p. 68). The World Bank in its 1989 report on Africa noted that 'more and more Africans are going hungry. Severe food shortages were exceptional in 1960; now they are widespread. It is estimated that about one-quarter of sub-Saharan Africa's population – more than 100 million people – faces chronic food insecurity' (World Bank, 1989, p. 7). The report also noted that unemployment had become a major problem in Africa, and perhaps more worrying was the view that 'a growing sense of hopelessness', a 'crisis of confidence' and growing 'pessimism' have become the trend in the continent (ibid., p. 23). The net result is that adjustment has had adverse social impacts on Africa and the promises of recovery have hardly materialized (see, for example, Lancaster, 1989; Sandbrook, 1990; Shaw, 1988, 1993). It is in reaction to these deteriorating conditions and deepening tensions and repression in the continent that policies aimed at protecting vulnerable groups are directed. It is now increasingly thought that only a viable political environment can make room for the reform measures to be effective and sustainable. The debate over 'political conditionality' is therefore a precipitate of this new realization not only of the need to protect vulnerable groups and mobilize the people in support of reform, but also the need for some serious political reforms to broaden the support base for adjustment and recovery.

POLITICAL RESTRUCTURING IN AFRICA: ISSUES AND DEBATES

Traditionally the World Bank and the IMF saw and interpreted the African crisis as a purely economic problem. It was believed that economic responses would put African economies on the path to recovery. The ECA on the other hand argued along with the Organization for African Unity (OAU) that the crisis was as political as it was economic. The ECA contended that the 'authoritarian implementation of the unpopular orthodox stabilization and adjustment programmes was possible only because of the sporadic lack of people's participation' (Adedeji, 1990a, p. 19). In its documents the ECA contended that the African crisis was reproduced in large measure by the widespread degree of authoritarianism, repression of popular forces, human-rights abuses, the harassment of students, youths, workers and intellectuals, the suffocation of civil society, and the total absence of democratic values and traditions. Under such conditions it is impossible to sustain reform measures, mobilize popular support and enable people to be innovative and creative. In the ECA's *African Charter for Popular Participation in Development*, the organization argued that the political context of the African crisis has been characterized by 'an over-centralization of power and impediments to the effective participation of the overwhelming majority of the people in social, political and economic development'. Consequently, the Charter argues, reform and recovery cannot take place 'unless the structures, pattern and political context of the process of socio-economic development are appropriately altered' (ECA, 1990b, pp. 17, 18).

In its 1989 report the World Bank shifted its position substantially away from a purely economic interpretation of the crisis. Not only did it give substantial weight to the need to build the protection of vulnerable groups into adjustment programmes, it also called for major political and institutional reforms. These reforms included empowering ordinary people, especially women, good governance, a reliable judicial system, efficient public service, an accountable administration, participation of the people in 'designing and implementing development programs', 'genuine delegation of responsibilities', and political renewal as 'part of a concerted attack on corruption from the highest to the lower levels' (1989, pp. 1–15).

As part of the call for political restructuring, donor agencies and Western governments have joined the call and linked future assistance to the extent of efforts at democratization, the guaranteeing of human rights and the protection of vulnerable groups. As the British foreign secretary, Douglas Hurd, rather bluntly put it, 'Aid must go where it can clearly do good'. For the British government, recipients of Western aid must be seen to be moving 'towards pluralism, public accountability, respect for the rule of law, human rights and market principles' (*West Africa*, 25 June–1 July 1990). On another occasion Hurd was emphatic on the preparedness of the West to 'use aid as a lever for better governance' (quoted in Lone, 1990b, p. 3). This position has been supported by the European Community, President Mitterand of France, Herman Cohen, the US assistant secretary of state for African affairs, Barber Conable of the World Bank, Michael Camdessus of the IMF, and other multilateral organizations. Japan also declared recently its preparedness to tie future aid to political reforms. This call for political restructuring has generated different reactions from scholars and policy-makers within and outside the African continent.

There is no doubt that by trying to set the political agenda for economic reforms in Africa it would appear that international finance institutions, Western governments and donor agencies were interfering in the internal affairs of African states. Having set the political agenda through adjustment and stabilization measures, all that was left was the political agenda to ensure the success of complete integration of African economies into the Western sphere of influence and global capitalist economic relations. It would also appear that the West was attempting to impose Western political models and values as well as patterns of power and politics on Africa with little or no recognition of the specificities and contradictions of African social formations. The OAU vehemently opposes the imposition and cross-linkage of these political and economic conditionalities. Let us briefly examine the arguments of the OAU and African leaders.

It is contended that Western governments and international finance institutions were responsible for the rise or sustenance of repressive and authoritarian regimes in Africa. To suddenly acknowledge their negative roles in the process of recovery without isolating such governments immediately was a mere excuse to divert attention from the continent and justify the already reduced aid to Africa. The OAU also contends that with the developments in Eastern Europe it has become obvious that foreign assistance, investment and political support have shifted from Africa to Eastern Europe. The civil war in Liberia, in which over 30 000 people were killed, and the devastating conditions in Somalia and the Sudan were mentioned only occasionally in the Western media. Incursions into the Front Line States by South Africa attracted less than a tenth of the attention given to Iraq's invasion of Kuwait. The implementation of United Nations resolutions on South Africa were pursued with a third of the vigour with which the West pursued the case of Kuwait.

One lesson is clear from these recent developments: Africa has become very marginal, almost unimportant to the economic and geostrategic calculations of the West. The changes in Eastern Europe were not brought about by Western-dictated political conditionalities but resulted from the gradual strengthening of civil society and the eventual internal challenges to the state and its custodians. Nonetheless the West is imposing new conditionalities on Africa's process of recovery. This has been interpreted by the OAU as not only unfair but as a ploy to rationalize the diversion of aid away from Africa.

In addition to the above, the OAU has contended that today Africa is the 'world's neediest and most crisis-ridden region' (in Lone, 1990a). It is currently implementing very dangerous and difficult economic reforms that cannot be implemented without some political and social costs. It is rather unfortunate that the West was disengaging from the continent at a time when these nations were 'pursuing politically risky economic policy reforms that were urged on them by donors as prerequisites for increased assistance and investment' (ibid.).

Of course there are African leaders who 'challenge the right of donors to impose particular forms of democratic government as a condition of further aid, particularly in the absence of any parallel moves to democratize the international system' (Lone, 1990b, p. 3). The prices of Africa's exports have continued to decline, the prices of imports have continued to rise, and interest rates as well as debt-servicing obligations have continued to increase. There have been limited attempts to make concessions to Africa's demands on these problems, including the debt issue, which is fast crippling African economies. This perspective has made the OAU question the motivation behind the new conditionality at a time when Africa is facing increased competition from other regions of the world for the limited concessional financial resources on offer. Western governments, in their demands, appear not to understand the complexities of democratizing regimes and societies that have been subjected to decades of authoritarian rule. If democratization is required to go hand in hand with economic reform, African leaders will be forced to make superficial reforms and concessions to civil society and Africa will not progress from its current situation.

Perhaps the best articulation of the response to the West was by Salim Salim, the secretary-general of the OAU, who, at the recent international conference on 'Africa in the 1990s', argued that the call for political restructuring 'is diversionary and a device to introduce irrelevances' into Africa's deepening crisis and increasing marginalization in the global system. According to Lone (1990a, p. 3):

> democracy is not a 'revelation'. How it is expressed, how it is given concrete form, of necessity, varies from society to society. Consequently, one should avoid the temptation of decreeing a so-called 'perfect' model of democracy and of exporting it wholesale or of imposing it on another society.

More importantly, Lone argued that,

> More misleading is the emerging notion that multi-partyism, in a magical way, can bring about development. For no matter how many political parties an African state has or may have, that will not alter her economic fortunes. It will not change the price of coffee, cocoa, cotton, sisal or copper.... Africa is responding to international situations created by others; and quite often without much possibility to manoeuvre. Africa, in a very real sense, is a victim of an international order which is not that democratic or just. Democracy must also apply to the international system ... Africa must democratize, our efforts will be

hamstrung by the non-democratic international economic system in which we operate and which militates against our development (*Africa Recovery*, 1990, p. 29).

The above, then, represents the position of the OAU.

It is certainly correct to complain about international double standards on political and economic matters, the collapse of commodity prices, declining foreign aid and investment, and the support of Western powers for repressive and extremely corrupt governments in Africa. Yet these are mere rationalizations and excuses for internal mismanagement, the lack of political will to undertake reforms, corruption, the marginalization of the masses in the process of development, the unproductive disposition of the African elite, and the general inability to provide responsible and accountable leadership since political independence. If African leaders had sustained the nationalistic fervour of the preindependence nationalist era and carried out structural changes both internally and in their relations with external interests, things might be different on the continent today.

However the negative developments in the global system have not been directed only at Africa – Africa was not the only continent to be colonized – and the oil price shocks of the early 1970s affected all developing countries. Nonetheless many developing countries with fairly stable and predictable political systems have succeeded in attracting foreign investments, while in the case of Africa 'foreign investment has not flowed in, and ... even the trickle that has come in has dried up' (Obasanjo, 1990). Africa has remained the most vulnerable to external pressures and manipulations. The ability to attract foreign aid and investment and prevent donors from diverting their interests to other regions cannot be divorced from the degree of internal changes and the visible commitment of the state and social forces to production. Africa has hardly moved in this direction since political independence. It has been all too easy to complain about the international environment and external exploitation, even when the majority of African states, without being coerced or prompted, deliberately initiated policies that eroded their autonomy and reproduced dependence and subservience to external interests.

The OAU cannot pretend that it is unaware that fundamental changes and donor sympathies are unlikely to occur in international economic relations in the very near future. Rather than make internal structural changes, check corruption, waste and misplaced priorities, and mobilize the people for self-reliant development, African leaders have found it more convenient to complain about commodity prices, declining foreign aid and so on. Rather than respect human rights, ensure accountability to the public, democratize their societies and expand political spaces in order to strengthen civil society and involve the people in the process of decision-making, African leaders have engaged in some of the worst cases of repression, human rights abuses and the suffocation of civil society.

In the *African Charter for Popular Participation* the ECA was clear that the crisis on the continent, as well as continuing authoritarianism and human-rights violations, was the result of decades of 'gross mismanagement of the economy, massive capital flight, unproductive use of resources, anti-rural bias, poor resource mobilization, distorted priorities ... and an absence of effective popular participation in decision-making' (Adedeji, 1990a, p. 19). As Douglas Hurd rightly put it, 'Poverty does not justify torture, tyranny' (quoted in Lone, 1990b, p. 28). There is no way African leaders can link to commodity prices the suffocation of civil society, corruption and waste that has characterized political competition and political relations since political independence. The little they have earned in their foreign trade relations has been looted out of the country, wasted on defence and grossly mismanaged. If external forces are now dictating the political tunes for political restructuring, it is the inevitable cost they are paying for largely running down their economies, increasing the continent's vulnerability to external pressures, and sacrificing the independence and autonomy of their respective states.

CONCLUSION

It is obvious that Africa currently has no alternative but to institute drastic internal political reforms. In virtually all African states the pressures for reform can no longer be contained. To be sure, the movement has been penetrated by opportunists in several countries. In others there is evidence of a very narrow definition of democracy and democratization to mean the mere existence of more than one political party. Yet in other countries regimes are making tricky concessions to opponents and civil society as a way of holding on to power in the hope that the commitments of the people will wane in the near future. But these are initial and inevitable developments in the struggle for change.

One can contend that the African crisis is first and foremost a *political crisis*. It is a crisis of the lack of democratic space, the non-involvement of the people in decision-making and the general brutalization of the masses. The non-empowerment of popular organizations and the strengthening of the structures of personal rule and corruption have contributed to the erosion of possibilities for democracy on the continent. The use of the state for private accumulation, the conversion of politics into a business, an investment from which political power is to be used for personal enrichment, as well as the manipulation of ethnic, regional and religious differences have also contributed to the delegitimization of the state.

It is these negative developments and political attitudes and positions that have led Africa into its present predicament. As a result of the irresponsibility and non-accountability of the majority of African leaders, who run their countries like personal estates, the continent has become characterized by 'highly centralized governments, rule by single men surrounded by cliques of courtiers, constitutions reduced to paper documents, cowed judiciaries, easily disposable laws, ubiquitous and intimidating security services, large and inefficient state bureaucracies, restricted freedoms of thought, assembly and organization, and widespread corruption' (Joseph, 1990, p. 17). Under such conditions, it is difficult to see how the continent can recover and become relevant in the geostrategic and economic calculations of other nations without serious, viable and sustainable political reforms.

At the very minimum certain changes must and should be visible before donor agencies advance further aid to African countries. These should include the existence of a free press, guarantees of trade union rights, academic freedom, decentralization of governmental operations, empowerment of popular organizations, and freedom of organization, speech and other fundamental rights. Further, there must be visible and enforceable checks on corruption, free and fair elections and multiparty political systems formed freely by the people, drastic cuts in defence expenditure and the dismantling of existing security organizations that are used to harass social critics, intellectuals and trade unionists. The protection of the environment and vulnerable groups, the promotion of gender equity by involving women in decision-making, and the implementation of previous protocols and agreements, such as the *African Charter for Human and Peoples' Rights* and the *African Charter for Popular Participation in Development*, to which all African states are signatories but which have never been respected or implemented, are essential actions. Not until these steps are taken will the continent recover from its economic and political crisis. Africa will remain almost irrelevant in global relations. It will continue to be marginal in the calculations of foreign investors and donor agencies will experience increasing frustration at the inability of the continent to show any positive results for decades of assistance.

It does not matter where the call for empowerment and democratization comes from. African governments and popular organizations can relate such externally generated calls to their specificities and struggles without sacrificing their autonomies. If African leaders are willing to implement foreign-inspired adjustment programmes and continue to call for foreign aid and other forms of assistance, why are they opposed to externally generated calls for popular empowerment, accountability and democratization? Olusegun Obasanjo has been very clear on the fact that Africa cannot continue to blame external forces for its predicaments because 'other countries equally disadvantaged by the colonial experience have recovered much better. The bold fact is that in Africa we have squandered over 30 years of nation building' (Obasanjo, 1990). If Africa is to survive the 1990s it must take urgent steps to open up the 'political process to accommodate freedom of opinions, tolerate differences, accept consensus on issues as well as ensure the effective participation of the people and their organizations and associations' (ECA, 1990b, p. 19). This is the only way to ensure popular mobilization, the willingness of the people to accept the pains of change and reform, and the entrenchment of accountability and democratic attitudes on the continent.

9 Reflections on the State, Democracy and NGOs in Africa

Julius E. Nyang'oro

INTRODUCTION

Today Africa stands at a political and economic crossroads. Politically, the majority of the countries on the continent are facing a renewed push towards opening up the political system through a concerted effort by advocates of pluralism, or multiparty systems. The push for political pluralism received new impetus with the collapse of state socialism in Eastern Europe in 1989–90. We may recall that the government of General Jeruzelski in Poland, the communist government in Hungary, the Honecker government in East Germany, the Zhivkov government in Bulgaria, the Husak government in Czechoslovakia and the Ceausescu government in Romania all fell in a space of only a few months in late 1989. The changes in Eastern Europe ushered in a new era in global politics because, for the first time since 1945, it was no longer possible to talk of an 'Eastern bloc'. But much more important for Africa was the fact that Eastern Europe provided an example of results that could be achieved if a united populace was organized against a perceived authoritarian system. Arguably the push for pluralism that we have seen in as diverse African countries as Zambia, the Ivory Coast, Benin and so on can in part be seen as a global movement away from state-centred political arrangements, which some of us have called 'state corporatism' (Nyang'oro and Shaw, 1989).

But it would be a mistake to suggest that the now overt pressure for political change is something new in Africa. We should recall that the nationalist struggles that culminated in the independence of African countries were part of a historical process that has always pitted centralizing forces of a non-democratic state (such as the colonial state), on the one hand, and the forces of resistance to this centralizing tendency – forces that

130

have attempted to pull away from the state – on the other hand. While independence was won in the early 1960s, for most of the population of African countries the qualitative difference between the colonial state and the post-colonial state has been minimal. At the political level, instead of having the colonial officials dictate action, the citizens were now faced with corrupt officials of a sole political party demanding total allegiance to the state. In the 1980s there was evidence of popular 'disengagement' from the state by civil society, resulting in contradictions in the relationship between these two important elements of society (Rothchild and Chazan, 1988; Ergas, 1987). Thus part of the crisis in Africa today is significantly of a political character. At the economic level the story of Africa's dismal record is a familiar one. The economies of Sub-Saharan African countries have performed extremely poorly in the last two decades. A World Bank report flatly stated that '[o]verall Africans are almost as poor today as they were 30 years ago' (World Bank, 1989). The same report notes that after an initial period of growth in the early years of independence,

> most African economies faltered, then went into decline. There were some exceptions, but sub-Saharan Africa as a whole has now witnessed almost a decade of falling per capita incomes, increasing hunger, and accelerating ecological degradation. The earlier progress made in social development [has] now [been] eroded (ibid., p. 1).

Of course the result has been the now ubiquitous structural adjustment programmes (SAPs), which African countries have adopted in order to continue receiving foreign capital. Whether SAPs have succeeded in arresting the decline of African economies is still a hotly debated issue. The World Bank and the IMF clearly see SAPs as the only way out of the economic crisis (World Bank, 1989).

The United Nations Economic Commission for Africa (ECA) does not seem to think so (ECA, 1989). All are agreed, however, that the implementation of these economic reforms necessarily will create hardship, at least in the short run, for large segments of the population, especially urban wage earners (Onimode, 1989; Nelson, 1989).

In terms of other economic indicators, the overall picture for Sub-Saharan Africa continues to be discouraging. The export sector has for the most part either stagnated or declined, reflecting the general slowdown in the world economy (World Bank, 1989, p. 2). In per-capita terms, GDP in Sub-Saharan Africa actually fell by 0.2 per cent in 1990. These figures led the ECA's retiring executive secretary, Adebayo Adedeji, to conclude that 'this means in effect that the average African continues, for the twelfth successive year, to get poorer' (Harsh, 1990a, p. 1). The poor performance of the export sector has also led to a poor profile of Africa's external debt, with mounting debts increasing the pressure on governments to borrow even more to meet payment obligations. World Bank figures released in December 1990 projected Sub-Saharan Africa's debt at $161 billion in 1990, an increase of more than 9 per cent over the $147 billion of the previous year. However the ECA, totalling the debt for all of Africa, estimated that it had risen to $271.9 billion in 1990, or 4.7 per cent higher than the year before (Harsh, 1990b, p. 42).

Coupled with the poor performance of the economy, Sub-Saharan Africa is also faced with the phenomenon of increased peripheralization in the global economy (see Chapter 2 above). The two processes are actually interrelated. As the African economies perform poorly, foreign capital becomes less interested in investing in the region, thus diminishing Africa's position in global competitiveness (ECA, 1989). The industrial sector has especially suffered because of the high import content of raw materials. The decline in social services and education is creating the impression that African labour is less skilled and therefore less attractive to multinationals that may be thinking of relocating from the developed countries in search of cheap, skilled labour, a process that led to the rapid industrialization of the Pacific Rim countries in the 1970s and 1980s (Gereffi and Wyman, 1990). The World Bank's conclusion with regard to Africa's economic performance tells the story:

> Africa's deepening crisis is characterized by weak agricultural growth, a decline in industrial output, poor export performance, climbing debt, and deteriorating social indicators, institutions, and environment. Agricultural output has grown annually by less than 1.5 percent on average since 1970, with food production rising more slowly than population. Although industry grew roughly three times as fast as agriculture in the first decade of independence, the last few years have seen an alarming reversal in many African countries where deindustrialization seems to have set in. With export volumes barely growing at all since 1970, Africa's share in world markets has fallen by almost half (World Bank, 1989, p. 2).

Given African states' high propensity for direct participation in economic production and in the marketing of the major export crops, the decline of the economy has had an almost instantaneous effect on state behaviour both economically and politically. At the economic level the state adopts policies that are bound to get it into trouble. For example, in many instances the state underwrites or subsidizes urban consumption and overvalues domestic currencies to maintain certain consumption levels for the most vocal segments of the population – the urban dwellers (Bates, 1981). This behaviour, although economically irrational, is politically expedient in the sense that the state is at least able to buy the allegiance and support of the potentially troublesome populations. This behaviour by the state is important in understanding the nature of political relations. The exclusivist character of African corporatist practice suggests that the consequences of exclusion are dire for those segments of the population that are either purposefully excluded by the state or themselves choose not to be included in the corporatist structure. They are excluded from the 'national cake'. The interaction between the state and the various segments of the population in the allocation of resources in society therefore defines the scope of politics – and thus of authoritarianism – in Africa (cf. Chapter 8 above).

NGOs, POLITICS AND DEVELOPMENT IN AFRICA

It would seem obvious that the failure of African states to effect economic development has resulted in the need for the population to find alternative ways in which to organize for purposes of meeting everyday socio-economic needs. Aiming at long-term development, however, is difficult when people are busy trying to survive from day to day, given the combination of bad government policy, natural disasters such as drought and famine, civil unrest, which has led to military conflict in some countries, and the general structure and consequence of underdevelopment. At one level, societal response to this ongoing crisis has been the now ubiquitous informal economy (*magendo*) in many African countries. Due to its very nature the informal economy is less structured and not easily subjected to standard economic measurement, although this sector of the economy may have been responsible for the saving of millions of lives in strife-torn countries such as Uganda in the 1980s and currently in Ethiopia, Somalia, Sudan and Mozambique.

At another level, non-governmental organizations (NGOs) have been the other response. The evolution of NGOs can be seen to reflect concerns at three levels: local, national and international. At all three levels NGOs have played a significant role in harnessing economic development efforts with the intention of positively affecting those people who under normal circumstances would not benefit from government policy. In other words, while the effects of government development policy may be an elitist development posture, thus limiting its impact on the majority of the people, NGOs at all levels would push for the 'democratization of development' (Clark, 1991; cf. Chapters 7 and 14 of this volume). As James Wunsch has noted, '[n]early all independent African states have pursued a largely statist and centralized strategy of economic and political development during the past thirty years' (Wunsch, 1990, p. 43).

Obviously the statist and centralized strategy of economic development has not worked. The introduction of SAPs is an indication of the failure of government. Michael Bratton has provided a convincing thesis as to why the emergence of NGOs was a direct result of government policy failure:

> Experience with poverty programming in the 1970s revealed that the public policy environment was not often conducive to the economic viability of individual development projects. Moreover, the established international aid bureaucracies and fragile African governments were organizationally ill-equipped to deliver services and respond to felt needs at the rural community level. Centralized agencies lacked information about, and the flexibility to adapt to, local conditions. As a consequence, a phalanx of non-governmental organizations (NGOs) with programmes in relief and rural development arose to fill gaps left by governments. By default as much as by design, these NGOs have been able to capture the lead in devising treatments for rural poverty in Africa (Bratton, 1990, pp. 87–8).

But in no way does the emergence and proliferation of NGOs suggest a retreat by the state. Indeed the continuing struggle between centre and periphery in Africa is a reflection of the desire by the state to have a substantial say in what happens in rural areas. Of course the question is how effective the state will be in establishing a preeminent role in rural development. The continuing problem for the state is its shallow penetration of society and its weak institutions, which allowed NGOs, at least in this case, to emerge in the first place. In some ways the relationship between the state and NGOs may define the scope of development in rural Africa for some time to come.

If, then, we are to envisage an important future role to be played by NGOs in rural development in Africa, we have to confront Michael Bratton's question regarding the debate about development in Africa. Bratton, like many others (for example Leonard and Marshall, 1982; Hyden, 1983), has noted that the critical issue in African development is institution building; but instead of casting the question in a 1970s mode as to the best way for state development agencies to reach the poor majority, the 1990s question is going to be 'how can the poor majority reach the makers of public policy?' (Bratton, 1990, p. 89). This question of course makes the assumption that NGOs can sufficiently develop and organize themselves to make them influential enough at the level of the state. This influence presumably would translate itself in terms of the state adopting policies preferred by the NGOs.

Thus the existence of NGOs would provide one avenue for political action by the rural poor, not only for purposes of influencing public policy in the area of economic development, but also in a larger sense of wider political participation in terms of the classic political rights of voting, freedom of association and the like. One may wonder how this could be achieved in the context of African politics where action by any group in society may be perceived by the state as a challenge to its authority (Macdonald addresses a similar question in the context of Latin American development in Chapter 14 below). This issue is unavoidable and must be addressed at the outset. As Bratton (1990, p. 91) notes, the construction of organizations, at least in the development field, is an unavoidably political act: 'it involves the exercise of power. It consists of efforts to maximize control over the factors that affect the realization of shared goals, and seeking to influence – through lobbying or alliance building – those factors which cannot be directly controlled'. But as he further notes, this organizational enterprise need not be confrontational with the state. Indeed, a 'smart' NGO that selectively collaborates with the state is likely to be more successful in achieving its goals:

> Effective leaders of NGOs in Africa have generally sought to identify openings in the administrative system and to cultivate non-adversarial working relations with the politically powerful. They have been most able to articulate the needs of the poor in the context of a declaration of loyalty to national development goals. Even if they have not been able to control the policy environment, they have been able to influence it. In this way the powerless have sometimes been able to achieve at least part of what they want (ibid., pp. 95–6).

But it should be pointed out that not all NGOs have the capacity to organize themselves to influence government policy in the way just described. The majority of NGOs would hardly have influence beyond their locality. The immediate difficulty for NGOs (and their benefactors) then would be how to reconcile two interrelated contradictions: first, the apparent cooptation by the state, which in turn would effectively make the NGO a non-NGO by virtue of its close association with the state; and second, the hierarchy within the NGO system, which would create the appearance of favouritism by the state, bilateral donors and IFIs of certain NGOs over others (see Chapter 7 above). One solution of this difficulty would be to raise questions (in order to satisfactorily answer them) in a long-term study that would address issues such as how NGOs perceive themselves in terms of both their membership and in relation to the state, the direction they would prefer to take and so on (Denham concludes with just such a list; see Chapter 7). If indeed some NGOs have accumulated enough experience to engage in public policy advocacy, as Bratton suggests, then, as both Denham and Macdonald suggest in this volume, the political nature of the NGOs themselves may require further scrutiny.

IS THERE A FUTURE FOR STATE-LED DEVELOPMENT?

The current debate about African development is in most cases conducted within a surprisingly unrealistic political context, especially if the debate is framed as free market vs state-led development. To a large extent the phony nature of the debate is perpetuated by the different interests that stand to benefit or lose in the event of a particular strategy of development being adopted. In these debates the poor are never really represented because they lack influence at higher levels of government in the state capitals or at powerful financial centres in London, Paris or Washington – hence the need for effective NGOs. I wish to make a few observations that strike me as important when considering the current debates.

It is difficult to see how successful IMF/World-Bank inspired reforms will be in limiting the role of the state in African economic development. This assessment is made for the following reasons. First, state-centred development strategy is not an invention of the postcolonial regime in Africa. All colonial states in one way or another participated in economic policy, ranging from the taxation of peasants in the growing and marketing of cash crops (Rodney, 1974) to the introduction of import substitution industrialization after the Second World War (Rweyemamu, 1972; Nyang'oro, 1989). With this long historical record of active participation in the economy, it is difficult to see how the state in Africa would so quickly cease to be an important actor in the economic realm (see also Bates, 1981). And, indeed, as Stubbs points out in Chapter 11, a strong state has in every case been a prerequisite for the phenomenal growth rates of the Asian NICs and near-NICs.

Secondly, in their dealings with African countries, international financial institutions for the most part deal with states qua states. Indeed most of Africa's external debt is publicly owned and guaranteed debt, which makes the state the central actor. This fact inevitably raises the question whether economic liberalism, as pushed by the World Bank and the IMF, can succeed under conditions of uncertainty in the political realm as state-makers grapple with popular demands for more political space and a greater voice.

Furthermore, while individual entrepreneurship is advocated by the international financial institutions, there is little evidence that these institutions are willing to lend money to individual entrepreneurs in Africa without the state acting as guarantor.

Thirdly, it must be noted that welfarism has become an essential feature of the modern state, both in developed and underdeveloped countries. Even the most repressive world states are theoretically committed to some socio-economic agenda, which makes state participation in the economy inevitable. In African countries, commitment to universal primary education and health care, for example, have been goals that have furthered the legitimacy of the state. In most instances, however, there has been a considerable gap between commitment to these goals and their actual implementation. Yet it is inevitable that African states will – as all bureaucratic institutions have a tendency to do – continue to push for what they perceive to be their important role in society. The issue therefore is not whether the role of the state is important, but rather the fact that the state perceives that it has a role to play.

NGOs AND STATE-LED DEVELOPMENT

This brings us full-circle to the question of NGOs. Theoretically, one would assume that global capitalism would be in favour of the free market in African countries, but the historical reality in the evolution of capitalism in Africa requires that the state play an important role; just how important that role should be is, however, still an open question. This fact, then, would suggest that in order to ensure that the voices of the poor in rural areas are heard, NGOs will have to speak for them. However, they will have to confront the reality of the struggle for resource allocation in society. The confrontation with this reality would of course mean raising the question not only of economics – development, opportunity and redistribution – but also the political question of participation. These are the two key questions facing NGO activity in Africa in the 1990s.

Part V

Asia

10 New Regionalisms in Central Asia in the 1990s

Kiaras Gharabaghi

INTRODUCTION

The disintegration of the Soviet Union in 1990–1 resulted in the emergence of fifteen newly independent states. Most media and academic publications refer to these states collectively as the 'former Soviet Union' (FSU) or individually, as 'formerly Soviet republics' (FSRs). Such terminology raises the question as to how one is to perceive the territory of the FSU: is it one region composed of fifteen states, or are there several, differentiated regions, defined along parameters bearing no relevance to the states' collective 'formerly Soviet' identity?[1] The characterization of regions has always been a contested issue in the relevant literature. While there is general agreement that regions involve an element of geographic contiguity (Duffy and Feld, 1980, p. 510), there is also considerable disagreement pertaining to the nature of factors determining the boundaries of individual regions, not to mention the principles according to which such factors can be sequenced in terms of importance.

This chapter seeks to determine the utility of applying a conceptual framework of regionalism to one particular territorial area of the FSU: that consisting of Turkmenistan, Uzbekistan, Tajikistan, Kyrghyzstan and Kazakhstan, collectively known as Central Asia.[2] Characterizing Central Asia as a region, and therefore as a meaningful analytical construct, is not an obvious choice, and thus requires justification. That, in turn, necessitates two quite distinctive methodologies: one is to examine closely the political, economic, social and religious elements of national *and* transnational character *within* Central Asia. The other is to determine the nature of the relationship of Central Asia as a region with its external regional environment. The former constitutes an issue-area approach to determine the degree of commonality between the individual Central Asian states; the latter constitutes a systems approach premised upon a framework of regionalism.

141

The central argument of this chapter is that Central Asia does indeed constitute a distinctive region, and as such is subject to a set of newly emerging regional issues. The future of Central Asia with respect to political and economic development as well as national sovereignties and security will depend not so much on fortuitous regional system dynamics, but instead on contrived policy choices based on the recognition of regional options.

NATIONALISM AND TRANSNATIONALISM IN CENTRAL ASIA

The very conception of Central Asia as a region has traditionally rested on two factors: religion and ethnicity. Four of the five states in the area are predominantly Muslim (of the Sunni branch of Islam), and all but Tajikistan are ethnically of Turkic origin.[3] Not surprisingly recent literature has identified Islam and ethnicity as potentially transnational forces in the development (political, social and economic) of the region. This perception rests on two fundamental assumptions: first, it assumes that there is no need to differentiate various types of Islam; and second, it assumes that the general ethnic characterization of Central Asia as Turkic is sufficient to determine mass allegiances. Such assumptions are misplaced. Neither Islam nor broad ethnic identification provide much of a basis for transnationalism in Central Asia, as will be shown below. Instead it is economic structure and dependency, on the one hand, and national security, broadly conceived, on the other hand, that render a regional perspective of Central Asia meaningful.

There is no question that Islam is an important element in the sociopolitical realm of individual Central Asian states. As Muriel Atkins points out, 'it remains influential not only in a strictly religious sense but also because people see it as an integral part of their own nationality's history, culture and customs and as a guide to proper social behaviour' (Atkins, 1989, p. 605). Although successive Soviet regimes tried very hard to curtail if not eliminate Islamic practices, 'Islam never died out in the Soviet Union' (ibid.). But neither under the Soviet Union, nor since independence, has Islam ever taken on a transnational dimension of any significance, nor is it likely to do so in the short or medium term.

One major reason for this is that Islam in Central Asia, at least at the mass level, is not of the orthodox, conservative or fundamentalist variety. Rather it is of the parallel (or folk) variety (ibid.). That is to say, while Islamic rituals and festivities are taken seriously, the linkage of Islam and politics is viewed with suspicion. Thus, it is Islam, not Islamicism (that is, politicized, ideologized Islam) that is prevalent in the region (Halbach, 1992, p. 382).

A number of scholars have emphasized in recent works that the trans-nationalization of Islam in Central Asia is secondary to the transnationalization of ethnic allegiances. For example, Hunter (1992, p. 36) states:

> The historic record indicates that, although very important, Islam is unlikely to replace ethnicity and ethnocentric cultures as the primary focus of national identity and loyalty. Therefore, overarching notions such as pan-Islamism may have even a lesser chance of success than their ethnically-based variants, such as pan-Turkism.

Similarly, Hyman argues that 'the ideal of a united Turkestan has staged a steady comeback in Turkic intelligensia circles' (Hyman, 1993, p. 297). But such observations are also misleading. The prospects for pan-Turkism are very poor in Central Asia: Tajikistan's society is not of Turkic origin, and in the other states ethnic diversity at the national level virtually ensures that any attempt on the part of national governments to advocate pan-Turkism would meet with firm opposition from the large Russian and other non-Turkic minorities, not to mention external intervention on the part of Russia and possibly even the Ukraine. More fundamentally, the notion of pan-Turkism assumes that popular allegiances to Turkic ethnicity necessarily and uniformly supersedes other allegiances, such as to locality, clan or social class.

Ultimately both religion and ethnicity will play an important role in the development of nationalism within the individual Central Asian states. There may well be a transnational character in the religious and ethnicity-based social and political dynamics of the region, but any such character should not be exaggerated. The prevalence of these elements in the literature (particularly in the media but also in academic publications) is due primarily to a 'monolithic or at least inadequately differentiated perception of the region' (Halbach, 1992. p. 382).

Economic structures, much more so than religion and ethnicity, provide the Central Asian states with common ground. Contrary to intuitive logic, whereby regional cooperation is facilitated by complementary economic structures among the units, in Central Asia it is the *congruence* of economic structures throughout the region that provides much of the impetus for transnationalism. Having been relegated to raw-materials suppliers under the centrally commanded Soviet economic system, all five states share a set of fundamental structural economic problems. So, typical of many other Southern-based regional experiments it is the nature of their underdevelopment that provides the rationale for regional cooperation, in spite of potential (and likely) inefficiencies (see Chapters 6, 8, 12, 13 and 15 of this volume).

As Table 10.1 indicates, the economies of all five Central Asian republics are primarily agriculturally based and crop diversity is minimal. Cotton is the dominant crop in all five republics, so much so that in Uzbekistan and Tajikistan it is reasonable to speak of an agricultural monoculture (IMF *et al.,* 1991, p. 218). Because of the low industrial output (as well as the lack of diversity in industrial production), all five republics are subject to very high interrepublican trade dependency, especially with Russia.

Table 10.1   Origin of net material product (NMP), 1990 (per cent)

	Industry	Agriculture	Other*
Turkmenistan	15.7	47.9	36.5
Uzbekistan	23.8	44.3	32.0
Tajikistan	28.6	38.3	33.2
Kyrghyzstan	32.0	43.0	25.0
Kazakhstan	27.6	39.9	32.6

Note: *Other = construction, transportation, communication and miscellaneous.
Source: IMF, 1992a; condensed from separate publications for each republic.

Under the central command of the Soviet Union, this system of trade dependency was, although terribly inefficient, at least functional. Since the disintegration of the Soviet Union, however, interrepublican trade has faced numerous obstacles, many of which are explicitly political in nature. As a result all five states are now actively pursuing trade diversification. That, in turn, cannot be accomplished without increasing crop diversity in the agricultural sector, as well as the output of the industrial sector relative to agriculture and other sectors (see Table 10.1). To further that end, both physical and social infrastructural improvements will be required. It is particularly in this context that Central Asia becomes clearly identifiable as a region, as all five states were consistently short-changed under the Soviet system relative to most of the other republics. For example, education and training levels of the national labour forces show that, on average, the number of specialists and scientists within the Central Asian labour forces constitute only 68 per cent and 48 per cent respectively, of the numbers for the averages of the other republics (IMF *et al.*, 1991, p. 222). Social indicators also point to commonalities within Central Asia when compared with the rest of the FSU (see Table 10.2).

Table 10.2   Social indicators, average Central Asia vs FSU, 1989

	Average family (number)	Birth rate (per 1000)	Infant mortality (per 1000)	Doctors (per 10 000)	Hospital beds (per 10 000)
C. Asia	5.2	32.1	38.7	35.5	119
FSU	3.6	17.4	16.4	45.4	121

Source: IMF *et al.*, 1991, p. 232; data for FSU excludes Russia.

Faced with fundamental shortcomings not only in the actual structures of their respective economies, but also in their potential capacity for structural reform, the Central Asian states have sought common solutions to common problems. Regional policy coordination amongst the Central Asian states, and more generally regional cooperation in dealing with common problems, has been steadily moving to the top of the national policy agenda. Economic structure alone, however, tells only half the story; a rationale for Central Asian 'regionalism' can also be found in the context of national (in)security.

There is no question that in the interest of regime stability, issues of religion and ethnicity (as discussed earlier) must be contained at the national level. The emergence of pan-Islamic or pan-ethnic social mass movements in Central Asia would call into question the legitimacy of the ruling regimes and elites, the composition of which, after all, has not changed much since the disintegration of the Soviet Union (Olcott, 1992, pp. 255–9). Uneven development across the region, or disparate development strategies, may well create vulnerabilities within the civil societies of the less successful states, providing an opportunity for the transnationalization of ideological, religious or ethnicity-based social movements. It is therefore this insecurity of the respective Central Asian elites/regimes that provides a rationale for regional cooperation.

Environmental disaster, like economic underdevelopment, is a powerful motive force for regional cooperation in Central Asia (see Gharabaghi, 1994). Martha Olcott has summarized candidly the environmental problems in Central Asia:

[F]ifty years of Soviet economic planning has left Central Asia with an acute water shortage and a general ecological crisis. Its environment is so contaminated (especially with defoliants, chemical fertilizers, and airborne salts from the Aral Sea) that much of the population suffers from environmentally induced or exasperated health problems (Olcott, 1992, p. 253).

Of particular concern with respect to environmental degradation in Central Asia is the disastrous condition of the region's major waterbodies. Thirty-five years ago the Aral Sea was the world's fourth-largest lake. Then, in the early 1960s, the central government of the Soviet Union, in an attempt to increase the cotton output in Central Asia, commenced diverting the Aral Sea's water into two rivers, which were to serve as irrigation channels. By the mid-1980s the lake had shrunk by almost 50 per cent and salinity had nearly tripled (World Bank, 1993, p. 14). As a result of this rapid shrinkage, 'thirty miles separate some coastal towns from the water. If recent trends continue, the sea will largely disappear within another decade or two, existing only in old maps and geographic memory' (Brown, 1991, p. 22).

In broad terms, one can identify four consequences of the Aral Sea ecological disaster. First, as a result of the increased salination, fish populations have decreased to almost nothing. This, in turn, has uprooted the entire fishing industry in the region. Second, as a result of the high volumes of water diverted from the lake into the cotton fields, the water table of the soil has risen to the degree that 'deep-rooted crops cannot develop properly in the waterlogged soil' (ibid.). Third, the Aral Sea is increasingly losing its function as 'climatic thermostat' for the region. As its size decreases, so does its influence on the climate, making for extremely cold winters and extremely hot summers (ibid., p. 24). This, in turn, also affects negatively the capacity for future crop diversification. Finally, because the cultivation of cotton in Central Asia has traditionally been accompanied by the heavy use of pesticides and chemical fertilizers, the tap water in surrounding areas is becoming increasingly tainted, thereby exposing the affected populations to severe health risks (ibid.). According to Lester Brown,

> the Aral Sea basin is the planet in microcosm. It is one of the first regions where environmental degradation is reducing economic output, leading to a steady fall in living standards. The people living there have only a few years to reverse this trend (ibid., p. 27).

Unfortunately the Aral Sea represents only one part of the story of the deteriorating ecological conditions of major waterbodies in Central Asia, with a similar crisis brewing in the Caspian Sea (Golub, 1992).

There has been at least a recognition of the disastrous consequences of the ecological crisis pertaining to the Caspian and Aral Seas. Thus separate conferences were held in Baku and Nulivs, Karakalpak, respectively, designed to discuss possible solutions to the problem. In addition, the World Bank, the United Nations Environment Programme and the UN Development Programme, in conjunction with the governments of Kazakhstan, Uzbekistan, Turkmenistan and Tajikistan, launched the Aral

Sea Environmental Assistance Programme in April 1993, aiming to develop and implement a series of specific measures designed to stabilize and eventually reverse the crisis in the Aral Sea (World Bank, 1993). Further ecological deterioration in Central Asia will undoubtedly be accompanied by social dislocation, migration, obstacles to crop diversification, rising costs in health services due to the spread of environmentally premised diseases and so on.

Clearly these transnational issues have come to threaten the very viability of Central Asia's states, and therefore present themselves as issues of national security. Mutual threat from transnational forces therefore may spur the development of a Central Asian 'regional' mentality. At the same time, however, contending trends are at work to weaken regional cooperation. The new sovereignty of the individual states is difficult to reconcile with the imperative of effective – and not merely rhetorical – regionalism. Furthermore, although the transnational character of religion and ethnicity have been discounted here, it should be recognized that Central Asia is still a relatively new region (as a separate entity from the Soviet Union), and the various local, national and transnational socio-political, ethnic and religious dynamics have not yet played themselves out. In fact it is quite likely that at least a possibility that the transnationalization of religion and other factors will remain intact for some time to come.

The final section of this chapter considers three sets of *potential* regionalisms that may emerge in the Central Asian context. It is by no means clear which of the three forms will come to dominate regional relations.

CONTENDING REGIONALISMS IN CENTRAL ASIA

The Commonwealth of Independent States

The *Declaration at Alma-Ata on the Creation of the Commonwealth of Independent States* (CIS), devised jointly by Belorussia, the Ukraine and the Russian Federation in December 1991, was an attempt to maintain the cohesiveness of the FSU via a formal regional organization. The declaration states that the parties to it have agreed to 'carry out coordinated radical economic reforms aimed at creating feasible market mechanisms, transformation of property and ensuring the freedom of entrepreneurship' (IMF, 1992b, p. 29). The document then proceeds to list twelve further aims, among them 'to abstain from any actions economically harmful to each other', 'to conduct coordinated policy of price liberalization and social protection', and 'to undertake joint efforts aimed at providing for a single economic space' (ibid.). However since then, rather than improving trade relations and economic cooperation and coordination, the newly independent states have created 'an incentive structure that *discourages* trade among [them] ... and without the necessary institutions to facilitate trade, trade relations have been thrown in disarray, at times verging on collapse' (Michalopoulos and Tarr, 1993, p. 22).

These obstacles are not the result of poor decision-making within the individual states; instead they are symptomatic of the lack of legitimacy of the CIS. From the very beginning the CIS encountered resistance, particularly from the Baltic states (Estonia, Latvia and Lithuania) and Georgia, none of which ever joined the Commonwealth (Migranyan, 1992, p. 11). Outside Central Asia, Armenia is the most ardent supporter of the CIS, principally for strategic reasons. At war with neighbouring Azerbaijan, Armenia has to worry about the possibility of Turkish or Iranian intervention. In that event Armenia's only ally capable of containing either Turkey or Iran would be Russia. Maintaining close ties with Russia and the CIS has therefore been an important element in Armenian foreign policy.

The Central Asian states have been the most consistent supporters of the CIS, although both motivations for and intensity of support varies considerably.

Turkmenistan and Kazakhstan are furthest apart in their respective views of the CIS: the former has distanced itself considerably, while the latter has sought to reinforce the legitimacy and effectiveness of the CIS as much as possible. Turkmenistan's position is captured well by the following statement of President Niyazov:

> There is talk about some sort of coordinating executive body within the Commonwealth's framework. We are against such a decision. I think that such a step would also resuscitate the former ... principle of managing the economy, and at this point we cannot entirely rid ourselves of it in any case; that is, we would again be allotted the role of a raw-materials base (Portnikov, 1992, p. 5).

Turkmenistan's capacity to distance itself from the CIS is enhanced by two factors: first, unlike most other republics, Turkmenistan has not experienced ethnic unrest, and the Russian minority in the country has not organized and therefore is not applying pressure on the Niyazov regime to cooperate closely with Moscow. Second, the country's budding oil and gas industries are providing desperately needed foreign exchange, thereby reducing dependency on the CIS framework.

Kazakhstan faces a very different situation. According to Migranyan (1992, p. 13),

[President] Nazarbaev is faced with a difficult situation, despite an outward appearance of stability. He has to reckon with the fact that the Kazakhs, like the Russians, make up 40% of the population, while other groups account for the remaining 20%. That is why he is pursuing an aggressive ... policy to preserve the CIS. This is not for the long run, not a geopolitical necessity but a tactic. The Kazakh leader needs to gain time. To leave Russia now would mean losing Russian-speaking East Kazakhstan.

As a result of potential ethnic volatility, President Nazarbaev has consistently supported the continuation and greater institutionalization of the CIS.

Tajikistan, Uzbekistan and Kyrghyzstan are all members of the CIS, albeit reluctant ones. Tajikistan depends on Russia for security (especially in the context of its civil war) as well as for economic survival. By far the poorest of the Central Asian states, with virtually no industrial capacity, a cotton monoculture and an unstable regime enjoying no legitimacy, Tajikistan has little control over its foreign policy and is likely to continue its participation in the CIS for as long as it exists. Kyrghyzstan's position vis-à-vis the CIS is also based entirely on economic dependency. As President Akaev has pointed out (quoted in Bayalinov, 1992, p. 7):

Kyrghyzstan is destined to follow Russia's lead.... [A]ll of our industry depends 100% on Russia – the metals and components are there. By ourselves, we could only return to the past – to the mountains, to yurts, to flocks of sheep ... Russia is an icebreaker. If you don't follow its lead, the ice will crush you!

Uzbekistan's stance toward the CIS is much closer to that of Turkmenistan than that of Kazakhstan. As Central Asia's most populous state, and with a modest export capacity in the energy sector (natural gas), Uzbekistan has attracted more foreign investment than any of the other states (excluding foreign investment in the oil industries of Turkmenistan and Kazakhstan), particularly from East and Southeast Asian states as well as Pakistan and Iran. The country therefore has at least a moderate capacity to loosen ties with the CIS and seek out alternatives. Although not openly opposed to the CIS, President Karimov's commitment to the Commonwealth appears to be premised mostly on rhetoric.

The CIS itself is a fragmented regional framework with very little *formal* institutional infrastructure and a set of rather disjointed informal relationships. The difficulties of the CIS as a viable regional framework for the states of the FSU have been summarized well by Lapidus, Zaslavski and Goldman:

The former Soviet republics find themselves at very different stages of social and economic development. A highly repressive political regime would be required to keep together regions as different as the Baltic states and Central Asia, which are characterized by an enormous and growing gulf in their economic, political, and demographic behaviour and in their industrial and political culture. The human and material resources to maintain such a regime have by and large been exhausted. Whether even a loose economic federation – a common market or commonwealth – is now viable is in question (Lapidus *et al.,* 1992, pp. 18–19).

Regionalism Within Central Asia

The relationships between the five Central Asian states have been marked by both cooperation and conflict. Territorial disputes in particular have been a source of conflictual relations throughout the region:

Potentially the most contentious dispute is between the Uzbeks and the Tajiks. Central Asia's two main Persian-speaking cities, Samarkand and Bukhara, were included in Uzbekistan, leaving the Tajiks with the backwater town of Dushanbe for their republic capital. For their part, the Uzbeks have periodically staked a claim to all of the Ferghana Valley, which includes Kyrghyzstan's Osh oblast, and part of the Khojent [formerly Leninabad] ... oblast in Tajikistan. The Uzbeks also argue that part of southern Kazakhstan and eastern Turkmenistan ... rightfully belongs to them as well. The republics of Kyrghyzstan and Tajikistan disagree not only about where their border should be but even where it is, and briefly came to blows over this question in the summer of 1989 (Olcott, 1992, p. 256).

A further concern for all the Central Asian states is the escalation and potential proliferation of the civil war in Tajikistan. Not surprisingly therefore, virtually all summit meetings held between the leaders of the five states have involved discussions on this topic. The region's states have expressed their preparedness to cooperate fully in the resolution of the Tajik conflict, but ultimately very little concerted action has been taken.

The creation of these new states has led, understandably, to conflictual regional economic relationships, as each state attempts to improve its position in the global division of labour. Trade barriers were created randomly, export quotas were imposed, and payments in rubles were often refused due to the instability of the currency. National economic policies were not coordinated in any way, and the pace of reforms varied widely from state to state. In an attempt to overcome these difficulties, on 4 January 1993 the leaders of the five states established the Central Asian Commonwealth (BBC, 1993).

It is important to recognize that this Commonwealth results from the failure of the CIS. At the January 1993 summit meeting in Tashkent, 'the Presidents [of the five states] noted unanimously that, for all practical purposes, not one document agreed upon and signed within the framework of the CIS is being implemented' (CDPSP, 1993, p. 3).

The aims of the new Commonwealth go well beyond the financial sector, however: coordination in customs regulation, pricing, tax system, and defence are envisioned (ibid.). Furthermore, 'priority in reciprocal deliveries of scarce raw materials is to be given to the countries' nearest neighbours' (ibid.).[4]

The establishment of the Commonwealth also calls into question the viability of maintaining the ruble zone. Although only Kyrghyzstan has actually introduced its own currency (in Central Asia), the other states held out in the hope that monetary policy could be coordinated under the auspices of the CIS. Kazakhstan's President Nazarbaev candidly explained what it will take for the Central Asian states to remain in the ruble zone:

> The republics of the region will continue to support a single ruble space if the ruble remains a supranational currency, if a single banking union made up of the executives of all the national banks is organized, with each of them having a full vote, and if a common investment policy is established (ibid., p. 2).

None of these conditions are likely to be fulfilled within the framework of the CIS. Instead, some form of monetary policy coordination is much more likely to occur within Central Asia, where the possibility of a dominating party (such as Russia) is minimized. If the institutionalization of the new Central Asian Commonwealth proceeds as planned, then the abandonment of the ruble in favour of national currencies combined with monetary policy coordination at the regional level will become inevitable.

Regionalism within Central Asia continues to be fragile, both formally and informally. Formally, the institutional infrastructure is new, unproven and based on frustration with the CIS rather than the acceptance of Central Asian regionalism as the most desirable policy orientation. Informally, many of the territorial and political disputes between the Central Asian states have remained unresolved. As such, political tensions can still override the 'regionalist consensus' so dramatically proclaimed by the leaders of the five states at the Tashkent meeting in January 1993.

Finally, it should be noted that all the regionalist rhetoric in Central Asia so far has been entirely state-centric; in part because of the relatively slow rate of privatization (compared with Eastern Europe, the Baltics or Russia), but also because of the authoritarian, 'democracy-from-above' style of government in all the states. The strengthening of Central Asian regionalism via the transnationalization of civil societies is thus far, at least, a concept for the future.

The Middle Eastern Dimension

The emergence of the five Central Asian states following the disintegration of the Soviet Union has considerably altered the foreign policy orientations of a number of Middle Eastern states, most prominently those of Turkey and Iran. There is no question that Turkey and Iran are competing for influence in Central Asia; at the same time, however, it is misleading to represent their interests in power-political terms alone.

For Turkey, the emergence of six Muslim states (included here is Azerbaijan) represented an opportunity to undertake a fundamental shift in foreign policy orientation away from Western Europe – where relations with Turkey, especially in the context of NATO, have always been based more on 'utility than on friendship' (Ruehl, 1992, p. 295; my translation) – and toward Central Asia.

As a secularized Muslim country in which regime legitimacy continues to be fragile, Turkey's foreign policy options are limited. Its relation to the Arab Middle East, though for the most part not hostile, never did present many opportunities either, in part because of Turkey's moderate stance on Israel, and also because the various Turkish regimes have sought to prevent activist Islamic influences within Turkish society. When the six Muslim republics in Central Asia became independent states, themselves uncertain about the role of Islam within their states and societies, Turkey seized the opportunity and undertook a major diplomatic effort to establish its own sphere of influence in the region.

Turkish initiatives over the last two years have included active material support to change from cyrillic to Latin script by sending books, typewriters and printing presses, making Turkish media publications available throughout most of Central Asia, broadcasting Turkish television in Baku, as well as offering scholarships to students from all the Central Asian states (British Information Office, 1993, p. 2).

The Central Asian republics, in turn, have responded positively to Turkey's overtures. No doubt pleased with Turkey's material assistance, the Central Asian republics also seek to balance Iran's aggressive pursuit of influence in the region. Since the overthrow of the Shah, Iran has been treated as a pariah in the international community. But under the leadership of Hashemi Rafsanjani, Iran has been aggressively seeking to (re)establish relations with all willing parties.

R.K. Ramazani has identified four clusters of interests driving Iranian policy toward Central Asia: (i) to consolidate the dissolution of the Soviet Empire and prevent its reemergence; (ii) to 'contain the contagion of ethnic revivalist movements in Azerbaijan'; (iii) to gain economic benefits via cooperation with the Muslim republics; and (iv) to establish a land route to China through Kazakhstan, and gain access to the Black Sea through Azerbaijan and Georgia (Ramazani, 1992, pp. 403–5).

The difficulty for the new Central Asian states' is that given Iran's international reputation, close ties to Iran could present more of an obstacle than a benefit to these states. On the other hand, Iran does indeed have much to offer, both economically and culturally. In the context of the former, Iran represents at once a source of cheap energy for those republics lacking energy resources, and a transportation route to the Gulf for those seeking to export oil and gas in order to earn much needed foreign currency.

Thus Iran has received positive responses from the Central Asian republics as well. When, for example, the Iranian foreign minister, Ali Akbar Velayati, visited Tajikistan early in 1992, he was reportedly greeted by a high-ranking Tajik official with the words 'we are two nations of the same blood, two divided brothers who should once again discover their unity' (*Der Spiegel*, 1992, p. 110; my translation).

The establishment of the Economic Cooperation Organization (ECO), and its development over the past two years, indicates that there may well be a basis for regionalism in spite of the more traditional, power-seeking, foreign policy postures of Iran and Turkey. The original membership of ECO consisted of Iran, Turkey and Pakistan. ECO is a successor to the Regional Cooperation for Development (RCD) organization, which was established in 1964 to help coordinate economic and cultural issues (Hoeppner, 1977). Although the RCD was never officially dissolved, it was abandoned following the Iranian revolution of 1978–9. Following the termination of the Iran–Iraq War, the RCD was revived as the ECO. Political circumstances prevented the organization from taking on a precise mandate, or even a stable organizational form. With the emergence of independent states in Central Asia, however, efforts intensified to shape the ECO into a viable organization (both on the part of the original members and the new states of Central Asia).[5]

In November 1992 membership was officially expanded to include Afghanistan and the six Muslim, formerly Soviet, republics (including Azerbaijan). Turkey has been making overtures on behalf of the Northern Republic of Turkish Cyprus (NRTC), while Rumania is reportedly also seeking admission (Ibrahim, 1992, p. A16). The organization is still in its formative stages, with Iran and Turkey disagreeing on the direction it ought to take. While Turkey is seeking an organization modelled after the European Community, Iran is pursuing a sort of 'Islamic Commonwealth'. At a meeting in February 1992, Iranian President Rafsanjani stated as his objective the formation of 'un grand marche commun islamique de 250 millions d'habitants et de 4 millions de kilometres carres' (de la Gorce, 1992, p. 38).

At this point the ECO is nowhere near becoming a viable focal point for Central Asian regionalism. The organization itself is structurally fragile, vulnerable to major political differences among the strongest members and, very importantly, composed of members that even under optimal circumstances could not come up with sufficient resources (investment capital, technology transfers and so on) to satisfy the development needs and/or objectives of all the members. That does not mean, however, that the ECO has no potential benefits to offer its Central Asian members.

First, the ECO provides alternative trading routes to the Central Asian states, whereby access to the Gulf via Iran is particularly important. Second, coordination in the energy sector, involving especially the more-efficient distribution of Central Asian electricity surpluses and Iranian oil resources, will be a fundamental first step in the improvement of much-needed infrastructure. Third, with a combined market of approximately 250 million people, the small goods manufacturing sector stands to benefit in all member countries. Fourth, many informal economic activities of transnational proportion, such as border area black markets and unrecorded cross-border trade could be controlled more effectively under the auspices of the ECO for the purpose of extracting revenue through taxation.

The basic ingredients for a significant impact on the economic development prospects of all the member states are still missing, principally, of course, investment capital and foreign exchange. On the other hand these issues are specific to the region and will have to be addressed through measures that are appropriate to it; in other words, measures that are sensitive to the prevailing cultural, religious, ethnic and, more generally, civil dynamics. The ECO, given its membership composition, is much more suited for this task than externally based development agencies.

CONCLUSIONS

This chapter has examined three potential regionalisms pertaining to Central Asia: the CIS, Central Asia itself and the Middle East northern tier. In all three cases it was noted that difficulties persist. The CIS's future is highly uncertain. Indications are that this regional grouping may not survive much longer. At the same time there clearly are important benefits to be derived from the continued association between the former Soviet republics, particularly in the area of trade. In the specific context of Central Asia, however, an institutionalized framework may not be required, as bilateral relations with the CIS's largest member, Russia, combined with regional cooperation within Central Asia, would by and large yield the same results as an optimally functioning CIS.

Central Asian cooperation holds much promise, in spite of the congruence of the states' economies. Not to be underestimated are the political benefits, particularly with respect to conflict management, that such intraregional cooperation would yield. The danger lies in the statist character of the region's efforts to cooperate; social forces, whether motivated by religion, ethnicity or economics, may eventually derail the process of institutionalizing or intensifying Central Asian cooperation, unless substate linkages are developed in addition to state linkages. A number of strategies could be employed to further this end. In the economic sphere, privatization and the encouragement of enterprise-to-enterprise transnational trading would significantly strengthen regional economic linkages and cooperation. Alternatively, in the social sphere, the Central Asian governments could allow for a transnational non-governmental organizational framework to develop to deal with transnational issues such as refugees, ecology, food security, and so on.

Finally, both opportunities and dangers are presenting themselves with respect to cooperation between the Central Asian states and their neighbours to the south. While the prospects for enhanced cooperation within the framework of the ECO are presently good, they are vulnerable to the political manouevring of regional powers (especially Turkey and Iran). An intensification of the Turkish–Iranian competition in Central Asia could have disastrous consequences for the Central Asian states, as such a development could lead to the mobilization of extremist groups within the region. Turkish–Iranian cooperation, on the other hand, will undoubtedly benefit all parties involved, both because of economic opportunities and the stabilizing impact on the region as a whole.

Ultimately none of the three regionalisms discussed above are individually sufficient to serve the needs of the Central Asian states. Abandonment of the CIS would likely do little harm to them, whereas the enhancement of regional cooperation within Central Asia as well as the ECO appear prudent from the Central-Asian perspective. It is crucial, however, that the latter two regionalisms do not inhibit the development of bilateral relations with extraregional actors, particularly those that can provide desperately needed capital investment, technology and foreign exchange.

Notes

1. It is interesting to note that despite the Soviet Union's transcontinental size, there was never any question prior to its disintegration that it did in fact constitute one region by itself. See, for example, Cantori and Spiegel, 1970, pp. 1–41.
2. The spelling of these countries' names varies considerably in English-language publications. For the sake of consistency, this spelling will be used throughout this Chapter.
3. It should be noted that there are significant variations among the Central Asian states: Turkmenistan, for example, is almost homogeneous with respect to both religion and broad ethnic origins, while the characterization of Kazakhstan, where Kazakhs are a minority, as a 'Muslim country' is not an obvious choice.
4. Kazakhstan, for example, will send its crude oil to refineries in Uzbekistan and Turkmenistan, as opposed to Russia.
5. As Ramazani (1992, p. 406) points out, 'anxious to affirm their newly won independence, the Muslim republics have sought Iran's championship of their membership in the ECO'.

11 Malaysia and Thailand: Models for Economic Development at the Margins?

Richard Stubbs

INTRODUCTION

In the new international division of labour/power, much talk centres on the performance of the NICs and near-NICs, especially as potential models for other Third World state economic development. This chapter addresses the question of whether or not it is possible to use the relative success of Malaysia and Thailand as a model for other developing countries in their search for economic development. Malaysia and Thailand have in recent years been singled out by a wide variety of analysts as next in line to become 'newly industrializing countries', or NICs. They have a high rate of economic growth, their economic prosperity is driven by a rapid expansion of the manufacturing sector and like the Asian NICs – South Korea, Taiwan, Hong Kong and Singapore – they have become significant exporters of manufactured goods. Moreover, unlike the Asian NICs they appear to be more closely akin to the general population of developing countries. They are not, like Hong Kong and Singapore, Chinese-dominated city-state entrepots that turned to export-oriented industrialization out of a lack of an internal market. Nor do they at first glance appear to have the set of prerequisites for success that are often cited in the cases of South Korea and Taiwan: advantages accruing from the period of Japanese colonial occupation, massive US aid and support for key policy changes, timely entry into the US market place, strong central governments and a relatively homogeneous population with cultural values that facilitate economic development. Indeed, noting that unlike the Asian NICs Malaysia has a vibrant agricultural sector and an ethnically divided society, Appelbaum and

Henderson (1992, p. 9) argue that 'If Malaysia is successful in its late industrialization strategy, it will, therefore, be a much more apt model for the Third World societies than the East Asian NICs could ever be'. Hence the interest in promoting these two near-NICs as development models for others outside the developed world.

Among the advocates of neoclassical economic theory interested in economic development in the Third World, the Asian NICs, and more recently Malaysia and Thailand as near-NICs, have been especially popular as models for economic development. They have been keen to emphasise that the key to the success of the Asian NICs is that they have provided the necessary public goods and allowed the market to operate in a suitably unfettered fashion (Hughes, 1989). Importantly, a significant number of these neoliberal economists are associated with the World Bank and have, therefore, been able to promote their views at a practical level (Balassa, 1981, 1988; Riedal, 1989). A number of World Bank reports in the last decade or so have advanced the argument that all Third World governments should look to the experience of the Asian NICs and near-NICs in order to understand how trade liberaliza-tion can be the salvation of their economies (World Bank, 1987, 1991a, 1991b).

But is this the total picture? In terms of the four Asian NICs, the neo-liberal economists have recently been taken to task by a number of analysts (Amsden, 1989; Rodan, 1989; Wade, 1990, 1992, 1993). And what if the two near-NICs are put into the equation? Can the experience of Malaysia and Thailand buttress the argument that the Asian successes should be transferable to the wider developing world?

The argument to be developed in this chapter is that neither Malaysia nor Thailand should be considered a model for the economic develop-ment of other Third World states. It will be shown that there were three sets of events that together, and most importantly in sequence, allowed both countries to enjoy rapid economic development; that is, US involvement in the post-Second World War period, the emergence of strong central governments and, more recently, massive Japanese investment. The confluence of these sets of events – or their equivalent – is most unlikely to be repeated in other areas and in other countries around the world. Indeed in many ways the history of the development of Malaysia and Thailand has been closer to that of the Asian NICs than that of other developing countries. Hence, just like the case of the four NICs themselves, the experience of rapid economic development in Malaysia and Thailand can not be transferred to other regions of the world.

US HEGEMONY AND GEOPOLITICS

One of the key factors in the economic development of the Asia–Pacific region, and one that is too often ignored, is the pervasive impact of the US strategic containment policy. Some attention has been paid to the impact of US aid on the South Korean and Taiwanese economies (for example Cumings, 1987; Krueger, 1979; Mason *et al.*, 1980) but overall it has not been given the consideration it deserves. This point is highlighted by the fact that not only is geopolitics a significant factor in the successes of Japan, South Korea and Taiwan, it is also key to the eventual rapid economic growth of Malaysia and Thailand.

In Malaysia, or Malaya, as it was known then, the Korean War and the US determination to stem the tide of Asian communism had an indirect but nevertheless considerable impact on the fortunes of the Malaysian economy. As a result of the crisis produced by the outbreak of the war, the price of natural rubber rose fourfold and that of tin more than doubled. These two commodities were the twin pillars of the Malaysian economy at the time and the resulting prosperity was felt in every quarter of Malaysia. Most importantly, profits in the rubber industry rose from 6.9 Malayan cents per pound in 1949 to 53.3 cents per pound in 1951. This allowed the government to revise corporate taxes and export duties and expand its income tax base. The overall result was that government revenues went from M$235.5 million in 1948 to M$735.4 million in 1951 at the height of the Korean War boom (Stubbs, 1974).

The windfall revenues garnered by the government were used to expand the country's economic and social infrastructure. Roads and railways were built, electrical capacity developed and the educational and health systems substantially augmented and revamped. Nearly five hundred thousand rural Chinese were also resettled, creating a large pool of labour near the main urban centres. The political will to embark on these development programmes also arose out of the security situation in the region. The Malayan government was faced with a guerrilla campaign, which started in 1948 and was waged by the Malayan Communist Party (MCP). At least in the first few years of the fighting the MCP were fairly successful and the government was fortunate to have the Korean War boom revenues on hand in order to regain the initiative (Stubbs, 1989). Overall, then, the boom gave a kick-start to an economy that had sunk into the doldrums after the Second World War and enabled the government to put in place an economic and social infrastructure upon which future economic development could be built. In particular it allowed for investment in the expansion of a relatively well-educated and trainable workforce, ways of diversifying the economy

and, during the 1960s and 1970s, the selective opening up of the economy
– especially the manufacturing sector – to international capital.

In Thailand it was not the Korean War but the threat of internal communist subversion and most particularly the Vietnam War that provided the
boost to its economic fortunes. After the war in Korea the attention of the
US administration turned to Southeast Asia with the recrudescence of the
fighting in Vietnam after the grace period created by the Geneva Agreement of 1954. Thailand was viewed as not only significant as a possible
future falling domino; it was also an important base area for US forces in
the region once the US campaign in Vietnam began in earnest.

Accordingly, from the mid-1950s onwards US aid to Thailand increased.
Security considerations led to a particular emphasis on improving the
transportation and communication infrastructure. A high proportion of aid
funds was spent on highways, airport facilities and deepwater ports. By the
mid-1960s Thailand had developed a national road system where none had
existed before and, as an indirect consequence, had acquired a relatively
capable civil engineering sector (Caldwell, 1974, p. 44; Benoit, 1971,
p. 628; Muscat, 1990, pp. 94–107). The major impact of US aid, however,
was experienced from the mid-1960s to the early 1970s. The construction
and operation of a number of bases (which housed as many as 48 000 at the
height of US involvement in the fighting), the spending by US personnel
on leave, the increased exports to Vietnam and aid disbursements combined to raise the total annual amounts pumped into the Thai economy
from around US$27 million in 1963 to about US$318 million in 1968
(Myint, 1971, pp. 75–6; Economist Intelligence Unit, 1968, p. 9; Muscat,
1990, pp. 149–84).

Overall the United States injected into the Thai economy US$650
million in economic aid between 1950 and 1975; US$940 million in
'regular military assistance' between 1951 and 1971; US$760 million in
'operating costs' in the acquisition of military equipment, and in payments
for the Thai division in Vietnam; US$250 million for the construction of
US bases; and US$850 million in expenditure by US military personnel
(Girling, 1981, pp. 235–6). This amounts to nearly US$3.5 billion spent by
the United States in Thailand over the period from 1950 to the closing of
the US bases in Thailand in 1976. While this was not the only reason for
Thailand's major economic boom during the 1960s, it was clearly a key
contributory factor. And just as the Korean War boom had enabled Malaysia to build up its economic and social infrastructure, so the economic
boom in Thailand allowed very much the same pattern of events to unfold.
Thus, even though the Thai economy suffered a number of major setbacks
in the mid-1970s, including the cutting back of US aid and military expen-

diture, the closing of its borders with Indochina and the oil-price crisis, it showed a remarkable resilience. Indeed the US aid and expenditure injected into the Thai economy had a long-lasting impact and set the stage for future economic development.

STRONG CENTRALIZED STATES

One of the major arguments that has been put forward for the economic success of the NICs has been the capacity of the state to direct economic policy (Amsden, 1989; Johnson, 1987; Onis, 1991; Rodan, 1989; Wade, 1990). Again the similarity of the Malaysian and Thai experiences with the history of the NICs is instructive. In all cases the fact that these countries were on the front line in the Cold War and the battle against Asian communism set the stage for a greater centralization of government authority. As Migdal (1988, p. 4) has pointed out, in most Third World countries the societies are strong and the central states are weak, making it very difficult for a country's leaders and central government to 'penetrate society, regulate social relationships, extract resources, and appropriate or use resources in determined ways'. As a result of colonialism and the penetration of Western capitalism, argues Migdal, most Third World governments are incapable of autonomous action, being beholden to regional strongmen who jealously guard their interests and shackle the actions of the central leadership. In both Malaysia and Thailand the state has not encountered these problems and has in the main been able to implement economic policies that have promoted export-oriented industrialization and economic growth more generally.

The Malaysian case is particularly instructive in this respect. Prior to the Second World War the British colonial administration had developed a rather odd patchwork of political authority, in which a great deal of power was vested in the states that made up the area governed by the British colonial administration. Directly after the war the British tried to impose a more centralized administration on the people of Malaya in the form of the Malayan Union, but after large-scale protests it was overturned and replaced by the much more decentralised Federation of Malaya. However the necessity of fighting a coordinated campaign against the communist guerrillas gradually allowed for the transfer of more and more power from the states to the central government in Kuala Lumpur. This transfer of power was reinforced, and indeed entrenched, by the country's constitution, which was drawn up in the months leading up to the granting of independence in 1957. With the guerrilla war and the fight against communism still a preoccupation, the constitution conferred extensive powers on the federal government so that it could finally defeat the MCP and ensure that communism did not return to Malaysia. On top of this the Alliance Party, which had become and was to continue as the dominant force in Malaysian politics at both the federal and state levels, compounded the centralizing tendencies arising out of the security situation in the country by ensuring that the state governments run by the Alliance Party were essentially controlled from the centre. Hence the exigencies of the guerrilla war against the communists and the success of the counterinsurgency campaign during the 1950s transformed Malaysia from a colonial society with a typically decentralized form of government to an independent country with a central government having extensive powers.

It is also important to make the point that the federal government had the capacity to make use of these extensive powers. The Malaysian government inherited at independence a substantial security apparatus with a large police force; an efficient, if relatively small, locally-manned army; and a Special Branch that had developed the reputation of being an excellent intelligence-gathering agency. The guerrilla war also produced a rapid expansion of the civil administration. After initially adopting an essentially coercive military approach to fighting the MCP, which proved to be unsuccessful, the government moved to an approach that sought to reimpose administrative authority throughout the peninsula and to address many of the grievances that fuelled support for the communists within the population (Stubbs, 1989). In order to do this, the total number of administrative employees at the federal, state and municipal levels climbed from 48 000 in 1948 to 140 000 in 1959. By 1965 the civil administration in West Malaysia had grown to about 228 000 and, as Milton Esman has noted, by 'international standards this was a high figure comparable to such countries as the United Kingdom and Denmark' (Esman, 1972, pp. 70–1). Hence the guerrilla war, or 'the Emergency' as it was called, set the stage for Malaysia's own version of 'soft authoritarianism' (Johnson, 1987). Most particularly, the Emergency paved the way for the central state structures to put in place, in stages, an expansionist, export-oriented economic policy.

The situation in Thailand was rather different. Thailand, of course, had never formally been colonised and the central government had maintained its authority. The monarchy and, after the 1932 coup, the military were able to exert a reasonable level of control over the country. Added to this, in the years following the Second World War the bureaucracy emerged as a key institution in Thai politics and policy-making. The state structures in Thailand were, then, relatively powerful in the immediate post-War period. However they did not have the resources or skilled manpower to plan and implement economic development policies. All this changed from the mid-1950s onwards as the United States began to send aid to Thailand in an effort to shore up what was thought of in Washington as the next line of defence in the further encroachment of communism into Southeast Asia. Most importantly from the point of view of the argument being made here, Thailand's public administration was a significant target of aid funding (Muscat, 1990, pp. 123–35, 256–71). Budgeting, financial and accounting procedures were modernized, and a school for upper-level bureaucrats was set up. Departments were created that allowed the Thai government to play a relatively strong role in the aid process. For example, two key agencies proved to be the National Economic Development Board, which was established in 1959 and which evaluated aid programmes, and the Foreign Loans and Supervisory Committee, which was put in place to screen foreign loans for their degree of necessity. Essentially the US aid programmes were able to build on the bureaucracy's long tradition of initiative and leadership. The results were fairly impressive. One observer noted in 1967 that Thailand had a 'strong and effective government and one of the most efficient civil services in Southeast Asia' (Caldwell, 1974). Hence, like Malaysia, Thailand developed its own form of 'soft authoritarianism' based on the dual pillars of the military and the bureaucracy.

It is perhaps instructive at this point to make a comparison between Malaysia and Thailand on the one hand and the Philippines on the other. While the Malaysian and Thai states have been relatively successful in sponsoring economic growth the same cannot be said of the Philippines, despite the fact that, like Thailand, the Philippines had received a great deal of aid from the United States as a result of US anticommunist campaigns in the region. Why, in contrast with Malaysia and Thailand, has the Philippines been unable to make effective use of this inflow of funds?

Much of the answer clearly lies in the fragmentation of society and authority in the Philippines. The colonial experience, first with the Spanish and then the US, left a weak and divided state. As Hawes notes, 'the lack of a strong state leadership and the complementary tendency of the state to respond in preferential, partisan fashion to demands from segments of the bourgeoisie, characterised the Philippines after independence' (Hawes, 1987, p. 32). The fact that family clans and provincial barons with regional power bases have fought and continue to battle with the centre has all but paralysed the government's ability to set the country on a course for economic development. McBeth (1989) points out that because of institutional weaknesses at the centre there is a 'chronic inability to disburse funds and services, with some US$2 billion in foreign economic assistance currently tied up by sheer disorganisation.' The result, as McBeth points out, is pork-barrelling and provincial-level patronage.

Hence, while in the Asian NICs and near-NICs social dislocation, mostly produced by wars of one sort or another or the preparation for wars, weakened the societal actors and strengthened the hand of the state, in the Philippines the state has remained weak and has had to consistently defend itself against incursions by regional strongmen. As a consequence the impact of US aid has been negated and economic development in the Philippines severely retarded.

One final point needs to be made here. The emergence of strong centralised states in Malaysia and Thailand has gone hand in hand with the adoption of what may be called a hegemonic project that has tended to solidify the government's control and enabled it to mobilize significant portions of the population behind its development programmes. In Thailand the government, rather like the governments of the Asian NICs, has been able to use the threat of communism to mobilise support. The battle against the communist guerrillas in the northern parts of the country and the threat posed by communist Vietnam have given the government the rationale for strong directive action and at the same time made the general population ready to accept strong central leadership. Certainly the government has recognised that the best way to keep communism at bay is to build up the economy and give people reason to support it.

In Malaysia there have been essentially two goals. The first is to ensure that communism does not return to the peninsula. The Malaysian government learnt during the Emergency that a prosperous economy is one of the best antidotes to communism. The second goal is to expand the economy so as to give the two competing social groups, the Malays and the non-Malays (mostly Chinese) the chance to meet their economic aspirations. As each of the governments of the NICs and the near-NICs has discovered, a rapidly growing economy is one of the best ways of keeping the population generally supportive and mobilized behind the government's programmes.

Overall, then, both Malaysia and Thailand have had strong central governments that have had the capacity to implement development programmes. In this sense they have been more fortunate than many other Third World countries, which, because of their colonial past and the way in which Western capitalism penetrated their economies, have had, as Migdal (1988) puts it, 'strong societies and weak states'. In these circumstances, having other countries adopt the Malaysian or Thai economic development model would not be very helpful if indeed it were possible at all.

JAPAN AND GEOECONOMICS

The third set of events that sets Malaysia and Thailand apart from other developing countries is the massive influx of Japanese investment that has taken place since the mid-1980s. In order to attempt to deal with the growing trade deficit between the United States and Japan, the G-5 (the United States, the United Kingdom, Germany, France and Japan) finance ministers signed an agreement in September 1985 that gave the central banks the responsibility of raising the value of the yen and lowering the value of the dollar. The rapid appreciation of the yen allied to structural changes that were taking place in the Japanese economy forced a number of Japanese manufacturing companies to relocate outside Japan.

Initially Japanese companies targeted South Korea and Taiwan, but their currencies also appreciated during 1986 and 1987 and so the ASEAN region quickly became an alternative destination. It is significant, especially given the argument being presented here, that Japanese investors were seeking to invest in areas that were close by, had a reasonable level of economic and social infrastructure and possessed a relatively competent state bureaucracy with which they could deal. Because of the sets of events outlined in the previous sections of this chapter, the Japanese found that first Thailand and then Malaysia suited their purposes admirably. The economic infrastructure that had been put in place as a consequence of the prosperity produced by US involvement in the region allowed Japanese companies to use the two countries as export platforms for manufactured goods and to compete with companies from South Korea and Taiwan in the important US and European markets as well as in the Japanese market, which was slowly opening up to imports. In particular Japanese firms were able to integrate their Thai and Malaysian operations into regional networks of production (Aoki, 1992). The Japanese also valued the presence of strong centralized states that could ensure that economic policies conducive to developing an export-oriented industrial base were implemented.

The actual figures for Japanese foreign direct investment (FDI) in the two countries are quite startling. Investment in Thailand went from US$48 million in 1985 up to US$1.28 billion in 1989 (ASEAN Centre, 1992). From 1988 to 1991, inclusive, Japanese companies invested approximately US$4 billion or the equivalent of US$73.00 per capita. Japanese investment in Malaysia did not rise so dramatically but has steadily increased from US$79 million in 1985 to US$880 million in 1991. Over the same period Japanese FDI amounted to US$2.67 billion or US $152 per capita (ASEAN Centre, 1992). No other developing country in the world – apart from the Asian NICs – has experienced such a massive inflow of investment funds in so short a period of time. And Japan is not the sole investor. According to *The Economist* (14–21 February 1992), Taiwan was reported to have invested US$1 billion in Thailand in 1991 alone. (This can be compared with the *outflow* of private capital from Africa and Latin America over much of the 1980s; see Chapter 15 below.) It is no wonder that these two countries have grown so rapidly over the last few years.

It is important to note that the recent reduction in the amount of Japan's FDI and the predictions that Japan is unlikely to reach the levels of the late 1980s in the short or even medium term suggest that Japan will not be in a position to give any other developing country the boost to its economy that it has given to Thailand and Malaysia. While a substantial amount of Japanese money has gone into Indonesia, the sheer size of the Indonesian economy suggests that the investment will not have the dramatic impact that it has had on Thailand and Malaysia. Moreover Japanese companies have in the main stayed away from the Philippines because of the problems outlined in the previous section (making the Philippines more representative of the African case than that of its immediate geographic neighbours).

At the same time that the Japanese private sector has been pumping large amounts of money into Thailand and Malaysia, the Japanese government has been doing much the same thing in the form of aid. Indeed a significant proportion of this aid is geared to helping the two governments provide Japanese industry with an efficient export base. For example, special emphasis has been placed on building roads, railways, ports, airports and electricity-generating capabilities. Complementing this approach has been the provision of bilateral structural adjustment loans to expedite policy reforms (Rudner, 1989). These further bolstered the export-manufacturing sector. Again, the extent to which Malaysia and Thailand have been major beneficiaries of Japanese largesse should be stressed. During the period 1982 to 1986 Malaysia received US$576 million from Japan in aid. This constituted 62 per cent of all the bilateral aid received by Malaysia and worked out to US$36.50 per capita. During the same period Thailand received US$1.17 billion from Japan, which was 65 per cent of all bilateral aid it received and worked out to US$22.20 per capita.

With the flood of Japanese FDI into both Thailand and Malaysia after 1987 came a sharp increase in the amount of Japanese aid reaching the two countries, especially Thailand. Aid to Thailand rose from US$260 million in 1986 to US$489 million in 1989 and US$419 million in 1990. While aid to Malaysia has been more sporadic, in 1990 it received US$373 million from Japan. The point of all this is, of course, that very few if any developing countries are likely to benefit to the extent that Thailand and Malaysia have done from Japanese aid and FDI. Certainly no South Asian, African or Latin American country seems destined to be in a position to emulate the two near-NICs in terms of the way in which they have benefited from such a flood of external capital.

Overall, then, it seems clear that the advantages that accrued to Malaysia and Thailand, first from the United States' pursuit of its geostrategic interests and later from Japan's pursuit of its geoeconomic interests, add up to a set of concatenating circumstances that are highly unlikely to be replicated elsewhere in the developing world. Hence to use the Malaysian and Thai experiences as models for economic development in other countries can only be said to be grossly misleading.

Part VI

The Caribbean and Latin America

12 Structural Change in the Caribbean Compared: Graduation or Marginalization in the World Economy?

Helen McBain

INTRODUCTION

The 1980s has been referred to as the 'lost decade' for most developing countries, largely because they failed to experience sustained economic growth and a relatively large proportion of their population remained below the poverty line. Many countries in the Caribbean and Latin America experienced high unemployment, inflation and debt, and low levels of production, productivity, savings and growth as well as persistent foreign-exchange shortages.

The cause of these ills has been attributed to, among other things, insufficient integration into the world economy due to the pursuit of inward-oriented development strategies. The remedy prescribed by the international financial agencies and endorsed by developed countries is economic adjustment based on an outward-oriented development strategy. This is expected to put these countries on a path similar to that taken by the newly industrializing countries (NICs) and near-NICs in East and Southeast Asia (see Chapter 11 above). But the question is whether and to what extent Caribbean countries can overcome the 'marginalization' that has been their historical experience and graduate into near-NICs and NICs through the pursuit of economic adjustment based on IMF and World Bank policy models. This chapter seeks to examine this question. But first we need to specify for the purpose of this chapter a working definition of the term 'marginalization'.

MARGINALIZATION

The concept of marginalization is used here to characterize the position of less-developed economies in the world economy in terms of the changing nature of that economy (see Chapter 2 above).

In the world economy, production has become more global and more concentrated in regions, trade has become more regional, and finance capital has become more quickly and easily mobile than goods and services. Industrialized and newly industrialized economies have moved up the production ladder in response to changes in demand and cost of supply. They have spun off labour-intensive and lower-technology-based components of the production process to less-developed countries, mainly in Asia, which have a comparative advantage in these areas, while focusing on developing exports based on capital and technology-intensive production. The less-developed countries in turn hope to move up the ladder by following the path of development of the NICs (cf. Stubbs, in Chapter 11 above, for a critique of this perceived 'path of development').

Countries in the Caribbean have found themselves on the periphery of the process of global production and the new technological revolution because of the structural features of their economies and their mode of insertion into the world economy. These economies specialized in the production of natural resource based commodities as part of the pre-war and immediate post-Second World War international division of labour. They maintained this specialization despite the changes that were taking place in the international division of labour. Domestic output was aimed at international markets and domestic demand was satisfied largely by imports from industrial countries. Some domestic demand was satisfied by domestic food production and by import-substitution manufacturing.

The preferential access to the European (mainly British) market as well as to the US market for traditional agricultural commodities, while guaranteeing higher than world market prices for these commodities, acted as a disincentive to technological innovation in their production (see Chapter 5 above). Incentives offered by government to import-substitution manufacturing, such as tax and duty-free concessions, had a similar effect. The result is that Caribbean countries have not responded to global changes in a way that would have allowed them to move up the production ladder and sustain their export-based economies.

World trade has been growing more than world production and has been liberalized more within regional blocs than within the world economy. This has resulted in the fast growth of intraregional trade. The trend towards increased intraregional trade has not been the experience of Caribbean and

Latin American countries. Intraregional trade accounted for about 10 per cent of total CARICOM trade in 1990. Latin American intraregional trade within the Latin American Integration Association (LAIA; formerly known as the Latin American Free Trade Association or LAFTA) is about the same level. In contrast intraregional trade grew to 60 per cent of EC trade in 1990 from a level of 35 per cent in 1960. Part of the reason for the low level of Caribbean and Latin American intraregional trade has to do with the import-substitution policies pursued in the region, the foreign-exchange problems that some countries experienced in the late 1970s, and the adjustment measures of the 1980s that have forced countries to liberalize extraregional trade.

Capital flows have been increasing significantly, but these have been moving more in the direction of industrialized and industrializing economies than in the direction of less-developed economies. The flows have been greater to the area of services than to primary products and manufactures. On the whole, net foreign capital inflows to most Caribbean countries declined during the 1980s. Some countries, such as Jamaica and Guyana, experienced net external transfers on account of significant debt-service payments to multilateral financial institutions (McBain, 1993). The Caribbean situation regarding low levels of capital flows is integrally related to the marginal position of the regional economies in global production and trade (the African case is similar; see Chapter 8 above).

To be marginalized is literally to be on the periphery or margin of events and processes. The synonyms alienation and maladjustment aptly describe the position of most Caribbean economies. The latter have failed to adjust to the changing global division of labour and have thus remained alienated from the benefits of higher stages of production. Moreover the failure to adjust has left Caribbean economies vulnerable to both external and internal economic shocks. It was to correct this weakness and facilitate greater integration into the world economy that a number of Caribbean countries such as Jamaica, Guyana, Trinidad and Barbados embarked on economic adjustment programmes, supported by the IMF and the World Bank.

THE CARIBBEAN IN THE WORLD ECONOMY

The major Caribbean countries, excluding Barbados and the Bahamas, have lagged behind many developing countries in Latin America and Asia in terms of their per-capita GNP since the mid-1980s. At the global level, developing countries have been growing faster than developed countries (except Japan) since the early 1980s. Developing countries in Asia have been responsible for most of the growth in output (see Table 12.1). In the Caribbean region only Barbados, the Bahamas, the Dominican Republic and most of the smaller islands in the Eastern Caribbean had growth rates of the world average (3.2 per cent) and above for the period 1975–84. Real output grew slowly or declined in many countries in the region during most of the 1980s. Growth increased significantly for a number of these countries in the 1990s, in particular Argentina, Guyana and Panama (see Table 12.1).

A similar situation obtains in the case of merchandise exports from the Caribbean. Developed economies accounted for 62 per cent of world exports in 1981 and 73 per cent in 1991. On the other hand developing economies accounted for 30 per cent of world exports in 1981 but only 24 per cent ten years later. Exports by LAIA represented 15 per cent of developing countries' world exports in 1981 and 13 per cent in 1991. On the other hand three countries in Asia – Korea, Singapore and Malaysia – accounted for 9 per cent of developing countries' world exports in 1981 and 20 per cent in 1991, 7 per cent more than the LAIA, which consists of eleven Latin American countries, namely Argentina, Bolivia, Brazil, Chile, Colombia, Ecuador, Mexico, Paraguay, Peru, Uruguay and Venezuela. The Central American Common Market, CACM, consisting of Costa Rica, El Salvador, Guatemala, Honduras and Nicaragua, was responsible for a small portion of developing countries' world exports – only about US$4 billion per year over the last ten years (IMF, 1993). The Caribbean Community, CARICOM, consisting of 13 countries in the English-speaking Caribbean, contributed about the same level of exports over the same period.

Export Structure

In 1970, 65 per cent of Latin American exports were primary commodities, 23 per cent were fuels and 11 per cent were manufactures. By 1990 only 41 per cent were primary commodities whereas 33 per cent were manufactures, with fuels at 24 per cent. Countries that have increased their exports of manufactures have also increased their foreign exchange earnings as manufactures have higher income elasticities. In the Caribbean and Latin America, three countries – Argentina, Brazil and Mexico – accounted for 64 per cent of the region's manufacturing exports between 1970 and 1974. Between 1985 and 1990 these countries' share of regional manufactured exports was 80 per cent. The major countries in the Caribbean region (excluding Trinidad and Tobago), the countries of Central America (excluding Mexico), and Ecuador and Paraguay in South America accounted for only 20 per cent of the region's earnings from manufactured

Table 12.1 Real GDP growth of selected countries (per cent)

Country	Average 1975–84	1985	1986	1987	1988	1989	1990	1991	1992
Barbados	4.0	1.1	9.6	3.8	3.1	3.7	-3.3	-3.8	-4.2
Guyana	-1.4	2.0	-0.9	0.9	-2.6	-3.3	-2.5	6.0	6.5
Jamaica	0.7	-0.9	4.6	1.7	6.2	3.0	6.2	2.8	0.8
Trinidad and Tobago	0.8	-5.6	-1.7	-5.0	-3.4	-0.2	0.7	3.0	0.2
Dominican Republic	4.0	-2.6	3.2	7.9	0.7	4.1	-5.4	-0.6	7.8
Argentina	-0.1	-1.7	5.6	2.3	-5.1	-4.6	0.4	5.0	7.0
Brazil	3.7	7.9	7.6	3.6	-0.1	3.3	-4.0	1.0	-0.9
Chile	1.8	2.4	5.7	5.7	7.4	10.0	2.1	6.0	10.4
Mexico	4.6	2.6	-3.7	1.7	1.2	3.3	4.4	3.6	2.7
Venezuela	1.8	0.2	6.5	3.6	5.8	-8.6	5.3	10.4	7.3
Korea	8.0	6.9	12.4	12.0	11.5	6.2	9.2	8.4	4.7
Malaysia	7.0	-1.0	1.2	5.4	8.9	8.8	10.0	9.0	8.7

Source: IMF, World Economic Outlook, May 1993.

exports in the period 1970–4. This was further reduced to 6 per cent in the period 1985–90 (IDB, 1992).

In most countries of the Caribbean the export structure has not changed significantly over the last two decades. In Jamaica, the main exports in 1970 were sugar, bauxite, alumina and bananas. This did not change until the 1980s, when furniture and clothing became significant items of export. By the end of the 1980s various items of clothing became the most significant exports after bauxite and alumina. Fresh vegetables and alcohols also became significant but represented less than 1 per cent of developing countries' exports of these commodities.

In Guyana the dominance of metal ores, sugar and rice, which together constituted over 80 per cent of exports in 1970, was reduced to less than 70 per cent at the end of the 1980s. Gold, chemical products and shellfish became significant exports in this period, although they represented less than 2 per cent of developing countries' exports of these products. For Trinidad, crude petroleum and petroleum products have remained the dominant export, accounting for over 70 per cent of total exports in 1970 and 60 per cent in the late 1980s. In the latter period, iron and steel, chemicals and fertilizers were significant exports.

In Barbados, sugar remained a dominant export product, although its share of domestic exports was reduced from 54 per cent in 1970 to about 15 per cent at the end of the 1980s. Petroleum products and electrical machinery became significant items of export. In the Dominican Republic sugar was the dominant export until 1980, when manufactured fertilizers became significant and sugar exports fell. By the end of the 1980s pig iron was the single dominant export, clothing was the second largest export and sugar the third largest export item. Coffee and cocoa were other significant export items. The smaller islands of the Eastern Caribbean have remained dependent on primary agricultural exports and on tourism services.

The Pattern of Industrialization

Industrialization has been taking place within the context of a production process that has become both global and regional; that is, parts of the production process are undertaken in more than one country but are concentrated within regions centred around the United States, the European Community and Japan (see Chapter 2 above). Foreign investment and transnational corporations have been at the heart of the process. The latter have established affiliates in a cluster of countries within a specific region, each specializing in production for a particular segment of an industry. This process has leds to increased intraindustry trade (United Nations, 1992).

In the Pacific region, Japan has been the dominant exporter of manufactured goods and the main source of foreign direct investment flows to NICs and near-NICs (see Chapter 11 above). As a result these countries have concentrated on producing in specific industry segments. The NICs have assumed the graduated position they now enjoy by moving into the leading export product areas where Japan has been dominant. And the so-called near-NICs are now moving into those areas as they emulate the performance of the NICs. UNCTAD trade data show the similarity in the changing export structures of Japan and the NICs and near-NICs of the Pacific region. A look at four types of products is instructive.

Ships and boats

Japan's exports of ships and boats in 1970 was its second largest export, after motor vehicles, and represented 37 per cent of developed countries' exports and 33 per cent of world exports in this sector. This category was ninth among Korea's leading exports in 1970 but was relatively insignificant at US$2 million, representing only 7 per cent of developing countries' exports and 0.06 per cent of world exports of this product. By 1980 ships and boats (valued at $4681 million) were eighth among the top Japanese exports but still constituted a significant portion (38 per cent) of developed countries' exports of the product, although they now represented only 29 per cent of world exports. Korea's exports of these products ($614 million) moved to eighth position and represented 43 per cent developing countries' exports and 3 per cent world exports. By the end of the 1980s ships and boats ($4187 million) were fifteenth among the top sixteenth Japanese exports and represented 25 per cent of developed countries' exports and 20 per cent world exports. Korea's product remained significant ($1774 million) and constituted 48 per cent of developing countries' exports and 8 per cent of world exports. Malaysia began to export ships and boats in the mid-1980s but this represented only 2 per cent of developing countries' exports and less than 1 per cent of world exports. As Japan's share of world exports contracted, the share of the NICs (Korea) and near-NICs (Malaysia) expanded.

Transistors and valves

These were the third most important export for Japan at the end of the 1980s whereas they were not among the top exports previously. Together they were valued at $13 225 million and were 37 per cent of developed countries' exports and 25 per cent of world exports in this sector. In Korea, transistors and valves became the most important export items ($4279 million) in the late 1980s. They represented 28 per cent of developing countries' exports and 8 per cent of world exports. In Malaysia, these products also became the most important export items ($3358 million), representing 22 per cent of developing countries' exports and 6 per cent of world exports.

Motor vehicles

This product was the most important export (valued at $38 737 million) for Japan in the late 1980s, representing 28 per cent of developed countries' exports and 27 per cent of world exports in this sector. In Korea this was the third most important export item ($2692 million), representing 53 per cent of developing countries' exports and 2 per cent of world exports.

Telecommunication equipment and parts

These products were the third most important export item for Japan in the 1970s, representing 28 per cent of developed countries' exports and 25 per cent of world exports in 1975 in this sector. It became the second most important export in the 1980s, increasing its share of developed countries' exports to 42 per cent and world exports to 32 per cent. In Korea, this export was the second major export in 1980, representing 17 per cent of developing countries' exports and 5 per cent of world exports. In the late 1980s this became the tenth most significant export, representing 19 per cent of developing countries' exports and 3 per cent of world exports. In Malaysia in the 1980s this export ranked ninth, representing 5 per cent of developing countries' exports and 1 per cent of world exports.

The last three products are fast-growing world exports and Japan, the NICs and near-NICs have all been increasing their world market shares.

In the Caribbean and Latin American region, the US position is analogous to Japan's position in the Pacific region. The United States has been the main source of investment in the former region, although Japanese and European investment has become increasingly significant.

The US export structure has been somewhat similar to Japan's. In the late 1980s, motor-vehicle parts were the third largest export category in the United States compared with Japan, where they were fifth among the leading exports. Automatic data-processing equipment was the fourth leading export both in the United States and Japan. Transistor valves were the sixth leading export in the United States but the third leading export in Japan. Motor vehicles have been the leading Japanese export since 1970. In the United States these were the leading export during the mid-1980s but had dropped to seventh place by the end of the decade. Telecommunication equipment was the number two export for Japan at the end of the 1980s whereas it was number ten for the United States during the same period. The internal combustion engine became a significant export for the United States at number thirteen, but was the eleventh leading export for Japan during the same period.

Argentina, Brazil and Mexico are considered to be the NICs of Latin America and the Caribbean. Their export structures have been developing in a manner similar to that of the United States. Mexico provides a good example of this trend. In 1970 Mexico's main exports were sugar, cotton, coffee, fresh vegetables and fish. Total exports doubled in 1975 and crude petroleum became the dominant export. By 1980 sugar became non-significant whereas motor-vehicle exports grew in significance, representing 12 per cent of developing countries' exports. By the end of the 1980s crude petroleum was still the single most important export, representing 30 per cent of total exports. However a number of new and significant exports emerged, such as internal combustion piston engines, which represented 47 per cent of developing countries' exports of this product; motor-vehicle parts, representing 15 per cent of developing countries' exports of this product; lorries and specialized motor vehicles, representing 28 per cent of developing countries' exports of this product; automatic data-processing equipment, representing 3 per cent of developing countries' exports; iron and steel products, representing 10 per cent of developing countries' exports; and electrical distributing equipment, representing 12 per cent of developing countries' exports. Other significant exports were copper, carboxylic acids and shellfish. Like the Asian NICs, Mexico has been increasing its share of world and intraindustry trade in products that form part of the globalized (and regionalized) production process.

From their manufacturing export performance, Colombia, Venezuela, Peru, Chile, Uruguay and Trinidad can be seen as the near-NICs and prospective near-NICs of the region. Their export of manufactures grew during the period 1970–90 by as little as 12 per cent (Colombia and Trinidad) and by as high as 20 per cent (Peru). Iron and steel was the most significant group of exports for Colombia, Trinidad and Venezuela. Plastic materials were significant high-growth exports for Colombia, Uruguay and Venezuela; essential oils and perfumes were high-growth exports for Chile and Uruguay; and clothing and textile yarn and fabrics were high-growth exports for Peru. The rationale for identifying these countries as the Latin American near-NICs or NEEMs (newly emerging exporters of manufactures) is that their export earnings from manufactures represented between 1 per cent and 5 per cent percent of Latin America's total exports and grew

180   *Structural Change in the Caribbean Compared*

by over 12 per cent during the 1980s (IDB, 1992). These countries have not yet significantly moved into high-technology manufacturing for specific industry segments.

What is interesting about the export structure of Latin America and the Caribbean is the primary position maintained by primary commodities and fuels such as food, leather, metal ores and petroleum. This is on account of the natural resource base of many of the countries in the region. And this has given rise to the significant export growth of basic manufactures by a number of countries, in particular iron and steel, chemicals and leather. Nevertheless exports of machinery and transport equipment have grown significantly, especially in Brazil and Mexico, as well as miscellaneous manufactured goods, which include clothing, footwear, and plumbing, heating and lighting equipment. The latter have become less significant relative to exports of machinery and transport equipment by Brazil and Mexico.

In the Caribbean and Latin American regions, the following countries are not yet considered to be approaching near-NIC or NEEM status: the Bahamas, Barbados, Bolivia, Costa Rica, the Dominican Republic, Ecuador, El Salvador, Guatemala, Guyana, Haiti, Honduras, Jamaica, Nicaragua, Panama and Paraguay. These countries have experienced a significant decline in their export earnings from manufactures between 1970 and 1990; and their export manufactures consist mainly of miscellaneous manufactured goods, particularly clothing. The diversification of export manufactures in the direction of clothing has been facilitated by the structural adjustment programme pursued by a number of countries, in particular Jamaica and the Dominican Republic since the early 1980s.

For a restructuring of production and exports, investment in new (manufacturing) industries is a necessary condition. It can be undertaken by either private investors (local or foreign) or the state. The policies of the 1950s to 1970s were geared towards encouraging foreign investment in import-substitution manufacturing activities. In some cases the state itself undertook investment, especially in basic industries. However adjustment measures adopted to address significant debt burden and fiscal deficits have constrained governments in this role. The adjustment measures are aimed at attracting foreign investment to export-oriented industries.

Adjustment policies pursued in the 1980s have led to increased foreign investment flows to a number of Latin American countries, in particular Argentina, Chile and Mexico. In Mexico the fall in the value of the peso from 1982 reduced the price of labour and increased foreign direct investment in assembly-type operations in the free zone or *maquiladora*. But whereas transnational corporations have been attracted initially by cheap labour, the changing nature of global production with increased emphasis on technology can lead them to upgrade the low-valued assembly operations in some locations to high value-added operations based on technical skills and other high-quality local inputs.

The requirement is of course the presence of technical skills, the development of which governments can facilitate. Mexico, Brazil, Argentina and Chile have encouraged the development of skills and technology through increased expenditure on training and research and development (R&D). For example, in the mid-1980s Brazil had 52 000 scientists and engineers while Mexico had 16 000. Brazil spent US$900 million on R&D whereas Mexico spent US$1 billion (IDB, 1992). This emphasis has resulted in the growing significance of machinery and transport equipment in the exports of these countries since the 1980s.

Foreign investment has also increased to the NICs and near-NICs of Asia during the 1980s. For example, in Malaysia foreign direct investment, mainly from Japan and Korea, grew as significantly as in Mexico (see Chapter 11 above). Malaysia has also been increasing its technical skills and its expenditure on R&D at a rate comparable to that for the major Latin American countries (IDB, 1992). The result has been the development of higher value exports from specific industry segments such as transistor valves and telecommunications equipment.

Foreign investment inflows into the Caribbean have not grown as significantly as for countries in South and Central America (see Table 12.2). Most of the inflows increased from the latter part of the 1980s. Foreign investment in Trinidad has been associated mainly with the petroleum industry whereas recent flows of foreign investment into Jamaica and the Dominican Republic are associated mainly with the growth of the apparel industry, which is located in export-processing or free zones. The time period of the recent adjustment measures undertaken by Guyana is too short to observe any significant changes in foreign direct investment and in the production and export structures of the country, although natural resource-based products, namely sugar, bauxite, gold, timber and rice, continue to dominate the production and export structures.

The transfer of technology through foreign investment in order to develop technology-intensive exports may not be any more feasible now than it was in the past. Furthermore, foreign investment has been associated with enclave operations and repatriation of profits. The strategy followed by Korea and Taiwan was to acquire the technology through imported machines, by training in science and technology and by sending their technicians to study the process in developed countries (McCarthy,

Table 12.2 Net direct foreign investment flows, selected countries, 1970–90 (US$ millions)

Country	1970	1971	1972	1973	1974	1975	1976	1977	1978	1979
Barbados	8	14	17	4	2	22	5	4	9	5
Guyana	9	-55	2	8	1	0.8	-26	-1	–	0.6
Jamaica	161	176	97	75	23	-1	-0.6	-0.9	-26	-26
Trinidad and Tobago	83	103	86	65	120	93	132	83	128	93
Dominican Republic	71	65	43	34	53	64	60	71	63	17
Argentina	11	11	10	10	10	–	–	145	273	265
Brazil	407	536	570	1341	1268	1190	1372	1687	1882	2223
Chile	-79	-66	-1	-5	-557	50	-1	16	177	233
Mexico	323	307	301	457	678	609	628	556	824	1332
Venezuela	-23	211	-376	-84	-430	418	-889	-3	67	88
Korea	66	29	63	93	105	53	75	73	61	16
Malaysia	94	100	114	172	571	350	381	406	500	573

Country	1980	1981	1982	1983	1984	1985	1986	1987	1988	1989	1990
Barbados	2	7	4	2	-1	2	5	4	10	5	na
Guyana	0.6	-1	4	4	4	1	na	na	na	na	na
Jamaica	27	-11	-15	-18	12	-9	-4	53	-12	57	93
Trinidad & Tobago	184	258	204	114	109	-7	-21	35	63	149	109
Dominican Republic	92	79	-1	48	68	36	50	89	106	110	133
Argentina	788	944	257	183	268	919	574	-19	1147	1028	2008
Brazil	1544	2313	2534	1373	1556	1267	177	1087	2794	744	
Chile	213	383	401	135	78	114	116	230	141	184	249
Mexico	2156	2835	1655	461	390	491	1160	1796	635	2648	2548
Venezuela	55	184	253	86	-3	57	-444	-16	21	77	96
Korea	-7	60	-76	-57	73	200	325	418	720	453	-105
Malaysia	934	1265	1397	1261	797	695	489	423	719	1668	2514

Note: = not available.
Source: IMF International Financial Statistics Yearbook 1993.

1993, p. 61). Nevertheless foreign direct investment has increased in these countries since the late 1980s.

The Caribbean would have to significantly increase technical skills in order to attract foreign investment in high-technology industries. In 1984 Trinidad had 275 scientists and engineers or 2.4 per every 10 000 persons and spent US$67 million or 0.9 per cent of its GDP on R&D. In contrast Jamaica had only 18 scientists and engineers in R&D in 1986 and spent only US$1 million in the same year on R&D (IDB, 1992, p. 215). The need to reduce the government deficit as part of the adjustment programme constrains increased investment in science and technology training and R & D. It also constrains a strategy of offering tax and other incentives to encourage the development of specific industries, which was the strategy adopted by Taiwan and Korea.

This brings us to the question of the relationship between economic adjustment and graduation in the world economy from primary producer to manufacturer status.

ECONOMIC ADJUSTMENT AND REPOSITIONING

Economic adjustment has been pursued since the late 1970s by a number of Caribbean and Latin American countries in order to satisfy certain objectives, namely greater integration into the world economy, balance-of-payments equilibrium, fiscal viability and debt-servicing capacity. There are two components: a stabilization programme usually supported by the IMF and geared toward adjusting demand to available supply in the short term; and a structural adjustment programme supported by the World Bank (and other agencies such as the IDB and USAID) aimed at increasing production and exports in the medium and long term. The overall goal is improved management of the internal and external accounts, which would be facilitated by greater outward orientation of the economy.

Stabilization programmes are adopted by countries with large and persistent balance-of-payments deficits. When growth in demand (for goods and services), which is reflected in an increase of the money supply, cannot be satisfied by existing domestic output then domestic prices will rise and imports will increase to satisfy demand. The deficit (difference between earnings and expenditure) can be financed by external borrowing and/or running down the country's international reserves. The inability of a country to obtain inexpensive financing usually leads to some arrangement with the international lender of last resort, the IMF. Jamaica and Guyana found themselves in this position in the late 1970s when their terms of trade deteriorated after the significant oil price increases. The Jamaican government aborted an earlier arrangement with the IMF and resorted to domestic credit creation by printing money to finance its operations. The resulting inflation and balance-of-payments disequilibrium eventually led to a series of arrangements with the IMF from 1981. The conditionality attached to the use of IMF funds to 'stabilize' or restore balance to the economy centred on demand-restraint measures: restricting the growth of credit and the money supply via high interest rates, reducing the government's deficit and adjusting the 'overvalued' exchange rate (cf. Ihonvbere in Chapter 8 above for the African comparative case; see also Black and McKenna, 1993, for the Guyana case).

The World Bank focuses more on the supply side of the economy and supports the strategy of export-led growth, which would allow developing countries to replicate the experience of the Asian NICs. Its conditionality centres on liberalization of trade and payments, privatization of state enterprises, deregulation of price and other controls and tax reform in order to induce increased output and exports. The devaluation mechanism usually advocated by the IMF is also supported by the World Bank as it is expected to lead to a switch of resources from import-substitution to export-oriented industries, whose output would increase on account of higher returns in local currency.

The adjustment measures that directly affect graduation to near-NIC or NIC status are currency devaluation, trade liberalization, privatization of public enterprises and reduction in government expenditure.

Exchange-rate changes, in particular currency devaluation, which has been a significant aspect of adjustment measures, functions mainly to alter factor prices. It tends to make labour-intensive exports more competitive and hence profitable and thus induces the relocation of the labour-intensive portions of global production to these countries. The main disadvantage with this type of operation is the relatively low value added. Moreover, global production has become more technology-oriented and hence low labour cost is no longer an advantage in attracting export manufacturing to developing countries (*The Courier*, 1993, p. 62). Significant currency devaluation also leads to price inflation, which affects manufacturing and other activities.

Trade liberalization and privatization may have an adverse effect on a policy of industrial development if they are pursued before primary and secondary import-substitution industries have been well established. In East Asia the strategy was to actively promote specific industries (via tax and interest-rate policies) and to pursue trade liberalization on a phased basis in conjunction with an export-substitution strategy. The maximum tariff rate in Taiwan was reduced to 58 per cent only in 1987. In Latin America, Mexico has significantly liberalized its foreign trade but the country had set up a number of manufacturing industries since the 1960s under high-tariff and non-tariff barriers. Brazil has only recently embarked on a trade-liberalization strategy (IDB, 1992). In Jamaica the significant reduction in tariffs before the footwear industry was restructured to face external competition has led to a decline in the industry and an increase in imports.

There are two major requirements for sustained economic growth and movement up the industrialization ladder. One is the growth of the world economy and international trade. The recession in the major industrialized economies has led to a slowdown in the growth of those economies and in world trade as a whole. This has resulted in the pursuit of protectionist policy measures. For example, clothing and textile imports are restricted by the United States through higher than average tariffs and through bilateral agreements, and by the EC under the Multi-Fibre Arrangement. Leather footwear is restricted by the United States through high tariffs and by the EC through quotas and voluntary export restraint (VER) by exporters. Iron and steel imports into the United States and the EC are restricted by VERs. Trade barriers – tariffs and especially NTBs – constrain the growth of trade among developing countries. The trade liberalization measures could be used to increase trade among these countries.

The second requirement is macroeconomic and political stability in the developing countries. In the Caribbean, instability has been the major problem for Jamaica and Guyana. In the latter country the elections of 1992 restored the functioning of political democracy, whereas the stabilization and structural adjustment measures pursued since the end of the 1980s have been geared toward correcting the imbalances in the fiscal and external accounts. Substantial currency depreciation and liberalization of the foreign exchange market have addressed the twin problems of high inflation and foreign exchange shortages by bringing demand into line with supply. However the need to reduce the debt burden and increase foreign exchange earnings has led to increased production and exports of primary commodities, sugar, bauxite, rice, gold and timber.

In Jamaica the problems of inflation and foreign-exchange shortages have remained acute despite the pursuit of stabilization measures since the early 1980s. Different instruments of stabilization have been used at different times with different effects. For example, currency depreciation was the major instrument used from 1983–5 whereas wages-and-incomes policy was a major tool for stabilizing prices until the end of the 1980s. Steps were also taken to reduce the government deficit, namely reductions in expenditure and increases in taxes. This resulted in relatively low inflation until the 1990s.

A return to orthodox stabilization measures in the 1990s has not yet led to price stability as the various policy instruments used have sometimes conflicted with each other. Confidence in the ability of the government to maintain a stable economic climate has been negligible and this in turn has affected the achievement of low inflation and increased foreign-exchange inflows. The government has had difficulty, as is the case with most developing countries, in applying stabilization measures in a consistent manner because of the nature of electoral politics and the need to respond to different constituencies at different times. Nevertheless the government that emerged from the 1989 elections has been willing to intensify the pursuit of orthodox stabilization measures. This seems to have been the experience also of governments that emerged from elections in some Latin American countries (Stallings, 1992; Nelson, 1992).

CONCLUSION

Caribbean countries that have not successfully altered or prepared for altering the production and export structures of their economies since the mid-1970s are in danger of being marginalized in the world economy in terms of its changing structure. The main requirement for restructuring is development and strengthening of the capability to produce goods with high value-added. This can be done by upgrading technical competence of workers, by expanding research and development and by upgrading infrastructure. Government has to play an active role in this development through its budget. Where government expenditure in the past has been inadequate in these areas, this is made worse under stabilization and structural adjustment programmes that require significant cuts in expenditure to balance the budget (see Chapters 8, 14 and 15 of this volume).

Reliance on foreign investment to undertake this type of expenditure is unrealistic as, in the changing production process, TNCs choose locations where skills and infrastructure are already available. Approaching adjustment through measures to reduce labour costs will result in the growth of labour-intensive manufacturing, from which only a relatively small portion of value-added accrues to the national economy. This would leave Caribbean countries at the margin of the globalization and regionalization process in the world economy, as TNCs operating in these areas would relocate to Mexico once NAFTA comes into effect, since they would enjoy both low wage cost and free market access to the United States (cf. Chapter

5 above). It would also worsen income inequality in countries such as Jamaica, where this has been a significant problem, and lead to internal marginalization of specific groups.

The sequence and pace of adjustment is crucial to the success of the attempts at restructuring the economy. The East Asian countries of Korea and Taiwan have pursued adjustment policies slowly since the mid-1970s. Currency depreciation and high interest rates were pursued at specific points in time and foreign trade was slowly liberalized. The most significant tariff reforms were adopted from the mid-1980s. Liberalization of capital has been the last adjustment measure pursued and has resulted in the growth of foreign investment and intraindustry trade in high-technology products during the last few years. What was important in the case of the East Asian NICs was their ability to maintain low inflation and to adjust their export structures in response to the changes in the world economy.

The NICs of Latin America, like their Asian counterparts, pursued primary-import-substitution strategies followed by export-substitution and/ or secondary-import and export-substitution strategies. This was facilitated partly by foreign investment and partly by state investment. These countries also invested in upgrading their technological capabilities. Structural adjustment measures have therefore resulted in increased foreign direct investment in high valued-added manufacturing; these countries are being linked into the global and regional networks of TNCs to produce and trade in specific industry segments. Governments have facilitated regional links through bilateral trade agreements such as that between Argentina and Brazil (1986), which has led to the merger of the two largest TNCs in the automotive sector and hence to the integration of production in these countries.

Where Caribbean countries such as Jamaica and Guyana have already adopted most of the adjustment measures (see Black and McKenna, 1993), the key determinant of both domestic and foreign investment is political and macroeconomic stability, which would also increase government's ability to invest in the development of human resources and infrastructure. In addition, success in overcoming marginalization would depend on the purposive behaviour of government in relation to the development of an industrial strategy.

13 Caribbean Trade Options: Playing the North American, European and Latin American Cards

Aaron Segal

INTRODUCTION

Since the first voyage of Columbus in 1492 the Caribbean has conducted most of its external trade through preferential arrangements with extra-regional powers. Throughout five centuries the assumption has prevailed that small, island economies could not compete in global markets. Therefore the negotiation and retention of preferential trade arrangements has been regarded by many as a matter of necessity, if not of survival.

Historically the dominance of preferential, extraregional trade has not precluded intraregional trade, much of it in the form of contraband. Extraregional imports, whether slaves or luxury goods, frequently found their way to prohibited Caribbean ports. However this lively non-preferential trade, whether licit or clandestine, has seldom represented more than a small portion of total Caribbean exports and imports. The thirteen-member Caribbean Community (CARICOM), after more than twenty years of troubled operations, still does not account for more than 10 per cent of the total trade of its members. Its decision to press ahead for a full common market is not expected to significantly increase trade between economies that are not complementary (see Figure 13.1; cf. Chapter 12 above).

Thus the persistent belief, seldom tested, that small, open, island economies must invest their diplomatic talents in the securing of extraregional preferences. Spectacularly the Caribbean, with the exception of Cuba, is the only region of the world to have negotiated extraregional, non-reciprocal trade agreements with the EC and the United States and Canada (Segal, 1991). Alone in the world most of the Caribbean enjoys privileged trade

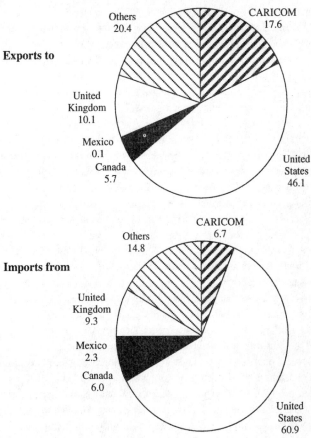

Exports to

Imports from

Note: Totals may not add due to rounding.
Source: International Monetary Fund, *Direction of Trade Statistics Yearbook*, various issues (Washington, DC).

Figure 13.1   CARICOM countries' direction of trade, 1990 (per cent)

access to the largest trading blocs in the world, approximately 52 per cent of the global market. Given the very limited political interest of the EC and its member states in the decolonized Caribbean, the construction of special trade ties to Western Europe and to North America is an impressive diplomatic achievement. The entry in 1989 of the Dominican Republic and Haiti into the now seventy-one-member Lomé Convention brought the entire independent Caribbean except Cuba into both the Lomé and CBI agreements. It also marked the unwillingness of the EC to accept in the Lomé Convention any Central American or other 'continental' Latin American members. Instead the EC reaffirmed its commitment to provide economic aid and technical assistance but not preferential trade to Central America.

The problem is that unique, preferential trade access to the two largest markets in the world is not paying off for the associated Caribbean. The EC provides preferential access and guaranteed prices for bananas, some sugar and other commodity exports. However its high and complicated rules of origin make assembly production in the Caribbean for export to the EC extremely difficult. The Lomé Convention, dominated by extremely poor African member states, has done little to improve erratic Western European air and transport links to the Caribbean, or the Caribbean share of European tourism. Financial aid to the Caribbean from the EC amounted to about 20 per cent of total aid to the Caribbean during the 1980s but lacked priorities or overall impact (World Bank, 1991, Table 20). EC private investment in the Caribbean has grown only slightly since the onset of the Lomé Convention and has limited presence in the critical service sectors of telecommunications and electronics.

Although Caribbean states have provided disproportionate leadership within the Lomé group of states, their needs are overwhelmed by the majority of debt-ridden, single-commodity-exporting African members (Segal, 1991).[1] Thus the four renewals for five years each of the Lomé convention have focused on stable commodity prices, increased financial aid and guaranteed market access. The Commonwealth Caribbean effort at Brussels has been directed at continuing preferential access and prices for high-cost Windward Islands bananas to part of the EC market. Approval of the Dominican Republic's entry into Lomé was conditional upon its agreement not to export bananas to the EC (OECD, 1974; *Times of the Americas,* 7 March 1991).

The Lomé Convention has not reflected the profoundly democratic nature of most of its Caribbean members in contrast with the majority of Lomé states. Nor has it reflected the greater diversification, service and tourism orientation, and higher skills levels of Caribbean economies.[2] Haiti is the only Caribbean member of the Lomé Convention whose socio-economic indicators resemble those of the majority of Lomé members. Even the poorest of the Leeward and Windward Islands have socio-economic levels well above most Lomé members. Only Mauritius, with its dynamic tourism and manufactured exports and its vibrant democracy, resembles the Caribbean members of Lomé.

The Caribbean has also lacked effective political support within the EC. Spain has championed Hispanic Caribbean interests as well as retaining some contacts with Cuba. France is a stalwart defender of its overseas Caribbean territories, who benefit from extensive EC aid through being legally part of a member state. The Netherlands has been content to channel some EC aid to the Netherlands Antilles and to independent Suriname. The United Kingdom, whose Caribbean trade and investments have noticeably declined, has lobbied for continued EC commodity preferences. Germany has mounted modest Caribbean bilateral aid programmes but has shown little interest in trade promotion. Pro-Caribbean private-sector groups in the EC continue to be organized around traditional commodity imports and lack influence.

Trade preferences with the EC have served to stabilize certain commodity prices and markets and to provide a modest flow of aid. These ties have helped to slow economic decline but they have done little to generate economic growth. They are designed to respond to the massive economic problems of Sub-Saharan Africa, and not to more sophisticated Caribbean economies.

THE CARIBBEAN AND CBI

The Caribbean Basin Initiative (CBI) was launched in 1983 by the US Reagan administration on a novel non-reciprocal basis. Its premise is that manufactured exports using US components can be catalyzed by duty-free preferences and private investment, both local and foreign. The geographic scope was extended to include Central America and Panama while excluding Cuba and Nicaragua, then under Sandinista rule. Non-tariff barriers and other restraints were used to limit exports of sugar, textiles, apparel, footwear and a few other items competing with US production.

The CBI has stimulated new manufacturing exports, which rose to $3.4 billion in 1991. Certain countries, such as Costa Rica, Belize, and Jamaica, have been quicker to take advantage of the CBI than others. The CBI is not an unqualified success but it has demonstrated the feasibility of diversified manufacturing for export.

The problems of the CBI have been extensively documented (*The Times of the Americas*, 13 December 1989; Griffin, 1990). The non-tariff barriers, like the domestic agricultural subsidies of the EC, represent a major loss of potential exports. Demands for the removal or reduction of these barriers surface at each five-year renewal of the CBI but are overcome by domestic producers. The US-dictated rules of origin limit downstream, vertical integration and use of local components. Lack of US aid limits development of trade-promoting infrastructure. A serious problem in smaller islands is the shortage of investment capital and entrepreneurial skills. The CBI is also charged with promoting environmentally harmful projects and ignoring trade union, occupational safety and other concerns.

Caribbean concerns are mostly directed at consolidating and extending the CBI. While there are some critics who advocate economic self-reliance based on food over export crops and other measures, there is more support for increasing the CBI and protecting it from the effects of NAFTA.[3] Table 13.1 on US–Caribbean Basin imports for January–July 1992 conveys the geographic extent of CBI involvement, which accounts for a high percentage of its manufactured and agro-business exports to the United States.

Dual preferential trade access through the CBI and the Lomé Convention has failed to produce sustained economic growth in the Caribbean. World Bank data indicate that most Caribbean states during the 1980s and into the early 1990s were barely able to keep economic growth above levels of population increase.[4] Social indicators, as reported by the United Nations, also fell during this period or were stagnant for most countries.[5] Export-oriented industrialization succeeded in increasing foreign exchange earnings in some countries but these were more than offset by inflation, increased imports and the costs of debt service.

There are many factors that account for extended slow economic growth in the Caribbean and trade preferences are probably not the most important (see Chapter 12 above). Essentially they have acted as partial safety nets for exports and some employment and foreign exchange earnings. They have facilitated some firms making the transition to becoming more competitive, at least in regional markets. The CBI has attracted US investment capital, transferred some technology and trained some workers. The EC has provided some concessional loans and technical assistance. It has also encouraged contacts between the independent Caribbean and the French and Netherlands Antilles.

Table 13.2 indicates that tourism, remittances and other forms of transfers have become nearly as important sources of foreign exchange for some Caribbean countries as merchandise exports. Formal trade preferences have little effect on service sector earnings under the Lomé Convention or the CBI. Neither agreement has any provision for encouraging the reinvestment of remittances by the Caribbean diaspora workers in North America or Western Europe. Investments in financial services such as offshore banks are also excluded from either agreement.

Thus during a period of weakening world economies dual trade preferences have slowed Caribbean economic declines. They have not been sufficient to catalyze and sustain growth. They have to a limited extent

Table 13.1   US $ trade with the Caribbean Basin, January–July 1992
(millions of US $)

	US Exports (F.A.S.)		US Imports (c.i.f.)	
	1991	1992	1991	1992
Anguilla	6.6	6.1	1.4	0.1
Antigua	42.9	41.1	3.3	2.6
Aruba	114.2	188.7	45.1	128.7
Bahamas	407.9	410.6	306.7	284.2
Barbados	97.1	72.5	18.0	18.9
Belize	67.6	68.2	35.2	43.1
Bermuda	137.4	146.9	6.5	3.4
British Virgin I.	25.9	29.9	1.9	2.1
Cayman Islands	75.2	205.3	12.7	8.9
Costa Rica	570.2	764.9	721.9	877.8
Cuba	0.8	0.6		
Dominica	24.6	20.4	4.5	2.4
Dominican Rep.	963.0	1189.3	965.9	1365.2
El Salvador	273.5	420.0	188.7	245.8
French Guiana	140.1	75.9		
Grenada	17.0	13.9	5.4	5.0
Guadeloupe	29.9	40.4	1.5	0.4
Guatemala	493.3	609.5	577.4	709.7
Guyana	40.2	65.4	55.6	73.9
Haiti	265.6	112.4	187.4	53.8
Honduras	339.6	451.1	345.4	467.4
Jamaica	570.5	531.0	358.4	363.9
Martinique	22.0	19.0	0.4	0.6
Montserrat	4.4	5.9	1.8	2.0
Netherlands Ant	343.4	276.1	398.1	358.5
Nicaragua	77.3	101.6	53.9	35.9
Panama	531.5	631.9	184.2	181.3
St. Kitts-Nevis	21.5	18.9	9.7	13.9
St. Lucia	50.1	48.8	14.5	17.2
St. Vincent + Gr	23.7	20.2	3.9	2.7
Suriname	71.9	79.5	31.3	34.3
Trinadad & Tobago	261.6	238.0	2.0	2.6

Source: Caribbean Update, November 1992.

compensated for some of the effects of structural adjustment policies in the Caribbean involving privatization, fiscal constraints and reduced social services.

Table 13.2   CARICOM countries' sources of foreign exchange, 1989 ($ millions)

	Merchandise exports	Tourism	Other services	Transfers[1]	Other	Total
Antigua and Barbuda[2]	28.5	188.4	0.0	18.7	−12.8	222.8
The Bahamas	259.2	1214.3	212.6	1.0	15.1	1702.2
Barbados	146.9	528.7	109.6	5.8	130.8	921.8
Belize	124.4	28.5	41.9	31.1	−5.9	220.0
Dominica	55.6	12.3	0.0	17.2	−16.0	69.1
Grenada[3]	32.8	47.5	1.5	21.6	−18.2	85.2
Jamaica	1017.0	593.0	244.6	296.3	74.8	2225.7
St. Kitts and Nevis	32.8	40.3	3.5	15.2	−9.8	82.0
St. Lucia	111.9	113.0	22.5	12.4	−12.1	247.7
St. Vincent	74.6	25.2	5.7	30.2	−22.4	113.3
Trinidad and Tobago[3]	1453.3	91.9	165.2	−29.6	66.2	1747.0
Total Exports[4]	3337.0	2883.1	807.1	419.9	189.7	7636.8
Per cent of Total Exports	43.7	37.8	10.6	5.5	2.5	100.0
Trinidad and Tobago Non-oil	508.2	−	−	−	−	−
Total Exports, excluding oil	2391.9	2883.1	807.1	419.9	189.7	6691.7
Per cent of Total Exports	35.7	43.1	12.1	6.3	2.8	100.0

Notes:
[1] Transfers are mainly remittances.
[2] 1987.
[3] 1988.
[4] CARICOM except Guyana and Montserrat.

Sources: International Monetary Fund, *Balance of Payments Yearbook* (Washington, DC: International Monetary Fund, 1990); and International Monetary Fund, *International Financial Statistics* (Washington, DC: International Monetary Fund, 1989).

OTHER PREFERENCES: CANADA/CUBA

A glance at other trade preference experiences in the region helps to understand the significance of these policies. CARICOM negotiated in 1986 a non-reciprocal trade agreement with Canada, replacing a series of earlier commodity preferences. The agreement excludes clothing to protect Canadian producers and has done little to increase CARICOM exports. Again Canadian foreign investment in the region, tourism, remittances, concessional aid and other transactions outweigh trade, which accounted for only 5.7 per cent of total CARICOM exports in 1990 and even less for the Dominican Republic and Haiti. Non-reciprocal trade preferences with a sympathetic partner with a domestic market more than twice as large as that of Mexico generated only a modest expansion of traditional exports.

The second relevant experience is that of Cuba, which for nearly 30 years until 1989 operated a bilateral series of trade-preference agreements with the former Soviet Union and to a lesser extent with Eastern Europe. These agreements were based on planned, semi-barter exchanges at non-market prices, primarily of Cuban sugar for Soviet oil. These exchanges contributed to the ability of Cuba to provide comprehensive educational and health services. When the agreements collapsed in 1989 and the Soviets either failed to deliver oil or demanded payment in foreign exchange, Cuban–Soviet trade, 85 per cent of all Cuban trade, fell from $5.5 billion in 1989 to $2.6 billion in 1991 (Segal, 1992). Cuba has had to drastically cut electricity, social services and private consumption. It is also avidly seeking to attract tourism and private investment, primarily from Western Europe.

The Cuban experience demonstrates both the generosity of a trade-preference agreement and its political vulnerability. Excluded from Lomé, the CBI and CARICOM, and denied the possibility of buying Mexican or Venezuelan oil at a discount, Cuba is totally isolated from a world that is moving into regional groupings. Its sugar monoculture makes it an unattractive candidate for membership in a regional scheme, even with a change of regime. Yet it is difficult to conceive how a democratic regime in Cuba could survive without some kind of preferential trade access.

NAFTA: IMAGE AND REALITY

The North American Free Trade Agreement (NAFTA) should be understood as an historic turning point for both Mexico and the United States. The initiative comes from a group of US-educated Mexican technocrats headed by President Carlos Salinas Gortari. Determined to end decades of import substitution and industrialization based on protection, these technocrats privatized state enterprises, joined GATT, slashed protection, reduced budget deficits and carried out other measures to reverse historic state domination of the economy. Once they realized that Mexico could not find major markets in Latin America, Japan or the EC, a strategic decision was taken to tie Mexico's economic future to that of the United States (see, for example, Hufbauer and Scholtt, 1992). This represented an historic break with the strategy of maintaining economic and political distance from the United States, which was seen as a dangerous adversary. Standard Mexican history books were rewritten to upgrade the image of nineteenth-century dictator Porfirio Diaz, who encouraged foreign investment. Another reason for seeking a permanent economic link to the United States was to guarantee markets and anchor the new Mexican market economy for the future.

The United States, under the Bush administration, responded favourably to the Mexican free-trade initiatives for several reasons. One was that Mexican–US trade has risen to nearly $60 billion a year, with Mexico representing an attractive, growing market. More important was US concern for domestic economic and political stability in Mexico and some way of generating stay-at-home development to eventually reduce the flow of undocumented Mexican migrants to the United States (Diaz-Briquets and Weintraub, 1991).[6] Mexico has increased in importance in US eyes, and traditional policies of non-intervention were ready to be replaced by phased interdependence. The eroding sixty-year domination of the single PRI party and the prospect of truly competitive Mexican national politics underlined the urgency of bolstering Mexico's capitalist economy and export orientation. Long-term favourable access to Mexican oil reserves may also have been a factor.

A complicating factor was the 1989 Canada–US Free Trade Agreement; still controversial on both sides of the border and yet to produce major economic benefits during a time of recession. NAFTA is necessarily trilateral, although Canadian–Mexican trade is less than 5 per cent of the North American total.

The format was easy. The full economic and eventual political union sought for the EC was unwanted. Each government sought to retain control over trade relations with third countries and to avoid long-term commitments. Joint political institutions were avoided and trade disputes are to be handled by mediation panels rather than by arbitration or international courts. NAFTA is not designed to grow into something else. It is an extremely asymmetrical free-trade area between a hegemonic state and two client states. Its combined purchasing power is slightly less than that of the EC; however, as a common market with extensive economic policy powers the EC is a much more powerful entity. NAFTA asymmetries are pronounced. Mexico has 30 per cent of the NAFTA population and less than 5 per cent of its total trade and gross domestic product. Lacking institutions for coordinating monetary, external trade, dispute-resolution and other policies it is not clear how NAFTA can work.

The dismantling of Mexican trade restriction, the Canada–US trade pact and GATT negotiations have lowered many North American tariffs. While a variety of non-tariff barriers have arisen as trade obstacles, trilateral trade has increased rapidly as tariffs have fallen. The stripping away of important licensing and other regulations has significantly opened the Mexican market.

NAFTA proposes to phase out tariffs sector by sector over a fifteen-year period. It leaves for last controversial sectors such as agriculture and citrus, where Mexican and US fears are strong. US tariff provisions favouring assembly plants using US components will be phased out in favour of free trade. Only a few sectors have been excluded from the negotiations. These include petroleum – a constitutionally nationalized industry in Mexico since 1938 that will be further opened to service contracts and procurements – and cultural and media products in Canada. NAFTA strives to preclude non-tariff barriers, although there is no rule preventing their being nationally legislated in the future.

The rules of origin or value-added for assembly products provoked intense debate in the NAFTA negotiations. US firms wanted to prevent Japanese or other companies from locating in Mexico, importing components and then exporting duty free to the United States. Mexico was anxious to attract foreign investment from all quarters. Canada was determined that its car plants would be able to use components imported from the United States on a duty-free basis, even if these components were first imported from a third country. The eventual compromise involves a high rules-of-origin standard, which is likely to be a continuing source of friction.

One of the most important features of NAFTA concerns intellectual-property rights, banking, insurance and other services such as telecommunications. Anxious for US investment and technology, the Mexican neoliberals scrapped a series of restrictionist banking, insurance, trucking, royalty, licensing, technology-transfer and other laws. Prior to the NAFTA negotiations the Mexican government had sold a 60 per cent share in the archaic National Telephone Company to a foreign consortium. These investment features contribute to a major improvement in the Mexican business climate for foreign firms, combined with a bustling Mexico City stock exchange.

Why did Mexico agree to these investment-related features? Faced with a youthful population growing at over 2 per cent annually, Mexico needs to create an estimated one million new jobs a year. Access to the United States for exports and capital is considered to be essential to a pro-growth strategy. This strategy is based on the business dynamism of Monterrey and other northern Mexican cities, with the impoverished south lagging even further behind (Trejo Reyes, 1984).[7]

Carefully excluded from the NAFTA negotiations was any discussion of migration, legal or undocumented. Instead a minor clause was agreed that should make it easier for foreign executives to be employed in Mexico. Although long-term stay-at-home development is an implicit premise of the NAFTA agreement, it receives no explicit mention. There is growing evidence that undocumented Mexican migrants in the United States are increasingly bringing their families and staying for longer periods.[8]

One unusual feature included in the NAFTA accord deals with environmental questions. Each country pledges to enforce its environmental laws, especially plant inspections, and to commit substantial new sums of money to environmental clean-ups at the border. The 'greening' of NAFTA stemmed from the pressures of US environmental groups, from the fear that US companies would move to Mexico in order to take advantage of lax environmental laws, and from recognition that much of the 2100-mile border has been seriously polluted. NAFTA uses commitments by each government to enforce environmental as well as occupational health-and-safety standards, without establishing any supranational authorities as in the EC. So, while protecting the environment has made it into the NAFTA accord, it remains problematic.

One suspects that this was done deliberately in order to protect sovereignty and the Mexican government from its left-wing opponents, who oppose NAFTA. The lack of a trilateral trade-dispute resolution mechanism may be a particular problem. The Canada–US agreement has encountered a number of unilateral disputes where mediation is not working.

NAFTA has a high symbolic value. It reorients Mexico towards its colossus neighbour and away from Latin America (see, for example, Noques and Quintanilla, 1992). It confirms the importance of Mexico in US geopolitics. It creates a new relationship between Canada and Mexico.

Through NAFTA, Mexico should be able to increase its exports to the United States, attract investment capital, improve its human resources and further open its economy. Regional and social-class inequalities may widen while the economic growth rate accelerates. A return to the import substitution strategy would be costly and inefficient.

Politically NAFTA should strengthen the PRI dominance if it accelerates growth and job creation. However, to open the economy and bring in new ideas is to further erode the domination of the governing party. The change in the state–private sector balance also increases the numbers of businessmen and professionals who do not depend on state favours. NAFTA should at least marginally contribute to Mexico becoming a competitive political system.

The impact on Canada, with its growing centrifugal forces, is quite different (see, for example, Lipsey, 1992). NAFTA will further North–South trade ties, between British Columbia and the state of Washington, Western Canada and the Rocky Mountains, Ontario and the US Midwest and so on. Thus an already fragmented Canadian market under free trade may further disintegrate.

NAFTA is likely to have only a limited impact on the United States. Jobs will be lost in unskilled, labour-intensive industries where jobs are already being lost to Mexico and overseas. Jobs will be gained in high-tech, capital-goods industries where the Mexican import market is growing. Much has been written and said about the need for trade-adjustment assistance but little is likely to happen. Existing US legislation to help displaced workers has been poorly funded and implemented. Retaining older workers is not easy; nor is fitting retraining to new jobs.

On the US side of the Mexican border there will be dislocations and gains. Unskilled workers may see their jobs move to Mexico in pursuit of lower wages. Engineering, technical services, health care centres and other professional services should prosper as the Mexican middle-class market grows. Perhaps Mexican and US border cities will learn to work together on shared environmental, air pollution and other problems.

Nationally Mexico stands to become more important in Washington. The risk is that NAFTA will become bogged down in recriminations, trade disputes, challenges and adverse media attention. This could reinforce the impression that Mexico is not a reliable or trustworthy trade partner. It will take much hard work and diplomacy to prevent the escalation of disputes. It is not clear that the existing joint US–Mexico congressional meetings and other mechanisms can do the job. Canadian–US relations operate primarily through low-profile diplomacy. The style of post-NAFTA Mexican–US relations has yet to be defined. Perhaps making them trilateral when possible will help? The troubled history of Mexican–US relations suggests that implementing NAFTA will not go smoothly (Meyer, 1984).

NAFTA: A THREAT

The most widely perceived threat that NAFTA poses to the Caribbean and other regions is that of trade diversion (Krugman, 1992).[9] This means that instead of generating trade creation and economic growth, NAFTA will cause the Caribbean to lose sales and markets to Mexico. This fear extends to Canadian markets, where Mexico will benefit from free trade previously confined to CARICOM.

Calculations concerning trade creation versus trade diversion as a result of economic integration depend on several assumptions. These include tariff levels, inflation, transport costs, consumer preferences, non-tariff barriers, exchange rates and the willingness of exporters/importers to absorb costs. For instance, Japanese automobile and electronics exporters are known for lowering prices in order to retain foreign market shares. Moreover trade-diversion analysis seldom considers, tourism and other services that are important to the Caribbean.

Several considerations apply to possible NAFTA trade diversion.[10] Caribbean exports to Canada and the United States for CBI members are already duty free, except for a few items. These items – sugar, apparel, footwear, textiles and so on – are scheduled under NAFTA to have tariffs phased out over extended periods. Mexico is already exporting to the United States and Canada most items subject to 5 per cent tariffs or lower. The phasing in over time of free trade will make only a nominal difference. Mexico must invest heavily in improved telecommunications, ports, roads and air freight to increase its penetration of North American markets.

The list of possible exports in which Mexico could take trade away from the Caribbean with the help of free trade is extensive. It includes tropical fruits and vegetables, canned fruits and juices, seasonal fruits and vegetables, spices, sportswear, footwear, textiles, leather goods, petroleum and by-products and other items. The list is similar to that faced by Brazil and other Latin American states from Mexican competition in NAFTA.[11] Textile exports are subject to the Multi-Fibre Arrangement, with its global quotas, rather than NAFTA free trade.

The evidence does not suggest that Mexico will become a major source of trade diversion for the Caribbean. Products subject to non-tariff restraints such as sugar will not be phased in to free trade for many years. The elimination of an already low duty on most Mexican exports to the United States, currently valued at ten times those of the Caribbean, should not make much difference. Caribbean exports will need to rely on quality control, marketing, costs and distribution to retain NAFTA markets, and market share.

Mexico is a more serious competitor for tourism (Caves, 1989). Opening its economy will mean more and lower-cost flights, additional foreign investment in a growing number of resorts, an improved image in North America and an ability to spread tourism throughout the year. Retaining the Mexican peso at a semi-float with the US dollar also encourages tourism.

Mexico is capable of tapping tourist markets in all parts of Canada and the United States while the Caribbean still relies primarily on the east coasts. While the Caribbean attracts approximately 10 per cent of its visitors from Western Europe, Mexico promotes off-season European tourism.

Competition for tourism may be more important than competition for NAFTA markets. Mexico has advantages of geographic proximity, frequent direct flights, extensive cultural sites, a warm-all-year climate, and new and uncrowded resorts plus price competitiveness. The Caribbean can respond with its own distinct cultures, aquatic and ecological tourism, diverse attractions, holding the line on prices, and cooperative marketing. Should NAFTA help to sustain Mexican economic growth, the tourist sector is likely to experience further investment.

The principal benefit to Mexico from NAFTA is likely to be in investments and technology transfer rather than trade. The repeal of Mexico's nationalist legislation of the 1970s on technology transfers removes an important obstacle to foreign investment. The assembly plants near the US border were already sheltered from those laws. The stipulations in NAFTA concerning intellectual property rights bring Mexico into line with Western country practices on copyrights, patents and related matters. The privatization of the banking industry and the NAFTA provisions for foreign investment in banking, insurance and financial services clear the way for a major expansion of foreign investment in a capitalist economy with legal guarantees.

Although Caribbean governments have been pursuing foreign investment for several decades with tax exemptions, credits, cheap labor and other measures, their legal paraphernalia falls short of what NAFTA contains. More significantly, NAFTA is a legal accord between three governments and any infringement of its clauses is a violation of international commercial law. A tax agreement between the government of Jamaica and the government of Canada has neither the same visibility nor the standing in law.

The prevailing impression is that North American capital is primarily attracted by low-cost labour in Mexico. What is forgotten is that Mexico requires employers to pay considerable fringe benefits, and that Mexican workers are well-known for rapid learning skills. Thus US firms, whether assembly plants or factories in the interior, have often transferred advanced technologies in order to achieve productivity gains. For instance, the Ford engine plant at Hermosillo introduced robots to a mostly skilled work force. Mexico is likely to attract much more capital per capita as a result of NAFTA and more advanced technologies than the Caribbean. The implication is that in the long-term Mexico in its manufacturing exports will have a better paid and more productive labour force than the Caribbean. The Caribbean may be compelled to compete with low-cost, unskilled labour in export-processing zones and assembly plants while Mexico upgrades its worker skills.

The most important characteristic of world trade is that it is dynamic and innovative. Mexico has gained a marginal trade preference through NAFTA. Its strategy will be to diversify and deepen its exports to reduce the cheap-labour component and to increase the value added. This is a Singaporean strategy relying on foreign investment to upgrade worker skills and wages rather than building-up local firms as in South Korea and Taiwan (Gayle, 1988). The fact that such a transformation has only partly occurred in the hundreds of foreign-owned border assembly plants indicates that assembling components for another plant is not enough. NAFTA provides an opportunity for Mexico to learn by engaging in the entire export industrialization cycle from product design to final delivery. The removal of tariffs takes away only one of the obstacles to exports.

CARIBBEAN TRADE OPTIONS

Given our analysis of NAFTA, image, reality and threat, and Caribbean ties to the CBI and EC, what are the available policy options? How should they be evaluated and what conclusions reached? While some policy options are mutually exclusive, can others be combined? How can thirty million people living in twenty-six independent and non-independent countries maximize their trade opportunities vis-à-vis the rest of the world? How can they use their universities and research institutes to analyze their options and then to explain the choices to their fellow citizens? How can they assist to convert these options into operational policies that will bring material benefits? What follows are trade-policy options discussed as pros and cons.

Keep the Status Quo

As members of the CBI and the Lomé Convention, Caribbean states have unique benefits and advantages. Both memberships are non-reciprocal and make limited demands on Caribbean states. The EC represents post-colonial ties, while the CBI provides a working relationship with the United States. The two memberships are compatible although the geographic areas are different. The EC has indicated its willingness to support closer contacts between the French Overseas Departments, the Netherlands Antilles and the rest of the Caribbean. The EC and the CBI have also provided some support for CARICOM, the Caribbean Development Bank and other regional institutions.

The problem with the status quo is that its contribution to Caribbean economic growth is too limited. EC preferences are confined to a few agricultural commodities and rules of origin eliminate most manufactured exports (see Chapter 5 above). The EC is not assisting the Caribbean services sector, especially tourism. The CBI non-tariff barriers bar important Caribbean exports and inhibit future growth. The CBI's lack of assistance for infrastructure is an impediment to exports. Rules of origin for the CBI discourage use of local components and value-added.

Modify CBI to Protect Against NAFTA

Lobby in Washington and through CARICOM to protect any CBI tariff concessions from being eroded or removed through NAFTA. This applies particularly to CBI non-tariff barriers, for example sugar and footwear, which could be subject to free trade. Whom in the US Congress will take up the cudgel on behalf of the Caribbean, especially if it involves renegotiating NAFTA? Why can't the Caribbean, which has enjoyed the non-reciprocal benefits of CBI since 1983, concede free trade to Mexico, which is making important reciprocal concessions? This policy option looks like a political non-starter.

Give Notice to Leave the Lomé Convention and Negotiate a New Caribbean–EC Agreement

The Lomé Convention is intended for the poorest of the poor states and is not suitable for the needs of the Caribbean, which is lost among its 71 members and cumbersome negotiating process. North Africa, Israel, Hungary, Slovakia and the Czech Republic have all negotiated separate trade agreements with the EC that reflect their particular interests. The EC Secretariat and the Commission might object to members leaving the Lomé Convention but they would be prepared to negotiate with the Caribbean as an entity, probably represented by CARICOM.

Leaving Lomé would hurt the agricultural subsidies and financial aid of the poorest Caribbean states: the Windward Islands, Haiti and the Dominican Republic. It would jeopardize Caribbean exports and subsidies in the EC and produce little in exchange. The EC is unlikely to agree to trade preferences for Caribbean-manufactured exports, which is against its general policy. The EC is also opposed to promotion of financial services such as offshore financial paradises and other service schemes.

The Lomé Convention is probably the best arrangement that the Caribbean can obtain from the EC, as witnessed by the entry of the Dominican Republic and Haiti with additional aid. The Caribbean provides more than its share of Lomé leadership and is well-placed to steer demands. Leaving Lomé would be risky, less than gracious, and could provoke splits among Caribbean states. The EC should be asked to do more for the Caribbean in terms of financial aid, trade, preferences and furtherance of contacts with the non-independent Caribbean.

Rely on GATT

The Uruguay Round of the General Agreement on Tariffs and Trade could conclude with agreements on tariff reductions, service-sector trade and reduction of agricultural subsidies. Caribbean GATT members have little influence on these negotiations but much to gain from a favourable outcome, especially if it also addresses non-tariff barriers (*The Economist*, 17 October 1992).

This is the moment for the Caribbean to renounce a history of tariff preferences and to opt for trade globalism. Although about half of Caribbean trade is with the United States, adherence to GATT will permit use of tariff and other reductions around the world. Since the Caribbean needs to be globally competitive, it should rely on GATT to open trade doors everywhere.

The GATT policy option is compatible with remaining in the CBI and the Lomé Convention. It implies that the Caribbean will abstain from joining the Enterprise for the Americas Initiative (EAI) or other regional schemes except for CARICOM. Opting for GATT does not mean abjuring regionalism; only being prepared to extend regional preferences on a most-favoured-nation basis to other GATT members.

GATT is too fragile an instrument for the Caribbean. It is dominated by the major powers and has little to offer small states. The impact of the Uruguay Round is in question. It is likely that it will produce little of value for poor, small countries. Specific Caribbean needs should be pursued on a regional basis through the CBI and Lomé.

Enter the Enterprise for the Americas Initiative (EAI)

Initiated by President Bush in 1990 as a follow-up to NAFTA, the EAI could encompass a series of overlapping free-trade agreements to include much of Latin America and the Caribbean (see the collection of essays in Saborio, 1992). Although the details are still vague, a series of framework agreements have been signed between the United States and other regions, including CARICOM, to prepare for eventual negotiations. It is not clear whether these would take a hub and spoke form with the United States leading, and what topics would be covered.

Joining the EAI would be a protective measure on the part of the Caribbean. Presumably it would receive free-trade benefits comparable to those of NAFTA members, although not necessarily identical. It would be asked to reciprocally make free-trade concessions to NAFTA and possibly to other EAI members.

Since the Caribbean already enjoys CBI and General Special Preference tariff concessions in the United States, EAI membership would add little. It could serve as a hedge and lead to the removal of some non-tariff barriers (Worrell, 1992). Chile and the Central American Common Market have expressed their interest in EAI membership and CARICOM has also been positive. Is there a good reason for the Caribbean to give up the principle of trade non-reciprocity to achieve nebulous benefits? The initial EAI package came with the promise of limited debt relief, and additional Inter-American Development Bank credits, but these are not yet firm.

Cultivate Mexico, Venezuela and Central America

Mexico and Venezuela provide oil at discount prices to many Caribbean and Central American states. Both countries have offered to negotiate non-reciprocal free-trade agreements with the Caribbean. Venezuela has conducted an active political and bilateral aid programme in the Caribbean, and Mexico has increased its Central American involvement. As middle-level powers, each of these countries offers the prospect of a generous and interested friend.[12]

Together Mexico and Venezuela account for less than 5 per cent of total Caribbean trade, mostly petroleum. Caribbean exports are negligible to each country, whose combined markets are less than half that of Canada. They are marginal trade partners although their sale of discount priced oil is most helpful. It is difficult to see the development of economic relations except on a further basis of export credits, and bilateral and multilateral aid, perhaps with some Mexican and Venezuelan tourism to the Caribbean. Mexican and Venezuelan influence is not available in CBI, Lomé or other negotiations. The idea of cultivating these countries as partners for the Caribbean encounters real resource limits.

The Caribbean, the five Central American states and Panama share membership in CBI. They have shared interests in NAFTA and the EAI. Hence regular meetings to discuss and coordinate positions make sense and have been taking place.[13] However the Central Americans are not members of the Lomé Convention and do compete with the Caribbean over EC markets for bananas and other exports. There is a conflict in principle between the Caribbean commitment to agricultural preferential exports and subsidies and the Central American desire for global agricultural free trade (Saborio, 1992).

Fragmentation

It is unlikely that the Caribbean will find a single voice for its external trade relations. Cuba faces US economic sanctions as it moves painfully from a planned to an externally trading economy. A post-communist Cuba will in all likelihood attempt to enter CBI and perhaps even Lomé and negotiate an observer status with CARICOM. Cuba's sugar monoculture and efforts to develop tourism make it a competitor to much of the Caribbean.

Puerto Rico is determined to retain its political and economic union with the United States while using tax credits to promote investment and trade with the Caribbean.[14] As Puerto Rico extends its political and economic influence in the Caribbean, it reinforces strategies based on export-industrialization and trade preferences.

The French Antilles, Guyana and the Netherlands Antilles benefit from a variety of EC subsidies and trade preferences.[15] Yet they remain on the periphery of the European market with many anxieties, especially in the French Antilles, about its impacts. Advocates of closer cultural, economic and even political ties with the rest of the Caribbean, these societies also wish to be fully integrated in the EC. Their trade options mostly revolve around retaining EC markets and subsidies.

Suriname would prefer a closer relation and more aid from the Netherlands and the EC. Its semimilitary regime and tense ethnic politics restrain its policy options. Next to Cuba it is the most isolated of all Caribbean societies.

The Dominican Republic and Haiti joined the Lomé Convention in 1989 after being founding members of the CBI. Haiti, since the 1991 military coup ousting President Aristide and the imposition of Organization of American States economic sanctions, has seen its economy crippled. Assembly plants exporting to the United States have mostly closed. Scarce foreign exchange has been used to import oil from Europe and the Netherlands Antilles, which did not adhere to sanctions. Similarly the EC refused to impose sanctions but has confined most of its aid to humanitarian purposes. The sanctions have cost Haiti much of its external trade without producing a change of regime. Ironically some of what Haitian trade remains takes place without the benefit of any trade preferences, suggesting that Haiti is a low-cost producer. It is hard to see how Haiti can renegotiate its external trade relations on any basis except charity.

The Dominican Republic as a member of CBI and Lomé has relied on tourism, remittances, export processing zones and merchandise exports to extend its foreign trade, predominantly with the United States. It has not formally joined CARICOM and its regional trade is primarily with Puerto Rico. Mexico's membership in NAFTA is perhaps more of a threat to the Dominican Republic than to any other Caribbean state, although still a minor threat. In spite of its Lomé membership the Dominican Republic has its trade policy fixated on the United States.

The 13 CARICOM member states are pressing towards a full common market but their regional trade remains less than 20 per cent of total trade (Worrell, 1992). Economies remain non-complementary, shipping costs are high, credits scarce and distribution poor. The CARICOM hard-won consensus continues to be Lomé and CBI plus regional integration. Some of the regional successes, as the multiple campuses of the University of the West Indies, have come in services rather than trade. However CARICOM-country politicians and diplomats do provide leadership for the Caribbean at the CBI and Lomé talks.

The above discussion of policy options and the perspectives of individual countries and blocs indicates why it is so difficult to arrive at a Pan-Caribbean view. Even the working out of a joint CARICOM position is a formidable task. National interests and differences are real and deeply felt. Foreign trade dominates these open economies and negotiations are high-profile and high stake.

CONCLUSION

This is an opportune moment to reexamine in academic centres and elsewhere the external trade ties of the Caribbean. NAFTA is a minor rather than a major threat to Caribbean interests. However, its formation extends the organization of the world economy into powerful, regional blocks (see Chapters 2 and 3 of this volume).[16] The Caribbean as a region that lives par excellence from trade needs to deal with these emerging blocks. Its relations with the EC and North America have not been particularly fruitful and perhaps need changing or at least revising; its economic relations with Canada, Mexico and Venezuela need reconsideration.

The task of intellectual analysis is not necessarily to predict what will happen tomorrow or next week or next year. Instead it is to provide the

208 *Carribbean Trade Options*

concepts and the empirical data to come up with alternate visions of the future. Students need to understand that there is more than one way to structure external trade relations. They need some tools for evaluating those alternative relations. They need to be able to build some alternative futures in which external trade becomes a vehicle of social change.

Notes

1.   Edwin Carrington of Trinidad and Tobago was elected secretary-general of the ACP group for one five-year term and nearly reelected for a second. Caribbean diplomats have consistently played leadership roles in the ACP group.

2.   Data on the 71 ACP member states is drawn from World Bank (1992) and United Nations Development Program (1992).

3.   Carmen Diana Deere (1990), for example, advocates self-reliance policies favouring local food production rather than export crops.

4.   Economic average annual growth rates for the 1965–90 period were 0.2 per cent for Haiti, 2.3 per cent for the Dominican Republic, –1.3 per cent for Jamaica and 0.0 per cent for Trinidad and Tobago. Figures for the Bahamas are 1.1 per cent, 2.3 per cent for Barbados, 2.6 per cent for Belize, –1.3 per cent for Guyana, 1.3 per cent for Dominica, and 2.9 per cent for St Vincent. Overall, during a 15-year period, per capita incomes in the Caribbean have barely exceeded population increases in spite of extensive emigration. The failure to expand export earnings has been a major factor in sluggish economic growth (World Bank, 1992).

5.   'Human development' includes health, education, nutrition and other data (UNDP, 1992).

6.   The long-run stay-at-home development strategy is presented with case studies in Diaz-Briquets and Weintraub (1991).

7.   Trejo Reyes (1984) compiled an early and influential study advocating export industrialization based on Northern Mexico.

8.   Rico (1992) provides an historical overview of migration issues in Mexican–US relations. Vermez and Ronfeldt (1991) is an excellent survey of recent trends.

9.   Krugman (1992) makes a case for regionalism producing trade creation, which may lead to multilateralism.

10.   See Worrell (1992) for a careful and balanced study of the possible accession by CARICOM to NAFTA and its effects.

11.   Erzan and Yeats (1992) use a simulation model to project possible trade gains and losses from free-trade proposals.

12.   Serbin (1982), for example, has long been an advocate of closer Caribbean–Latin American relations, especially with Venezuela.

13.   Lewis (1992a) is an example of the usefulness of Caribbean–Central American discussions.

14.   Lewis (1992b) presents the case for Puerto Rico as a source of investment capital, technology and markets for much of the Caribbean, using tax credits from US firms in Puerto Rico.

15. Several papers presented at a conference on the EC and the Caribbean in Paris in June 1990 discussed the situation in the French overseas departments and other non-independent territories.
16. A World Bank, CEPR Conference in April 1992 presented a series of papers on economic regionalism around the world.

14 Globalizing Civil Society: Interpreting International NGOs in Central America

Laura Macdonald

INTRODUCTION

The globalization of capital in the years since the Second World War represents a profound challenge to the dominant world order. The implications of globalization for production relations and the role of the state are subjects of considerable debate. The theoretical tools for understanding the impact of globalization on the structure of world order and the relationship between the individual, groups and the world system is, however, still underdeveloped. Recently emerging literature on a 'global civil society' represents one way of conceptualizing current transformations of world order. Most importantly, however, this approach permits the reinsertion of questions of agency and democracy into the study of international political economy which, at times, is overwhelmed by the seemingly implacable forces of capitalist economic expansion and the consequent bypassing of the authority of the nation state, the primary focus of most democratic political action in the modern world.

The questions raised by theorists of global civil society are thus essential ones for both global and local politics. The answers that have been provided so far are, however, less helpful. The current popularity of the concept of a global civil society is clearly inspired by recent debates over the relationship between state and civil society at the domestic level. However, the international relations debate fails to come to terms with the complexities that have been identified with evaluating the nature and significance of domestic civil societies. Moreover, in contrast with the subfield of comparative politics where some rich empirical studies of the dynamics of domestic civil societies have appeared, there has been relatively little concrete analysis of the agents of the emerging global civil society.[1]

One of the types of actors most commonly forming part of an evolving global civil society is the development non-governmental organization (NGO). Development NGOs claim to work on a people-to-people basis, linking civil societies in North and South. As a result of the polarization of civil societies in Central America in the 1980s, the actions of international NGOs working in the region were increasingly politicized. This, then, represents a good case study for examining the nature and significance of at least one actor in a global civil society. A few words of caution are in order, however. The problems of theorizing civil society at the domestic level are hardly inconsiderable. Application of the concept at the global level is even more problematic, particularly when the inherited power relations between North and South are entered into the equation, as they must be. Dominant approaches that view both domestic and global civil society as harmonious spheres of free association will be incapable of addressing this type of problem.

It is also important to avoid overly hasty applications of metaphors from domestic politics to the international level. While these two spheres are not completely separate, as the realist approach suggests, there are differences between them that mean that a global civil society would have somewhat different constituent elements, dynamics and significance than domestic civil society. Looking at the specific case of international NGO activity in Central America will help us avoid some of the idealism and abstractness of much discussion of the issue.

THEORETICAL ROOTS OF GLOBAL CIVIL SOCIETY

Discussions of global civil society are clearly indebted to previous attempts to understand the nature of ties between individuals and groups that transcend the system of states. The concept of global civil society is, of course, explicitly non- or anti-realist because of the emphasis on non-state actors, and ties between individuals and groups that transcend national boundaries (cf. Bull, 1977). One example of a previous attempt to conceptualize these relationships is liberal functionalism, particularly the work of the school's founder, David Mitrany. Like the contemporary discussion of 'global civil society', the functionalist concept of 'world society' focuses on non-state actors, and prescribes greater political participation by individuals and groups in international decision-making (Mitrany, 1966, pp. 121–8).

Although the origins of the idea of global civil society clearly can be traced to earlier versions of international relations theory, the contemporary debate is inspired by the recent resurgence of interest in civil society in both political theory and comparative politics. The concept of global civil society also represents a shift away from the sociological and anthropological conceptions of 'society' and 'community' to the more explicitly political 'civil society'. Like society and community, however, the use of the term civil society often hides widely differing ideas about what the term means, and how civil society interacts with the state and the economy. At least three different usages can be identified, linked with very different theoretical affiliations: neoconservativism, liberal-pluralism and critical theory (incorporating both neo-Marxist and post-Marxist approaches).

In the neoconservative vision, civil society exists as a sphere autonomous from, and morally superior to, the state. Part of the contemporary neoconservative attack on the state, then, includes a championing of the democratic potential of civil society, in both the Third World and the West.

Jean-Guy Saint-Martin, vice-president of the Canadian Partnership Branch of the Canadian International Development Agency, presents an example of this type of discourse. Saint-Martin contrasts the previous approach to development, which he calls the 'Newtonian universe' in which all development efforts are focused on the state, to the current 'Einsteinian era,' in which non-governmental groups, both for profit and non-profit, are seen as central:

> Recent developments in our way of seeing things suggest that politically, we are moving out of the era of Newton and into that of Einstein, thereby expanding the creative potential of the multiple groups that constitute civil society. Participatory democracy will take root more readily in a politico-economic culture that encourages the entrepreneurial spirit, that rewards the creative initiatives of a multitude of private entities which, each according to its own style, and mission aims at fulfilling the multiple aspirations of society [*sic*]. A liberalized economy will enable the laws of the market to more rationally determine the interplay of production factors (Saint-Martin, 1992, pp. 3–4).

Saint-Martin's definition of civil society includes microenterprises, credit associations, private corporations, bankers' associations, universities, professional associations, cooperatives, trade unions, urban popular movements and rural peasant movements (cf. Bowles and Gintis, 1987; Macpherson, 1973; Pateman, 1988). These diverse organizations are linked, in this view, by their alleged autonomy from the state.

In the neoconservative agenda for the Third World, NGOs play a crucial role in creating a 'civic culture' to restrain the potential excesses of unregulated mass politics. The contemporary neoconservative approach to civil society is also, in part, a response to the restructuring of the global political economy. By strengthening civil society in the Third World, international actors such as the IMF and the World Bank hope to contribute to the political sustainability of structural adjustment programmes. In fact, structural adjustment and support for civil society are presented as essentially the same project, as the quote from Saint-Martin indicates; they are both directed at weakening the power of the state and strengthening the form of choice and free association associated by neoconservatives with both the market and civil society.

While the neoconservative conception of the state–civil society divide has undergone a resurgence in recent years, it competes with and overlaps another theoretical approach that is enjoying renewed popularity at least in the study of underdeveloped societies, liberal pluralism. In this paradigm, organizations of civil society such as NGOs provide a focus for individual political participation in crosscutting associations and counterbalance the power of authoritarian states. Liberal pluralists thus share with neoconservatives the attempt to create an artificial division between state and civil society. NGOs take the place normally assigned to interest groups in pluralist theory, as intermediaries between the unorganized masses and the state. Grassroots and intermediary organizations, centred on specific issues, are encouraged to pressure the state to incorporate their input with regard to these issues. However this approach clearly does not call for broad-based social movements organized around class divisions and in a fundamentally antagonistic relationship with the state, capitalism, gender structures and so on.

The ideals of the liberal-pluralist perspective are apparently more appealing than those of the restricted democracy promoted by neoconservatives. However its silences on a number of crucial issues – the relationship between state and civil society, forms of oppression within civil society and the structural constraints on both state and civil society imposed by international economic factors – mean the outcome is the same. Meaningful participation in civil society is restricted to a few – the wealthy and well organized – while other groups are marginalized.

In contrast with the celebration of civil society seen in neoconservative and liberal theory, critical theorists underline the forms of oppression and constraint that exist in the realm of civil society. The thought of Antonio Gramsci is the principal influence on Marxist approaches to civil society. Gramsci (1971, p. 262) criticizes the liberal attempt to draw a clear distinction between state and civil society. He insists, instead, that state and civil society are integrally connected. State power is thus maintained not just through the formal organizations of 'political society' (government, political parties and the military), but also through many of the institutions of civil society. The attempt of neoconservatives and liberal-pluralists to distinguish between state and civil society is therefore misguided. However, in contrast with the 'direct domination' exercised by the institutions of political society, civil society is principally a sphere of indirect domination. The dominant class is able to exercise this hegemony when it comes to represent some of the interests of subordinate groups and to present its political project as embodying universal interests rather than narrow corporate interests.

More recently a post-Marxist perspective has emerged, which shares some elements of the liberal-pluralist approach, combined with the concern with exploitation and the espousal of a socialist project derived from Marxism. The concept of civil society has been found attractive by leftist theorists who reject the obsession with state power and class structures in traditional socialist theory and practice. Civil society is thus seen as the sphere of a political project of radical democratization. Once again, NGOs are called on to play a key role within this sphere in promoting democratization. However democratization is conceived of very differently than in previous conceptions, since it occurs not just at the level of state institutions but also within civil society itself, including the sphere of the family. Also in distinction to neoconservatism and pluralism, civil society is seen as a terrain of exploitation, discrimination and oppression. In contrast with traditional Marxism, however, daily struggles to combat these forms of oppression are seen as the essence of transformatory action. In another area of divergence from traditional conceptions, business organizations are either downplayed or excluded as elements of civil society. Civil society is thus sometimes conceptualized as a 'third sphere' distinct from both the private and public sectors. This is an area of frequent confusion, however, since exactly what is meant by civil society is often left undefined.

'GLOBALIZING' CIVIL SOCIETY: COMPETING PARADIGMS

The notion of global civil society has been raised as a new way of challenging the realist view of the (untheorized) nation state as the primary actor in international politics. Instead proponents of this approach theorize that the density of interactions between individuals and groups transcending state boundaries makes it possible to theorize an emerging global civil society comparable to that which exists within nation states. As indicated above, however, there is clearly no consensus on what is meant by civil society, even at the domestic level. Debates on global civil society largely replicate the divisions discussed above, although the neoconservative approach has not developed a theory of *global* civil society because of its strong affinities with realist thought.

Liberal-Pluralist Approaches

As within the comparative politics literature, liberal writers are primarily distinguished by their assertion of the analytic separation of civil society from the state, their view of civil society as a sphere of freedom, and by their lack of attention to class relations. M.J. Peterson asserts, for example, while recognizing that the state and civil society are 'intertwined,' that 'where the state does not completely monopolize the public sphere [as, for example, in Nazi Germany or the former Soviet Union], the autonomy of the state from the society is matched by an autonomy of the society from the state' (Peterson, 1992, p. 176). At the global level, the author argues, an autonomous political sphere has been established by transnational linkages among a wide variety of non-state actors: consortia of banks, international scientific associations, international associations of trade unions, religions, environmental groups, feminist groups and so on (ibid., pp. 378–9).

Martin Shaw asserts that groups, movements and institutions are making themselves felt within the international state system in a way comparable to that envisaged for domestic pressure groups in pluralist political philosophy:

> What is involved, however modestly and contradictorily, is the begin-
> ning of the development of what we may call global civil society, in
> which members of global society are starting to try to make the state
> system responsible – in the way in which national civil societies have, in
> the past, generated pressures to ensure the accountability of national
> states (Shaw, 1992, p. 431).

International NGOs are one of the main actors mentioned as shaping this transnational political space. Paul Ghils (1992) argues that international NGOs act in three principal ways: as 'pressure groups' or 'shapers of opin-ion' (for example, pressuring governments to reform foreign assistance programmes), as autonomous actors (for example, in the direct delivery of aid programmes), and as actors in competition with and critical of states and intergovernmental organizations.

Perhaps the most significant potential contribution of a liberal-pluralist approach to global civil society is the framework it offers for the promotion of democracy internationally. In liberal democratic theory, the existence of a civil society in which competing interests are organised is traditionally seen as the main guarantor of democracy. While the existence of a direct causal connection between civil society and democracy may be questioned (Fowler, 1991), the positing of a global civil society at least opens the door to a radical democratic project at the global level – one that rejects the common liberal assumptions that democratization must be implemented by elites and is limited to the national level. Yoshikazu Sakamoto thus asserts that a project of 'democratization from below' must include the 'globalization of democracy', by which he means 'the creation of a global perspective and values in the depths of people's hearts and minds, establishing the idea of a global civil society'. Thus, 'democracy can be deepened only if it is globalized, and it can be globalized only if it is deepened' (Sakamoto, 1991, p. 122). This vision represents a considerable advance over the restricted democracy of much liberal thought,[2] and moves toward the broadly participatory democracy promoted by post-Marxists. However class conflicts and economic processes, which are one part of the analysis of post-Marxists, are virtually absent here,[3] as are other structural sources of inequality addressed by post-Marxism such as gender and racial divisions.

Critical Theorists

These silences in pluralist approaches on the origins and manifestations of structural sources of inequality in global civil society are best addressed within critical theories of world politics. Just as Antonio Gramsci is widely recognized as the major theorist of civil society within the Marxist tradition, the application of Gramscian analysis to international relations by theorists such as Robert Cox provides a necessary starting point for a historical materialist analysis of global civil society. Cox replaces the realist conception of hegemony, based on the preponderant military power of the dominant state, with a Gramscian approach, in which hegemony, founded in civil society, is based on a combination of legitimation and force (Cox, 1983, p. 171). Cox thus differs from the liberal-pluralists in identifying the sphere of production and class relations as the primary constituent force in defining civil society. International capital becomes the prime actor in the creation of a global civil society. The Marxist approach thus permits an analysis of contradiction and conflict *within* civil society, rather than viewing the primary contradiction as lying between state and civil society (cf. Gill, 1990b, p. 305).

The danger here is the tendency to portray global civil society in one-dimensional terms (Abercrombie *et al.*, 1980) without recognizing the forms of contestation of transnational capitalist hegemony that already exist. And while some of these authors (for example Gill and Law, 1988; Gill, 1990b; Lipschutz, 1992) do speak tentatively of the possibility of the emergence of a transnational counterhegemonic movement that would deal with perceived problems such as militarism and inequality, they establish overly stringent criteria of evaluating success. The potential long-term impact of actors in global civil society lies not merely in their material resources, but also in their ability to create new identities, to contest established ways of thinking, and to create new linkages between peoples in different parts of the globe (Lipschutz, 1992). Existing international NGOs such as Amnesty International, Greenpeace and OXFAM are seen as 'prototypes' for transnational counterhegemonic networks, but they are described as often too specialized, small, temporary or poor to challenge the existing hegemonic order.

INTERNATIONAL NGOs IN CENTRAL AMERICA: A GLOBAL SOCIAL ACTOR?

One way of evaluating these competing concepts of global civil society is to look at whether transnational networks of various kinds have acted as a relatively autonomous force in responding to international events. The activities of international NGOs in Central America in the 1980s will be examined on this basis.

The crisis in Central America can be viewed as a clash between domestic class conflicts (which were overdetermined by the historical role of the United States in the region) and the power politics of the hegemonic state. Especially in a period of real and perceived challenges to its hegemony on a global level, the United States was unwilling to accept the emergence of alternative forms of state in its 'backyard', nor was it able to assist existing client regimes to accommodate and coopt internal pressures in order to establish hegemonic forms of rule domestically.[4] Direct economic interests were marginal to Washington's response, but Central American states were also subject to pressures from the international financial institutions that were demanding greater conformity with neoliberal principles in all Third World countries.[5]

As a result of the regionalized economic and military crises and the direct intervention in state policy by agents of both the US government and the international financial institutions, we can see a qualitative transformation of both state and society in Central America, and in their relations with the world system, which hold important implications for NGOs. The area has always been highly dependent but, because of backward production relations and underdeveloped civil societies, it was primarily the oligarchic state that was the point of contact with the metropolis (Torres-Rivas, 1989). In recent years, though, the United States has increasingly penetrated Central American civil societies in an attempt to reestablish order. Ironically, though, this penetration has had ambiguous results. Rather than enforcing passivity, forces for increased dependency have also resulted in the development of social movements that are challenging authoritarian regimes and external intervention. Both of these factors, external intervention and domestic political evolution, have shaped the nature and impact of international NGO assistance to the region.

There are several elements of the NGO response to the Central American crisis that would support liberal-pluralist visions of global civil society. NGO response to the crisis was certainly intense, visible and often highly critical of US policy, and had some impact on the eventual 'resolution' of the crisis. It was largely motivated by highly personal and moralistic responses to perceived domestic and international injustices, and involved the establishment of new relationships between Northern non-state actors and civil societies in a part of the world hitherto largely ignored.

Part of the impact of NGOs in Central America in the 1980s was purely quantitative. Traditionally weak civil societies saw the emergence of thousands of grassroots organizations and NGOs as people responded to the overlapping economic, political and military crises by devising new forms of cooperation and self-help. While these were largely spontaneous responses to the crisis, a typical strategy was to seek assistance from the hundreds of international NGOs that turned to the region in the 1980s. International NGOs were particularly attracted to Nicaragua because of the perception that the Sandinista regime was creating a new development model, based on popular participation and basic needs, goals with which development NGOs had traditionally identified. The new donors included not just established NGOs but also solidarity groups, trade unions, women's organizations and twinned cities. While figures are not available on the overall level of unofficial aid to Central America in the 1980s, it was undoubtedly considerable (particularly in Nicaragua, a country desperate for alternative sources of finance as a result of the US blockade and the freeze in IMF and World Bank assistance).[6] According to a leading Central American analyst, Xabier Gorostiaga, the non-governmental organization was the only institution in Central America, apart from the military, to expand during the 1980s. In the long term, this quantitative expansion of grassroots organizations and national NGOs (assisted by international NGOs) may represent a crucial element in the qualitative transformation of

Central American civil societies, seen by many as necessary for true democratization.

International NGOs were also seen by some Central Americans as playing an important role in modifying the perceptions and actions of individuals and governments in the North in their responses to the Central American crisis. Lesbia Morales, director of the office responsible for coordinating NGO assistance in the Nicaraguan Ministry of External Cooperation stated in 1988:

> The political impact [of NGOs] can be evaluated with reference to the situation of the Nicaraguan revolution itself – the fact that the Reagan administration has tried to isolate the revolution diplomatically, politically, and economically. In this respect, we consider that international NGOs, in their role of educators and information-providers for their own peoples, have succeeded in foiling all the machinations of the U.S. administration.... Obviously, this has a high political value – an incalculable value, I would say (interview, Managua, 1988).

As part of its strategy to prevent the consolidation of revolutionary Central American actors, the United States distorted the information available to the international media. NGOs thus offered one tool for penetrating the wall of official propaganda and providing alternative sources of information. Human rights NGOs such as Amnesty International, Americas Watch and some agencies of the Catholic Church (for example El Rescate in El Salvador) also provided invaluable independent information on human-rights abuses. The heavy-handed response of the US government to the Sanctuary movement, in which churches in the United States assisted Salvadorean refugees who had illegally entered the country, could be taken as evidence that this type of activity by an important actor in US civil society was seen as a considerable threat to its position.

The lobbying efforts of NGOs also played a role in convincing US allies not to fall in line with US policy in Central America, but to maintain economic assistance to Nicaragua, continue pressure on Guatemala and El Salvador, and support the peace process (North and CAPA, 1990). While none of these actions by international NGOs was a decisive force in shaping events in the region, it could be argued the international activities of NGOs acted to constrain the policy options of Northern states and increase public participation in foreign policy discussions.

There are certainly elements of international NGO action in Central America that would support the idealistic view of global civil society offered by the liberal-pluralist perspective. I would argue, however, that this depiction of international NGOs as international pressure groups provides an overly static approach to transformation of international politics and risks both overstating and understating the actual impact of nongovernmental actors. The debate over non-state actors in the international system often degenerates into a sterile discussion of whether state power is being eroded or not when the real issue is how the role of the state is changing in relationship to other actors. Brian Smith argues, for example, that NGOs present no challenge to nation state sovereignty:

> The [private aid] network preserves, at least in the short run, a differentiation among social classes within developing countries and among rich and poor nations, since it alleviates some of the pressures for more radical restructuring of the international economic system as called for by the NIEO. It also harnesses the energies of some middle class idealists and political dissidents both in the North Atlantic region and in developing countries and keeps them from more radical political or even revolutionary activities (Smith, 1990, p. 282).

While Smith makes some valid points, he, like others, prematurely forecloses on the possible long-term impact of NGO initiatives because they fail to directly challenge the existing world order in the short term. It is important to recognize the existing limitations of NGO initiatives while also assessing the possible germs of systemic transformation.

Unlike the liberal-pluralist approach, the critical theory approach to civil society helps alert us to the multiple dimensions of power inherent in NGO relations. Robert Wood's questioning of the imagery of aid as gift giving is as relevant to NGO as it is to official development assistance: '[T]he donor–recipient terminology reflects a basic asymmetry of power and status that lies at the core of the aid process' (Wood, 1986, p. 14). The emphasis on the division between state and civil society in liberal-pluralist approaches leads to fundamental misunderstandings about the nature of NGOs. In fact it has frequently been pointed out that the term 'nongovernmental' organization is misleading since most NGOs receive some type of state funding, and many would not exist without that funding (Jara, 1987, p. 4). They also enter into diverse relationships of cooperation with and dependency on governments in both North and South.

In Central America in the 1980s, far from representing a homogeneous sphere of free association, the NGO world was heavily polarized because of NGOs' diverse relationships with states in both North and South, and because of divisions within Central American civil societies themselves. Although many NGOs were extremely critical of US foreign policy, other NGOs were used as a tool of that policy. The so-called 'low-intensity conflict' (LIC) strategy adopted by US policy-makers was, despite the name, extremely broad-ranging and inclusive. Because of the nature of guerrilla warfare, no line was drawn between civilian and military targets; thus civil society was deeply implicated in the conflict.[7]

Both Central American and US-based NGOs were seen as one of the tools available for delivering economic assistance in support of counterinsurgency policies. The NGOs that received support cooperated with rightwing governments and military institutions, providing humanitarian and development assistance that served to legitimate the status quo. Some of these groups, such as those formed by right-wing fundamentalist churches, were ideologically committed to the anticommunist crusade. Others viewed themselves as apolitical but were lured by the availability of funding and were reluctant to examine too closely the political implications of their work (Inter-Hemispheric Resource Centre, 1988a, 1988b, 1988c) .

As a result, two main types of NGOs emerged and struggled for influence in Central America in the 1980s. More conservative NGOs were funded principally by the United States Agency for International Development (USAID). USAID established local umbrella groups in several countries of the region to channel its funds to NGOs. The goal was to reduce social tensions and support structural adjustment by channelling the poor into microenterprise projects or non-traditional exports. In the context of Guatemala, Carol Smith argues, such projects have contributed to the economic restructuring of the highland region. USAID projects help to open up a 'free' land market to allow the more efficient farmers to gain access to more land; introduce new, non-traditional export crops that require less land but more labour to produce; and provide loans for the technology and capital needed to produce new crops. All this has contributed to concentration of land ownership, proletarianization and internal migration (Carol Smith, 1990, pp. 23–6).

Another study of NGOs in Guatemala by AVANCSO–IDESAC notes the interconnections between NGOs and existing structures of power in both the state and private enterprise. The main 'interlocutor' or local partner for NGOs seeking to provide assistance in rural Guatemala are the neighbourhood improvement committees (*comités pro-mejoramiento de las comunidades*), which were established under the Ubico dictatorship of 1930–44. According to AVANCSO–IDESAC (1990, pp. 15–16).

These are grassroots organizations that lack networks for either horizontal or vertical integration.... This makes the work of NGOs difficult, because the levels of coordination and resource-use become very limited.... Also this style of organization limits the integration of strong social movements with the capacity to negotiate on a regional level. The phenomenon is even more complex because, as we will see, the NGOs themselves often contribute to the atomization of communities. This atomization arises from the communities but is fed and reproduced by the NGOs. This represents perhaps one of the key factors in the state's reconstitution of local power after the period of social emergency [my translation].

The Guatemalan military continues to attempt to strengthen the control of the state over civil society. However a modernizing component of the private sector, supported by USAID, is following a neoconservative strategy of privatization of civil society. Many newly emergent NGOs are thus funded by business groups and promote the type of economic activities described by Smith, often in collaboration with state agencies.

In contrast more progressive Central American NGOs (which sometimes call themselves 'historic NGOs' because they tend to have a longer trajectory of existence and ties with the popular movement) have been funded primarily by European and Canadian NGOs (and thus indirectly by the European and Canadian governments). The Concertation of Central American NGOs, a grouping of progressive NGOs, describes the conflicting tendencies:

What is the fundamental difference that distinguishes an NGO with a popular orientation from an NGO linked to the neo-conservative strategy? Both implement small projects; they both link themselves with the most vulnerable social groups. Both even display participatory pedagogical techniques and approaches to promotion which seek to consolidate a capacity for economic self-management. In reality, what distinguishes a neo-conservative wave of NGOs from an NGO movement committed to promoting the leadership of popular groups lies in how they view the problem of power. In the first case, the activity of the NGO is oriented at provoking changes in order to avoid modifications in the structure of power. In the second case, the NGOs try to promote changes in order to achieve transformations in the relation of social forces, in a manner which favours the majority (1988, pp. 24–5) [my translation].

The key factors distinguishing the progressive NGOs from their neoconservative competitors, then, are their transformational ideology and their attempts to strengthen social movements linked to the popular sector.

By directly addressing the relationship between the hegemonic state, the forces of international capital and global civil society, a historical materialist approach such as that of Cox and Gill helps us appreciate the contradictions at work in Central America (cf. Chapter 2 above). The fact that NGOs were often supportive of US policy does not indicate that non-state actors were insignificant; rather it alerts us to the intersections between state and civil society actors. A critical theory approach also helps us, however, to evaluate forces for change in the current system. International NGOs can be seen not just as creating linkages between actors in North and South and in pressuring/constraining state policies, but also in redefining identities, shifting allegiances away from the nation-state toward alternative modes of representation of interests. Within Central America, progressive NGOs were active in creating regional networks, forming linkages between popular-sector actors within these traditionally fragmented societies.

Attempts were also made to transform the traditional relationship between Northern and Southern NGOs. Partly as a result of their experiences in Central America, some Northern NGOs have attempted to transform their way of working, away from the traditional verticalist, paternalistic model toward more egalitarian relationships with partners in the South. This new model is sometimes referred to as 'accompaniment' and is based on respect for control by the local partner and an attempt to provide non-monetary forms of support for the struggles of local groups and a deeper form of commitment to the processes of social change in the Third World. Edwin Zablah, secretary general of the Fundación Agosto C. Sandino (FACS), a large Nicaraguan NGO linked to the Sandinista mass organizations, expressed his organization's goals thus:

> Over the years, we have succeeded in developing relations of a new type, which aspire to eradicating the verticalisms which existed between the NGOs which provide financing and their counterparts in the developing countries. Through an honest dialogue we have succeeded in pointing out the paternalistic and neocolonialist conceptions of some non-governmental sectors (FACS, 1990, pp. 2–3).

Agencies that adopt the accompaniment approach avoid direct implementation of projects; forms of support may include technical training, brigades and exchanges, and human rights advocacy, in addition to financial support. Development education and political advocacy work within the NGOs' home countries are viewed as crucial, both to support Third World struggles for autonomy and dignity, and also to promote social change within the North. This type of work attempts to break down stereotypical images of the South and identify shared interests between individuals in both South and North. While this is certainly not the dominant pattern among NGO programmes, it is a necessary model for constructing counterhegemonic global identities.

Globalizing Civil Society

CONCLUSION

Just as John Keane asserts with regard to domestic civil society, global civil society 'has no natural innocence; it has no single or eternally fixed form' (Keane, 1988b, p. 14). Global civil society interactions reproduce the conflicts and contradictions of the domestic civil societies from which they emerge and also create new ones, reflecting the dynamics of power at the international level. Despite all these ambiguities, however, the concept of global civil society is an important innovation because it opens up theoretical space for addressing the 'democratic deficit' within the current world order. As our examination of international NGOs in Central America in the 1980s illustrates, we can thus open the way for analyzing the interaction of agency and structure, avoiding the aura of inevitability that surrounds most discussions of globalization. Further analysis is needed of other forms of contestation in global civil society, including the international environmental movement, the women's movement, international trade union alliances in the post-Cold War era, and responses to NAFTA and the Enterprise for the Americas. Arguing that struggles within global civil society can play an important role in global democratization does not eliminate, however, the need for state action. In many cases the efforts of both domestic and global social actors must be directed at strengthening the abilities of nation states to resist the totalizing impact of globalization.

Notes

1. Stephen Gill's study of the Trilateral Commission (1990a) is an important exception.
2. For elements of a project of 'liberal retrievalism' see Pateman, 1988; Bowles and Gintis, 1987; Macpherson, 1973.
3. Sakamoto does recognize that the spread of liberal democracy in the West occurred simultaneously with, and indeed was facilitated by, the spread of empire. Western political development thus led to structural disparities between North and South that then stood in the way of democratic development within the latter (Sakamoto, 1991, p. 125).
4. Costa Rica was the only Central American state to have established a hegemonic regime, through its 'revolution' of 1948, at a time when US foreign policy interests were largely occupied elsewhere.
5. The interests of the United States in Central America were not completely compatible with the practices and policies of the IMF and the World Bank. For example, too stringent requirements for conformity to adjustment policies in El Salvador and Guatemala would have exacerbated the social unrest that the United States was hoping to diminish (Rivera *et al.*, 1986).
6. Total NGO assistance to Nicaragua has been estimated at $50 million per year – equivalent to about one fourth of the country's annual export earnings (Norsworthy, 1989, p. 79).

7.   According to Tom Barry, civic action programmes have three main objectives: (i) improving the public image of the military; (ii) improving rural socioeconomic conditions; and (iii) encouraging the formation of strong national institutions (nation building). These civic action programmes may involve the use of normally civilian activities such as public-relations work, humanitarian assistance and infrastructural development, but they are carried out by either US or surrogate military forces. The army often relocates entire villages to establish better control (Barry, 1986, p. 47).

Part VII

Conclusion

15 Survival in the 1990s: Rethinking the Political Economy of Foreign Policy in Africa, Asia, the Caribbean and Latin America

Timothy M. Shaw and Larry A. Swatuk

INTRODUCTION

[T]he world in the early 1990s looks different than it did a decade before, yet there are differences of opinion about which trends are worthy of note. We have chosen to focus on five trends ... as the core of the new international context of development. These include: the end of the Cold War; shifting relations among the capitalist powers; changing patterns of trade and production; declining availability of development finance; and new ideological currents.

Stallings, 1993, p. 2.

[N]o matter how important these concepts of new international division of labour and newly industrialising countries are, they do not include in their analysis of international stratification non-material aspects.... [B]oth material and non-material criteria of international stratification have to be taken into consideration in order to embrace the different facets of diversity existing within the Third World.

Korany, 1986, pp. 90–1.

Recent changes in the global political economy pose major challenges to the peoples of the South as state-makers and individuals alike seek to (re)define and secure their positions in the new international divisions of labour and power (NIDL/P). If the terms 'Third World' and/or 'South' were seen as overly simplified in the past, the end of the Cold War and the emergence of post-industrial processes of global production have now rendered these terms even more problematic. The emergence of new states, institutions, issues, political and economic relations, as well as new approaches that seek to make sense of these changes, have led many analysts to lament the passing of the 'old, bi-polar, world order' (Maynes, 1990).

Yet, as Jonathan Clarke has recently suggested, today's world is probably no more complex than that past. To be sure,

> [i]n an increasingly interdependent and multilateral world many of the problems are fantastically complicated... but the passing of the Cold War has stripped away one thick layer of complexity: superpower rivalry is no longer involved ... In one respect it is fair to concede that an additional level of complexity exists. This is in the field of analysis. *No longer do analysts have the luxury of a single lens through which they can scrutinize the world's problems* (Clarke, 1993, p. 60; emphasis added).

Clarke goes on to suggest that this perceived complexity is a good thing, for now 'problems can be approached much more on their merits ... [and] [t]o say that the diagnosis is more complex does not mean that the illness is too' (ibid.).

Similarly, we are suggesting that the end of the Cold War provides analysts with a unique opportunity to reexamine and perhaps redefine the 'South', taking into consideration not only extant, macro-level notions of 'Third', 'Fourth', and even 'Fifth' Worlds, but also the myriad regional, state, and sub- and non-state phenomena that help make this part of the world appear so bewilderingly complex today.

This chapter seeks to identify some of the many changes and challenges confronting the South as we move toward the next millennium. In this way we seek to draw some general conclusions about the forces and factors affecting the South, all of which were given more specific treatment in the theoretical and country case studies above.

Clearly, and as we have tried to demonstrate in this volume, any plausible explanation of foreign, strategic and/or development policies in the 1990s must begin by recognising and evaluating transformations in the global political economy, particularly in the South itself. This entails, in part, situating the South within the context of the following five factors:

- *New states*: from the Baltic to Central Asia in the former Soviet Union (FSU), and from former Yugoslavia to Eritrea and Somaliland, new states have mushroomed around the globe.
- *New relations*: the post-Cold War and post-industrial world has given rise to new methods and contexts of communication and production. The globalization of production has facilitated the emergence of the NICs and near-NICs as well as new notions of regionalism; similarly, the end of the Cold War has given rise to regional hegemons and numerous de facto and aspiring middle powers. At the same time, however, these processes have facilitated the swift decline of a number of the world's states and regions into 'Fourth' and 'Fifth' World categories.
- *New institutions*: the demands of economic and political security in a postbipolar world have given rise to diverse trans- and sub-national, inter- and non-governmental, regional and transcontinental organisations, all of which have, in turn, given rise to burgeoning new literatures on multilaterism, new regionalisms, and civil societies, to name but three areas of focus.
- *New issues*: varying widely from the environment, gender and informal sectors, to drugs, democracy, AIDS and migration, the proliferation of these issues and threats at the global level has led to a call for redefinitions of security, foreign policy and even political economy as constituted in the South.
- *New approaches*: this new global context has engendered a mood of revisionism in both analysis and praxis. Neither orthodox modernization nor orthodox materialism have been able to explain the causes and characters of the so-called 'developing world's' divergent political economies: from NICs to most seriously affected (MSAs); from recession-resistant to debt-distressed; and, particularly in the African context, from hitherto ubiquitous state 'socialisms' to contemporary state 'capitalisms'.

To be sure, some continuities of assumption and condition remain, yet, it seems to us, the emerging analytic response must be both postmodernization and postmaterialism, now reinforced by the series of democratic transformations and/or aspirations in Eastern Europe and the former Soviet Union (FSU). The new contexts confronting academic analysts and policymakers alike mean that established explanations and prescriptions are no longer valid. In particular, the orthodox paradigm of modernization is being seriously challenged by (i) more radical approaches that address gender (Palmer, 1991), ecology (Homer-Dixon, 1991; Williams, 1993), culture and informal sectors (Rathman, 1992), as well as constitutions, organisations, classes and formal sectors; and (ii) more pragmatic ideologies that advance agriculture, innovation and accumulation rather than industry, conformity and consumption (UNDP, 1991).

In contrast with the dominance of US political science and agendas over the course of the last three decades, and inadequate, often hopelessly idealistic Third World intellectual responses, the 'new' political economy for the South attempts to go beyond these two solitudes toward a mix of both materialist and non-materialist perspectives, combining policy with production, ideology with interest, and national with global interactions. Our discussion now turns to look at some of these issues and approaches.

FROM ORDER TO DISORDER: CHANGING STATE-CENTRIC HIERARCHIES

The postwar period, especially its 'golden age' from the mid-1950s to the early1970s, was marked by stability in the hierarchy of states. Following Western reconstruction of Germany and Japan, the incorporation of Eastern Europe into the growing Soviet empire, and the early dynamism of countries such as Brazil, India, Mexico and China, the Bretton Woods global economy experienced growth until the energy and debt 'shocks' of the early 1970s (see Chapter 4 above). It was during this period that the 'three-worlds' typology came into vogue.

The early signs of restructuring and reordering were disguised by 'triangular' OPEC–North–South liquidity in the mid-1970s. The First and Second Worlds clearly belonged to the superpowers (as represented in NATO/OECD and Warsaw Pact/COMECON axes); while the Third World began to exert pressure for new political and economic international orders through such alliances as the Non Aligned Movement and the Group of 77. However, by the early 1980s divergence within both North and South was undeniable as heavy borrowing and deficit-spending gave way to global recession, the debt crisis and radical economic restructuring. While some regions of the South benefited from the emerging new international division of labour (NIDL) – the so-called NICs and near-NICs of East and Southeast Asia – others, particularly in Africa, fell further behind (see Table 5.2 above). According to Stallings (1994, pp. 15–16),

> During the 1960s and 1970s, the East Asian economies became extremely successful. Per capita income rose from only $110 (South Korea) and $170 (Taiwan) in 1962 to $1620 and $2250 respectively in

1980. This trend continued where, in contrast with Africa's 'lost decade' of debt and structural adjustment, for East Asia the 1980s were a very successful period. ... East Asia's strong growth performance meant that it alone among third world regions continued to have abundant access to private sources of external finance.

This may be contrasted with the African case where, according to Kuhne (1991, p. 9), the continent's 'share of global foreign investment has fallen below 2% from 5.5% in 1960. Africa, unable to compete successfully on the world market, is undergoing a process of deindustrialization' (see Chapters 2 and 8 above). Hence the emergence of Third and Fourth World typologies.

Meanwhile the reorientation of Eastern Europe proceeded apace in the late 1980s, culminating in the disintegration of the FSU in the early 1990s. Newly emergent states in the FSU are now vying with other countries and regions of the South for the limited pools of Western investment capital and technology available to them (see Chapter 10 above). How they fit into current notions of the 'South' is not entirely clear. Certainly, on a per capita GDP basis or in terms of structures of production, much of the FSU seems to have a 'Third World' profile. But in strategic terms the FSU remains more central to the global political economy than most of Africa, South Asia or the Pacific (see Chapter 3 above).

'ORDERING' A NEW WORLD

To date, despite the burgeoning literature on the post-Cold War strategic system there is less debate and clarity about any post-Bretton Woods economic structures. While the United States may presently enjoy unipolar status as the sole global nuclear power, its economic 'hegemony' is clearly problematic (for example Rengger, 1993). As Boardman points out above, the United States is at once the world's leading debtor and trading nation. Its economic – particularly financial and technological – supremacy is increasingly challenged by both Germany and Japan. According to Jonathan Clarke,

> [T]he sole-remaining-superpower syndrome betrays a curiously old-fashioned mindset deriving from the 1950s.... Talk of a monopoly of power fails to take account of something Clinton himself has said: 'The currency of national strength in this new era will be denominated not only in ships and tanks and planes, but in diplomas and patents and paychecks' (Clarke, 1993, p. 62).

For Clarke, it is time the United States scaled down its aspirations:

> To accept responsibility for all the world's problems is to ignore the
> necessity for economic trade-offs. Foreign policy can no longer be for-
> mulated in a resource vacuum. In his inaugural address in 1989
> President Bush said that America had 'more will than wallet.' Four years
> and a trillion dollars of additional debt later, the time has come to align
> policy aspirations with resource realities (ibid).

Perhaps it is this triangular configuration of 'high-consumption countries',
to use Devlin's term in Chapter 4 – the United States, an enlarged EC and
Japan – that marks the new First World, and is symbolized by their novel
and controversial international peacekeeping commitments and mutual
support for democracy and capitalist economic development at a global
level (see Chapter 3 above).

A reconfigured Second World might include those elements of the FSU
that remain of particular strategic (including nuclear) importance to the
West – for example Russia and the Ukraine – and/or demonstrate a clear
commitment toward multiparty democracy and free-market economics –
for example the Czech Republic and Hungary.

Meanwhile the content of the Third World is no longer all the G-77,
which was an awkward typology at best, but rather the new, old and near-
NICs: Asian tigers and cubs, large Latin economies, China and India. The
Fourth World, then, would comprise most of those countries previously
defined as 'less developed' (LDCs): that is, the bulk of East, Southeast and
South Asian states, including the six Southern Turkic states of the FSU;
much of Latin America and the Caribbean; and a few countries in Africa,
but mostly those north of the Sahara (see, for example, Chapters 5, 8, 10,
11, 12 and 13 of this volume).

The Fifth World of the least developed countries (LLDCs) is also growing as crises and conditionalities impact and the downwardly mobile seek
the 'privilege' of access to International Development Association (IDA)
funds. As suggested in this volume, most of these countries are to be found
in Sub-Saharan Africa, that is, the 'hole in the doughnut of globalization'
(see Chapter 2 above). But it would also include some other, fairly obvious,
candidates: Bangladesh, Haiti, Pakistan, the Philippines.

Whilst the political expression and organisation of these emerging
'worlds' remains tentative, and overly statecentric, the location of international capital, communication, consumption, innovation and production, let
alone accumulation, is apparent: in China rather than Chad, Singapore
rather than Somalia. Moreover there is clearly a regional dimension to any

conceivable hierarchy, with Southeast Asia the most expansive and Africa the most vulnerable of the Southern regions (see Chapters 8, 11 and 12).

THE END OF BIPOLARITY AND THE 'PEACE DIVIDEND'

Analysts of Third World affairs have been speculating on the character of economic and strategic rumblings in the former Soviet Union and Eastern Europe and their potential effects on peace, development and security in the South. Many Third World sympathizers suspect that much of the developing world will become increasingly marginalized from the North-dominated global political economy, as events in the former Soviet Union, in Eastern Europe and in East–West relations in general continue to dominate the North's global agenda. Some scholars, however, do not fear but rather welcome such developments, arguing that heightening political–economic contradictions will finally topple unjust and largely authoritarian regimes, regimes that Ihonvbere has labelled 'booty capitalist' (see Chapter 8).

To be sure, the waning of the Cold War and the dismantling of the Iron Curtain as discrete political events of 1989–90 have had forceful effects on many regions and regimes of the South. Two of the more salient effects warrant elaboration: (i) the end of superpower competition globally; (ii) the emergence of a 'new hegemony' in the form of Western pressure for economic and political liberalization.

First, the end of the Cold War has led to the removal of an artificial, oppressive, Cold War-dictated 'stability' in many Southern societies. In the face of growing domestic pressures for multiparty democracy, authoritarian regimes now find themselves unable to turn to their 'superpatron' for support. The removal of this Cold War option, therefore, has added, in many parts of the globe, political uncertainty to increasing economic instability.

It has also facilitated the emergence of newly unrestrained 'middle powers', not all of whose regional aspirations will be taken so seriously or taken up so swiftly as Saddam's Iraq. Blight and Belkin (1993, p. 715), quoting Stanley Hoffman, explain 'why collective security, as practised in the Gulf War, is unlikely to be repeated soon or often':

> The new world order may ... remain just a slogan or, worse, a sardonic label applied to a situation far more chaotic than the world of the cold war.... If, in a world of shaky regimes, contested borders, ethnic upheavals and religious revivals, every act of aggression requires the mobilization of three-quarters of a million troops, many sent across the seas to

face well-armed troublemakers and obtain their unconditional surrender, there will be very few cases of collective security.

And, one might add, very few cases of unilateral attempts by the US to make peace around the globe. So, less Cold War-style intervention is likely to mean less order, as domestic and regional conflicts take on indigenous rather than superpower-proxy characteristics (see Chapter 6 above). The violent turn of events in Liberia and the Sudan, coupled with UN forces' ineffectuality in Somalia and world reluctance to become involved in the former Yugoslavia are all equally instructive in this regard.

Second, heightened Western pressure for similar political liberalizations as conditionality for continuing economic and political support may, in the end, prove contradictory. This points toward a return to corporatism and/or authoritarianism, perhaps even anarchy, especially in situations characterized by the absence of an entrenched middle class that derives its wealth independently of the state. As Huntington suggests (1993, p. 39):

> Democratisation occurs most frequently and also most easily in countries that have reached the upper-middle income levels of economic development. Economic liberalisation, however, is easier in countries at lower levels of economic development. Economic reform requires a strong, authoritative government. Note that I say 'authoritative', not 'authoritarian'. Economic liberalisation imposes special hardships on some groups in society: the political opposition will be strong. Opening up the political system first is likely to complicate reform.

In this way, newly democratic African states stand to lose the most. For there, unlike the Asian NICs and near-NICs, structural adjustment has caused contraction, rather than expansion, of the middle classes. The presence or absence of such a vibrant petty bourgeoisie is crucial for political stability as well as economic vitality. For example, the mounting political problems of Frederick Chiluba, whose Movement for Multiparty Democracy displaced incumbent Kenneth Kaunda in free and fair elections in 1991, are clearly tied to the continuing weakness of Zambia's copper-based economy.

Clearly the drama of events in Europe that culminated in a series of popular revolutions at the decade's end led, understandably, to a sort of 'premature triumphalism' in academic and popular analysis. Now that the initial euphoria has given way to harsh political and economic reality, present speculations tend to be much more pessimistic: more fragmenting Somalias, Yugoslavias and Georgias; as many reemerging old-style authoritarian regimes – for example Lithuania, Poland – as emergent liberal democratic ones – for example Benin, the Czech Republic, Zambia; and continuing civil wars, despite UN-brokered 'peace dividends' – for example Angola, Cambodia.

'SECURITY' AND 'FOREIGN POLICY' IN THE POST-COLD WAR SOUTH

To date, most analysis of security in the South has continued to be based largely on realist as well as statist assumptions, which emphasized great powers and Cold War on the one hand and national resources and capabilities on the other hand. Such a strategic perspective is quite uncritical and conservative, tending towards dependence: the South as target and arena for extracontinental power. It is also static and ahistoric, overlooking the inputs and impacts of a variety of non-state actors on security issues, both threats and responses: from guerrilla formations to security companies (cf. Shaw and Inegbedion, 1991).

Yet such a traditional approach in the 1980s had already begun to be revised by a few analysts at the frontiers of the school to incorporate novel factors such as economy, ecology and food; that is, security expanded to include new conceptions of non-lethal or non-violent 'high' politics. Thus, from a revisionist perspective, derived nonetheless from realist roots, conflict in the South is no longer treated as only a function of strategic issues but also of new concerns such as development, environment and nutrition. In short, basic human needs (BHN) via 'common' security (see, for example, Blight and Weiss, 1992; Chan, 1992). This reflects a global trend towards treating issues of economy and ecology as crucial, symbolised by the Brandt, Palme and Brundtland Commissions of the last decade. This in turn has led to the reconceptualization of related phenomena, such as, say, economic or environmental rather than merely strategic or political 'refugees'. So contemporary regional conflicts in the South, both on land and at sea, may have distinctive indigenous roots increasingly unrelated to extracontinental factors.

Furthermore, if the state in Fourth and Fifth if not Third Worlds is shrinking then increasingly foreign relations will also be among non-state actors: from informal financial exchanges to bourgeois professional associations. Governments may still go to war over boundaries and booty, as diversion or aggrandizement, but most crossborder interactions will be amongst companies and communities. Thus, in the late or post-adjustment period, foreign policy will be increasingly transnational, involving non-official actors in a routine manner outside the purview of the diminished state. This will pose challenges for both diplomats and students of diplomacy, leading away from realism over diplomacy and security and toward revisionism about economy and ecology.

Whether even diminished regimes can come to accept a more modest international posture in which such non-state relations are facilitated or even encouraged remains to be seen. But the decade of the 1990s, characterized by a proliferation of regional economic communities and civil societies as well as military–industrial complexes and middle powers, at least offers an occasion for reconsideration and reevaluation (see, for example, Edwards and Hulme, 1992; Korten, 1987; Moore, 1993; and Nyang'oro and Shaw, 1992). As such, Southern foreign policies may come to be both revisionist and realist before the end of the century, with promising possibilities in terms of revived and sustainable development: onto new forms of integration and industrialization for the next century appropriate for diminished states and expanded markets and civil societies?

Thus, the world of foreign policy and security studies in the 1990s has to begin to treat the twin phenomena of the erosion and proliferation of states as correlates of the NIDL and NIDP, respectively: erosion, especially in the North, and proliferation, particularly in the South. These trends are encouraged by powerful forces in the contemporary world political economy, notably economic and ecological globalization, and political and social liberalization. But the uneven incidence and impacts of these serve to advance transnational interdependence in the North and revived ethnic disputes in the South. Yet there are elements of transnationalism in the South – expansion of largely uncontrollable computer and satellite networks – and of ethnicity in the North – civil strife in Canada, Ireland and Spain, let alone Yugoslavia. Both trends point towards a possible global reordering: more micro 'nation' states but located within macro regional and global economic communities. The preceding chapters by Gharabaghi and McBain (Chapters 10 and 12) are particularly instructive in this regard.

Finally, a radical reformulation founded on a neomaterialist base would also recast security as 'state' or 'regime' or 'presidential' rather than 'national' security. And threats would likewise be reconceived as internal – from excluded or impoverished classes – as well as external – from corporate or collective interests challenged by a particular fraction in power. Similarly, such a neomaterialist approach would treat foreign policy as but the external expression of the interests of the ruling class or fraction whereas a more orthodox perspective assumes that such policy is on behalf of the community, even if it is about new issues such as debt and the environment (Swatuk, 1993).

Certainly the current conjuncture makes returning to and redefining comparative foreign policy as well as political economy and security policy in the South ever more imperative (Korany *et al.*, 1992). As indicated in the preceding chapters, this venture would have to take the variety of capitalisms as well as regionalisms and civil societies into account if they are to offer plausible explanations and directions into the next century (see Shaw and Okolo, 1994; Wurfel and Burton, 1991). We turn, in conclusion, to the major dialectic determining the nature of foreign and security policies in the South at the start of the twenty-first century.

DEMOCRATIC DEVELOPMENT, CORPORATIST COALITIONS AND REGIME MAINTENANCE

We conclude with a particular dichotomy – that between the now-fashionable democratic development and the new threat of corporatism or other forms of authoritarianism – which is all too easily overlooked by the prevailing, optimistic, adjustment paradigm, especially its governance correlates.

The South at the start of the 1990s confronts a contradictory set of options or conditions: liberalization and/or contraction in both economics and politics (see, especially, Chapter 4 above). Given its wide range of political economies and political cultures, some portions of the South may move in several of these directions at once. The primary tension that is emerging, particularly in Fourth and Fifth if not Third World states, is between economic contraction and political liberalization. This is a combination that is rather ominous for incumbent regimes that might prefer the alternative mix of economic expansion and political contraction; indeed that was the underlying basis of the post-colonial state-socialist model in most of the non-NICs.

The contrary condition of economic contraction, particularly in Africa and much of Latin America and the Caribbean, is quite familiar by now, induced by a mix of external, ecological and internal realities and policies (see the regional cases above). But the anticipated political correlates to economic liberalization – that is, democratization and popular participation – are proving more elusive and much more problematic. Incumbent regimes remain inclined toward domination in spite of internal and external pressures to democratize.

Nevertheless the emergence of democracy along with debt as a hegemonic ideological concept globally has encouraged not only formal constitutional changes, national conventions and multiparty elections. It has also facilitated the expansion of global NGO networks and the popularization of the notion of 'civil society' clustered around a set of current issues, from environmentalism and feminism to fundamentalism, both Christian and Muslim. Such energetic non-state actors now challenge regime authority, demanding accountability and transparency. But simple multiparty governance conditionalities may not be enough to sustain democracy in much of the South. The usurpation of the democratic process by well-entrenched elites, classes, fractions and even families throughout the South suggests that the term democratization will continue to ring hollow for most people seeking people-centred development (UN-ECA, 1989; African Leadership Forum, 1991). Indeed, a recent *Africa Confidential* report ('Africa: Democracy is not enough', 1992) suggests that where democratization means the emergence of truly people-centred movements – for example Mali, Ethiopia, Zambia, RSA – these may be the exceptions that prove the rule: 'It has become clear, for example, that in many countries the creation of new parties has not directly involved many citizens from outside the existing political elite, and particularly not in the rural areas'. And while *Africa Confidential's* correspondent labels this the 'Senegalese model of democratic politics', it is in no way unique to the African continent.

Thus continuous involvement of local and global civil society is imperative. International concern with human rights as well as human needs, women and development, and sustainable development, has expanded since the US presidency of Jimmy Carter. It has also developed away from notions of formal democracy towards those of democratic development or popular participation (cf. Clark 1991; Healey and Robinson, 1992; and Hyden and Bratton, 1992).

In contrast, given the state–society dialectic, many regimes' natural inclination is to look for arrangements that ensure their longevity. Notwithstanding its undermining of the middle class in Fourth and Fifth Worlds, the adjustment project is permissive, even supportive, of the rise of a national bourgeoisie – a crucial yet tenuous element in any process of sustainable democracy – alongside more bureaucratic, comprador, military, political and technocratic fractions. Therefore incumbent leaders have sought, in a period of declining, if not shrinking, resources, to replace the corruptive tendencies of cooptation with those of corporatism. They can no longer afford the expansive (and expensive) gestures of patronage; instead they have begun to rely on the less predictable but also less expensive arrangements of corporatism.

The latter consists merely of a set of structured social relations that both include and exclude central groups in the political economy. Normally it revolves around some understanding among state and economy, particularly labour and both national and international capitals; but it may also include connections with other major social institutions in the political culture: for example religious groups and universities, media and interest groups, professional associations and NGOs, women's and youth groups; that is, the leading elements in so-called civil society (Nyang'oro and Shaw, 1989).

The corporatist approach and formula, despite its distinctive roots, would seem to have resonance in the contemporary political economy of NICs and near-NICs in Southeast Asia as well as in some post-socialist states in Africa and Asia. Indeed the intrusion of Asian capitalisms as well as Asian praetorianism would seem to offer a distinctive opportunity to develop relevant new subcategories of corporatism appropriate to the Pacific Rim in the mid-1990s. Likewise, in the new South Africa, where inherited corporate concentration and high unemployment encourages national and sectoral forums, groups and summits, macro- and/or mesolevel corporatism is emerging. According to Maree (1993, p. 24) (cf. Baskin, 1993, p. 2):

> There is a remarkably strong corporatist current flowing in South Africa. The major actors – labour, capital and the state – are so caught up in it that they are hardly aware of the fact that they have become part of the current.

Surprisingly, then, corporatism as perspective or practice has received minimal attention in the South to date, except in Catholic Latin America. There has been some recognition that it helps to explain settler and post-settler states in, for example, South Africa or Zimbabwe. But in general a concern for trilateral or triangular relations among state, capital and labour has not been apparent, despite parallel, even compatible, notions of authoritarianism or exclusion, Bonapartism and commandism (Hutchful, 1988). Nyang'oro and Shaw (1989) have attempted to rectify this oversight by encouraging comparative analysis of a variety of corporatisms in contemporary Africa. Moreover it would seem that, in the African and Latin American contexts at least, the continual remaking of social relations under structural adjustment facilitates such analytic direction.

Indeed corporatism at the level of the state may not be incompatible with limited political pluralism at the level of society or market forces at the level of the economy – formal and informal forms of political economy – particularly in a period of adjustment. More formal, national-level arrangements amongst state, capital and labour may be compatible, then, with more informal, subnational activities of cooperatives, ethnic communities, interest groups, religions, NGOs and so on. In other words they mark somewhat compatible forms of post-adjustment self-reliance.

However the continuation of such a division of labour would require maturity on both sides – the state does not need to monopolize all social relations and, conversely, social groups do not automatically threaten the state. Thus far few leaders in the South have been prepared to countenance such real devolution and decentralization of authority and activity. So state–society relations are likely, in general, to be undermined by regime insecurity or social irrepressibility. Hence the ongoing and unstable state–society stand-off, which is likely to extend into the next century, when social restructuring will be even more apparent than today (cf. Rothchild and Chazan, 1988). In short, despite claims of democratic triumphalism there can be no simple, unilineal advance in the South to either democracy or development given its heterogeneity and inequalities (Sandbrook, 1993; Shaw, 1993b); a fact clearly supported by the case studies, particularly those in Chapters 11 and 12 above.

The corporatism–democratization dialectic constitutes a partial recognition of the fact that the combination of economic contraction and political challenge has not always led to a benign state. Indeed, in a rather contrary manner, the weakened state has come to rely on *coercion* rather than *cooptation* as resources for the latter contract; witness the extreme distortions in Myanmar and Somalia, for example. So, despite many tendencies toward political as well as economic liberalization, some regimes in the South have maintained, even expanded, their repressive capabilities in the 1980s and since (UNDP, 1991, pp. 81–3). To be sure, there is a wide spectrum of behaviour in the South, reflective of our Third, Fourth and Fifth World distinctions, which also vary among presidencies and time periods. But in general the tendency toward intolerance remains substantial, exacerbating debt as well as repression because of the high foreign exchange content of security expenditures other than labour (Klare, 1991).

The expansion of informal, popular participation, in addition to the spread of formal democracy outside the minority of states such as Botswana, the Commonwealth Caribbean, India and Mauritius, may limit the scope of official repression. But regular and continuing reports on the confinement of academics, activists, analysts, ministers, students and trade unionists by Africa/Asia/Americas Watch, Amnesty International and Index on Censorship are indicative of state preoccupations with and self-definitions of security.

Regimes have been particularly sensitive to any criticism of their adjustment programmes, conditionalities and performances, despite the linkage made by the IFIs and bilateral donors between economic and political liberalization, and now demilitarisation. Until the rule of law – especially freedom to organize and articulate, and fearlessness of arbitrary arrest or assassination – and regular elections prevail, as a minimum, the South will be neither democratic nor developed. And its capitalism as well as pluralism will be less productive and sustainable.

So, if the manifold claims of reinvigorated civil society cannot be satisfied by diminished states and economies, then a return to corporatist arrangements may be inevitable. The familiar cycle of one-party/military rule may thus be replaced by a multiparty/corporatist sequence, reflective of interrelated changes in national and global political economies. The presence and place of corporatism in the South as well as North – from Third (Singapore) and Fourth (Indonesia and Zimbabwe) to Fifth (Malawi) Worlds – remains an overlooked phenomenon that may yet become more familiar as regimes seek to manage often incompatible political (for example democratization) and economic (deindustrialization) reforms. In short, corporatisms may constitute a useful framework within which to manage tensions arising from uneven, sometimes incompatible, rates of economic and political change.

The apparent trend toward official, national multipartyism should not be exaggerated, then. As the studies in this volume demonstrate, economic liberalization has profound political and social implications, well beyond the purview of the World Bank and the IMF (Campbell and Loxley, 1989; Mosley, Harrigan and Toye, 1991; Nelson, 1989, 1990). Unless ecological, gender and informal sector elements are recognized and prioritized in any foreseeable democratic formulation, then sustainable development will remain elusive because the paradigm of adjustment will otherwise remain hegemonic, as it did throughout the 1980s – a decade regarded as 'lost' for the vast majority of peoples in the South (Shaw 1992, 1993a). Hence the imperative of truly popular and radical intellectual and political struggles and alternatives concentrated in burgeoning civil society that democratic pressures facilitate and require, but which authoritarian and corporatist regime machinations remain ready to repress: the ongoing dialectics of adjustment and change into the next century.

Bibliography

Part I   Introduction

Shaw, Timothy M. and Bahgat Korany (eds) (1994) 'Special Issue: The South in the "New World (Dis) Order"', *Third World Quarterly*, vol. 15, no. 1 (winter), pp. 1–144.
Shaw, Timothy M. and Julius Emeka Okolo (eds) (1994) *The Political Economy of Foreign Policy in ECOWAS* (London: Macmillan).
Swatuk, Larry A. and Timothy M. Shaw (eds) (1991) *Prospects for Peace and Development in Southern Africa in the 1990s: Canadian and Comparative Perspectives* (Lanham: University Press of America).

Part II   Changing Structures

'Address by President Carter to People of Other Nations' (1977) *Department of State Bulletin*, 14 February 1977, vol. 76, 123, quoted in Richard Falk, 1983, pp. 37–8.
Alves, Maria Helena Moreira (1988) 'Democratization versus Social Equality in Latin America: Notes for Discussion', paper presented to the conference on Comparative Politics: Research Perspectives for the Next 20 Years, City University of New York Graduate School, September.
Andreev, Yuri (1989) 'A New Foreign Economic Policy for the 1990s', in Gary Bertsch and Christopher T. Saunders (eds), *East–West Economic Relations in the 1990s* (Vienna: Vienna Institute for Comparative Economic Relations), pp. 223–30.
Anglade, Christian and Carlos Fortin (1987) 'The Role of the State in Latin America's Strategic Options', *CEPAL Review*, vol. 31, pp. 211–34.
Arrighi, Giovanni and Jessica Drangel (1986) 'The Stratification of the World-Economy: An Exploration of the Semiperipheral Zone', *Review*, vol. 10, no.1 (summer), pp. 9–74.
Ayoob, M. (1991) 'The Security Problematic of the Third World', *World Politics*, vol. 43, no. 2, pp. 257–84.
Banks, J.A. (1989) 'An Effective Demand Conception of History', *The British Journal of Sociology*, vol. 40, no. 2 (June), pp. 294–309.
Bell, Roger (1991), 'The Debate over American Empire in the Late Twentieth Century', *Australian Journal of International Affairs*, vol. 45, no. 1, pp. 78–88.
Berry, J.L. (1991) *Long-Wave Rhythms in Economic Development and Political Behavior*, (Baltimore: Johns Hopkins University Press).
Bienefeld, Manfred (1989) 'The Lessons of History and the Developing World', *Monthly Review*, vol. 41, no. 3 (July–August).
Blum, William (1986) *The CIA: A Forgotten History. U.S. Global Interventions Since World War 2* (London: Zed Press).

244

Boardman, Robert (1989) 'Ecological Security, the Oceans, and Common Security', paper presented to the XVII Pacem in Maribus Conference, Moscow, June.

Boardman, Robert (1993) 'The Middle East in the New International Order: Gorbachev, the Russian Federation, and the Rediscovery of the United Nations', in Paul Marantz and David Goldberg (eds), *The Decline of the Soviet Union and the Transformation of the Middle East* (Boulder, CO: Westview).

Boardman, Robert (1994) *Post-Socialist World Orders: Russia, China and the UN System* (London: Macmillan).

Bobrow, Davis, and Robert T. Kudrle (1991) 'Mid-level Power Strategies for Changing International Niches: Experience in the "Old World Order"', *Journal of East Asian Affairs*, vol. 5, no. 2. pp. 237–70.

Bonilla, Frank and Ricardo Campos (1985) 'Evolving Patterns of Puerto Rican Migration', in Steven E. Sanderson (ed.), pp. 107–205.

Bowles, Samuel and Herbert Gintis (1986) *Democracy and Capitalism. Property, Community, and the Contradictions of Modern Social Thought* (New York: Basic Books).

Brett, E.A. (1985) *The World Economy Since the War. The Politics of Uneven Development* (New York: Praeger).

Browder, John O. and Jose Antonio Borello (1987) 'The State and the Crisis of Planning in Latin America', *Journal of Planning Literature*, vol. 6, no. 4 (May), pp. 369–377.

Burris, Val (1984) 'The Politics of Marxist Crisis Theory', *Research in Political Economy*, vol. 7, pp. 237–67.

Calleo, David (1987) *Beyond American Hegemony: The Future of the Western Alliance* (New York: Basic Books).

Campanella, Miriam L. (1993) 'The Effects of Globalization and Turbulence on Policy-Making Processes', *Government and Opposition*, vol. 28, no. 2, pp. 190–205.

Campbell, Kurt C. and Thomas G. Weiss (1991) 'The Third World in the Wake of Eastern Europe', *Washington Quarterly*, vol. 14, no. 23, pp. 67–78.

Cerny, Philip G. (1993) 'Plurilateralism: Structural Differentiation and Functional Conflict in the Post-Cold War World Order', *Millennium*, vol. 22, no. 1, pp. 27–51.

Chenery, Hollis B. and others (1974) *Redistribution with Growth* (New York: Oxford University Press).

Chernoff, Fred (1991) 'Ending the Cold War: The Soviet Retreat and the U.S. Military Build-up', *International Affairs*, vol. 67, no. 1, pp. 111–21.

Clark, Ian (1989) *The Hierarchy of States: Reform and Resistance in the International Order* (Cambridge University Press).

Cole, Wayne S. (1993) 'United States Isolationism in the 1990s?', *International Journal*, vol. 48, no.1, pp. 32–51.

Cox, Robert W. (1987) *Production, Power and World Order: Social Forces in the Making of History* (Columbia University Press).

Cox, Robert W. (1989) 'Middlepowermanship, Japan, and Future World Order', *International Journal*, vol. 44, no. 4 (autumn).

Craig, Gordon A. and Alexander L. George (1983) *Force and Statecraft: Diplomatic Problems of Our Time* (New York: Oxford University Press).

de Janvrey, A. and E. Sadolet (1983) 'Social Articulation as a Condition of Equitable Growth', *Journal of Development Economics*, vol. 13, pp. 275–303.

Ekins, Paul (1992) *A New World Order: Grassroots Movements for Global Change*, (London: Routledge).

Evans, Peter, Dietrich Rueschemeyer and Theda Skocpol (eds) (1985) *Bringing the State Back In* (Cambridge University Press).

Falk, Richard K. (1983) *The End of World Order: Essays on Normative International Relations* (New York: Holmes and Meier).

Fröbel, Folker, Jürgen Heinrichs and Otto Kreye (eds) (1980) *The New International Division of Labour: Structural Unemployment in Industrialised Countries and Industrialisation in Developing Countries,* trans. by Pete Burgess (Cambridge University Press).

George, Aurelia (1991) 'Japan's America Problem: The Japanese Response to U.S. Pressure', *Washington Quarterly,* vol. 24, no. 3, pp. 5–22.

Gereffi, Gary and Donald L. Wyman (1990) 'Paths of Industrialization: An Overview', in Gary Gereffi and Donald L. Wyman (eds), *Manufacturing Miracles: Paths of Industrialization in Latin America and East Asia* (Princeton University Press).

Goldberg, Andrew C. (1991) 'Challenges to the Post-Cold War Balance of Power', *Washington Quarterly,* vol. 14, no. 1, pp. 51–60.

Goldstein, Joshua S. and John R. Freeman (1990) *Three-Way Street: Strategic Reciprocity in World Politics* (University of Chicago Press).

Gorbachev, M.S. (1987) 'Political Report of CPSU Central Committee to 27th Congress, February 25, 1986', in *The USSR and International Economic Relations* (Moscow: Progress).

Griffin, Keith and Azizur Rahaman Khan (1992) *Globalization and the Developing World: An Essay on the International Dimensions of Development in the Post Cold War Era* (Geneva: United Nations Research Institute for Social Development).

Halliday, Fred (1990) 'The Crisis of the Arab World: The False Answers of Saddam Hussein', *New Left Review,* vol. 184 (November/ December), pp. 69–74.

Halliday, Fred (1991) 'The Gulf War and its Aftermath: First Reflections', *International Affairs,* vol. 67, no. 2, pp. 223–34.

Herz, John (1950) 'Idealist Internationalism and the Security Dilemma', *World Politics,* vol. 2.

Hirata, Akira and Takashi Nohara (1989) 'Changing Patterns of International Division of Labour in Asia and Pacific', in Miyohei Shinohara and Fu-chen Lo (eds), *Global Adjustment and the Future of Asian-Pacific Economy* (Tokyo: Institute of Developing Economies), pp. 434–462.

Holsti, Kal J. (1985) 'The Necrologists of International Relations', *Canadian Journal of Political Science,* vol. 18, no. 4.

Hopkins, Terence K., Immanuel Wallerstein and associates (1982) 'Cyclical Rhythms and Secular Trends of the Capitalist World Economy', in idem, *World Systems Analysis. Theory and Methodology* (Beverly Hills: Sage).

Hough, Jerry F. (1988) *Opening Up the Soviet Economy* (Washington, DC: Brookings Institution).

Hughes, Thomas L. (1990) 'Pro Patria Per Orbis Concordiam', remarks at the Carnegie Endowment for International Peace Trustees' Dinner, Washington, 18 November.

Jacobson, H. K. and M. Oksenberg (1990) *China's Participation in the IMF, the World Bank, and GATT: Toward a Global Economic Order* (Ann Arbor: University of Michigan Press).

Keal, Paul (1983) *Unspoken Rules and Superpower Dominance* (New York: St. Martin's Press).

Kenway, P. (1980) 'Marx, Keynes and the Possibility of Crisis', *Cambridge Journal of Economics*, vol. 4, no. 1 (March), pp. 23–36.

Kleinberg, Robert (1990) *China's "Opening" to the Outside World: The Experiment with Foreign Capitalism* (Boulder, CO: Westview).

Kotz, David M. (1987) 'Long Waves and Social Structures of Accumulation: A Critique and Reinterpretation', *Review of Radical Political Economics*, vol. 19, no. 4, pp. 16–38.

Kotz, David M. (1990) 'A Comparative Analysis of the Theory of Regulation and the Social Structure of Accumulation Theory', *Science and Society*, vol. 54, no. 1 (spring), pp. 5–28.

Larson, David L. (1985) 'Security Issues and the Law of the Sea: A General Framework', *Ocean Development and International Law*, vol. 15, pp. 99–146.

Layne, Christopher (1991) 'America's Stake in Soviet Stability', *World Policy Journal*, vol. 8, no. 1, pp. 61–88.

Legault, Albert (1970) 'Le triangle URSS-Chine-EU et les perspectives d'une guerre Sino-Sovietique', *Etudes internationales*, vol. 1, no. 1, pp. 53–60.

Lembcke, Jerry (1991–2) 'Why 50 Years? Working-Class Formation and Long Economic Cycles', *Science and Society*, vol. 55, no. 4 (winter), pp. 417–45.

Lipietz, Alan (1987a) 'The Globalization of the General Crisis of Fordism', in John Holmes and Colin Leys (eds), *Frontyard Backyard. The Americas in the Global Crisis* (Toronto: Between the Lines).

Lipietz, Alan (1987b) *Mirages and Miracles. The Crisis of Global Fordism* (London: Verso).

Lukin, V.P. and A.A. Nagorny (1988) 'Kontseptsiia "treulgolnika" SSSR-SSHA-KNR i novye realnosti mirovoi politiki', *SSHA. Ekonomika, Politika, Ideologiia*, vol. 6, no. 222, pp. 3–13.

Ma, Zongshi (1991) 'China's Role in the Emerging Multipolar Asia–Pacific Scene', *Contemporary International Relations*, vol. 7.

MacFarquhar, Roderick (1989) 'The End of the Chinese Revolution', *New York Review of Books,* vol. 36, no. 12, pp. 8–10.

Macpherson, C.B. (1977) *The Life and Times of Liberal Democracy* (Oxford University Press).

Malthus, Thomas (1936) *Principles of Political Economy*, 2nd edn (London: William Pickering).

Martin, Dorothea A. (1990) *The Making of a Sino–Marxist World View: Perception and Interpretation of World History in the People's Republic of China* (Armonk: M.E. Sharpe).

Matthews, Jessica Tuchman (1989) 'Redefining Security', *Foreign Affairs*, pp. 62–77.

Mead, Walter R. (1991) 'The Bush Administration and the New World Order', *World Policy Journal*, vol. 8, no. 3, pp. 375–420.

Meeks, Philip J. (1993) 'Japan and Global Economic Hegemony', in Tsuneo Akaha and Frank Langdon (eds), *Japan in the Posthegemonic World* (Boulder, CO: Lynne Rienner), pp. 41–68.

Miller, Benjamin (1992) 'A "New World Order": From Balancing to Hegemony, Concert or Collective Security?', *International Interactions*, vol. 18, no. 1, pp. 1–33.

Miller, S.M. (1988) 'The Underconsumptionist Bias of Progressive Economics', *Social Policy* (summer), pp. 44–7.

Mittelman, James H. (1990) 'The Dilemmas of Reform in Post-Revolutionary Societies', *International Studies Notes*, vol. 15, no. 2, pp. 65–70.

Nel, Philip (1990) *The Changing Context of Soviet Policy towards Southern Africa* (Koln: Berichte des Bundesinstituts fur Ostwissenschaftliche und Internationale Studien), no. 16.

Nixon, Emerson M.S., Peter C. Ordeshook and Gregory F. Rose (1989) *The Balance of Power: Stability in International Systems* (Cambridge University Press).

Nye, Joseph S., Jr (1984) *The Making of America's Soviet Policy* (New Haven: Yale University Press).

Nzomo, Maria (1993) 'The Gender Dimension of Democratization in Kenya: Some International Linkages', *Alternatives*, vol. 18, no. 1, pp. 61–74.

Olsen, Gorm Rye (1991) 'Domestic and International Causes of Instability in the Horn of Africa, with Special Emphasis on Ethiopia', *Cooperation and Conflict: Nordic Journal of International Studies*, vol. 26, no. 1, pp. 21–32.

Organisation for Economic Cooperation and Development (OECD) (1989) *Programme of Research 1990–1992* (Paris: OECD).

Payer, Cheryl (1991) *Lent and Lost. Foreign Credit and Third World Development* (London: Zed Books).

Peet, Richard (1987) 'Industrial Devolution, Underconsumption and the Third World Debt Crisis', *World Development*, vol. 15, no. 6, pp. 777–88.

Pfaff, William (1991) 'Redefining World Power', *Foreign Affairs*, vol. 70, p. 1.

Rajmaira, S. and Michael D. Ward (1990) 'Evolving Foreign Policy Norms: Reciprocity in the Super-Power Triad', *International Studies Quarterly*, vol. 34, no. 4, pp. 457–76.

Rogers, Edward (1981) 'The Ethics of Security', in Nicholas A. Sims (ed.), *Explorations in Ethics and International Relations* (London: Croom Helm).

Ruggie, John G. (1982) 'International Regimes, Transactions, and Change: Embedded Liberalism in the Post-War Order', *International Organization*, vol. 36, no. 2, (spring), pp. 379–415.

Safire, William (1991) 'The New New World Order', *New York Times Magazine*, 17 February.

Sanderson, Steven E. (ed.) (1985) *The Americas in the New International Division of Labour* (New York: Holmes and Meier).

Shambaugh, David (1991) *Beautiful Imperialist: China Perceives America, 1972–1990* (Princeton University Press).

Shivji, Issa G. (1991) 'The Democracy Debate in Africa: Tanzania', *Review of African Political Economy*, vol. 50 (March), pp. 79–91.

SIPRI (1985) *Policies for Common Security* (London: Taylor and Francis).

Smith, W. (1991) 'Principles of U.S. Grand Strategy: Past and Future', *Washington Quarterly*, vol. 14, no. 2, pp. 67–78.

Spence, J. E. (1993) 'A Post-Apartheid South Africa and the International Community', *Journal of Commonwealth and Comparative Politics*, vol. 31, pp. 84–95.

Sunkel, Osvaldo and Gustavo Zuleta (1990) 'Neo-structuralism versus Neo-liberalism in the 1990s', *CEPAL Review*, vol. 42 (December), pp. 35–51.

Taira, Koji (1993) 'Japan as Number Two: New Thoughts on the Hegemonic Theory of World Governance', in Tsuneo Akaha and Frank Langdon (eds), *Japan in the Posthegemonic World*, (Boulder, CO: Lynne Rienner), pp. 251–64.

Tatu, Michel (1989) 'Le nouveau jeu triangulaire', *Politique internationale,* vol. 3, pp. 23–32.

'The "New Order" is a Tall Order' (1991), *New York Times,* 17 March.

Thomas, Caroline (1987) *In Search of Security: The Third World in International Relations* (Boulder, CO: Lynne Rienner).

Urquhart, Brian and Robert S. McNamara (1991) *Toward Collective Security: Two Views,* Brown University Occasional Paper no. 5, Thomas J. Watson Jr. Institute for International Studies, Brown University, Providence.

van Wolferen, Karel (1990) 'The Japan Problem Revisited', *Foreign Affairs,* vol. 69, no. 4, pp. 42–55.

Wallerstein, Immanuel (1993) 'The World-System after the Cold War', *Journal of Peace Research,* vol. 30, no. 1, pp. 1–6.

Weisskopf, Thomas E., Samuel Bowles and David M. Gordon (1985) 'Two Views of Capitalist Stagnation: Underconsumption and Challenges to Capitalist Control', *Science and Society,* vol. 49, no. 3 (fall), pp. 259–86.

Weston, Burns H. (1991) 'Security Council Resolution 678 and Persian Gulf Decision-Making: Precarious Legitimacy', *American Journal of International Law,* vol. 85, pp. 516–36.

Wilkinson, Frank (1988) 'Where do we go from here? Real Wages, Effective Demand and Economic Development', *Cambridge Journal of Economics,* vol. 12, pp. 179–91.

World Bank (1989) *World Development Report 1989* (New York: Oxford University Press).

World Bank (1990) *World Development Report 1990* (New York: Oxford University Press).

Part III   Present Trends and General Responses

Acharya, Amitav (1989) 'The Gulf Cooperation Council and Security: Dilemmas of Dependence: 1980–88', *Contemporary Strategic Issues in the Arab Gulf,* no. 2 (London: Gulf Centre for Strategic Studies).

Acharya, Amitav (1992) 'Regionalism and Regime Security in the Third World: A Comparative Study of the Emergence of the Association of Southeast Asian Nations and the Gulf Cooperation Council', in Brian L. Job (ed.), *The Insecurity Dilemma: The National Security of Third World States* (Boulder, CO: Lynne Rienner), pp. 143–164.

Aufderheide, Pat and Bruce Rich (1988) 'Environmental Reform and the Multilateral Banks', *World Policy Journal* (spring).

Axline, Andrew (1977) 'Underdevelopment, Dependence, and Integration: The Politics of Regionalism in the Third World', *International Organization,* vol. 31 (winter).

Banks, Michael (1969) 'System Analysis and the Study of Regions', *International Studies Quarterly,* vol. 13 (December).

Bayart, Jean-Francois (1993) *The State in Africa: The Politics of the Belly* (London and New York: Longman).

Beckmann, David (1991) 'Recent Experience and Emerging Trends', in Samuel Paul and Arturo Israel (eds), *Non-Governmental Organizations and the World Bank: Cooperation for Development* (Washington, DC: World Bank), pp. 134–54.

Bolling, Landrum R. with Craig Smith (1982) *Private Foreign Aid: U.S. Philanthropy for Relief and Development* (Boulder, CO: Westview Press).

Bratton, Michael (1989) 'The Politics of Government–NGO Relations in Africa', *World Development,* vol. 17, no. 4, pp. 569–87.

Brown, L. David and David C. Korten (1989) *Understanding Voluntary Organizations: Guidelines for Donors,* Policy, Planning, and Research Working Paper (Washington, DC: World Bank's Public Sector Management and Private Sector Development Division, Country Economics Department), September.

Bull, Hedley (1977) *The Anarchical Society* (London: Macmillan).

Buzan, Barry (1983) *People, States and Fear: The National Security Problem in International Relations* (Brighton: Wheatsheaf Books).

Cernea, Michael M. (1988) *Non-Governmental Organizations and Local Development,* World Bank discussion paper no. 40 (Washington, DC: World Bank).

Clark, John (1990) *Democratizing Development: The Role of Voluntary Organizations* (West Hartford, CT: Kumarian Press).

Cornia, Giovanni Andrea, Richard Jolly and Frances Stewart (eds) (1987) *Adjustment with a Human Face* (New York: Oxford University Press).

Davenport, Michael and Sheila Page (1991) 'Europe: 1992 and the Developing World', *ODI Development Policy Studies* (London: Overseas Development Institute), April.

de Silva, Leelananda (1984) *Development Aid: A Guide to Facts and Figures* (Geneva: Third World Forum in Cooperation with the United Nations Non-Governmental Liaison Service).

Deutsch, Karl *et al.* (1957) *Political Community in the North Atlantic Area* (Princeton: Princeton University Press).

Dewitt, David B. (1987) 'Confidence- and Security-Building Measures in the Third World: Is There a Role?', *International Journal,* vol. 52 (summer), pp. 509–35.

Duffy, Charles A. and Werner J. Feld (1980) 'Whither Regional Integration Theory', in Gavin Boyd and Werner Feld (eds), *Comparative Regional Systems* (New York: Pergamon Press).

Findley, Trevor (1989) 'Confidence-Building Measures for the Asia-Pacific: The Relevance of the European Experience', in Muthiah Alagappa (ed.), *Building Confidence, Resolving Conflicts* (Kuala Lumpur: Institute of International and Strategic Studies), pp. 550–74.

Fowler, Alan (1991) 'The Role of NGOs in Changing State-Society Relations: Perspectives from Eastern and Southern Africa', *Development Policy Review,* vol. 9, pp. 53–84.

Frimpong-Ansah, Jonathan H. (1991) *The Vampire State in Africa: The Political Economy of Decline in Ghana* (London: James Currey).

Gordon, Lincoln (1961) 'Economic Regionalism Reconsidered', *World Politics,* vol. 13.

Gorman, Robert F. (1984) 'PVOs and Development through Basic Human Needs', in Robert F. Gorman (ed.), *Private Voluntary Organizations as Agents of Development* (Boulder, CO: Westview Press), pp. 41–74.

Gross Stein, Janice (1985) 'Detection and Defection: Security Regimes and the Management of International Conflict', *International Journal,* vol. 40 (autumn), pp. 599–627.

Guazanne, Laura (1988) 'The Gulf Cooperation Council: Security Policies', *Survival,* vol. 30 (March/April), pp. 134–48.

Haas, Ernst (1964) *Beyond the Nation-State* (Stanford University Press).

Haas, Ernst (1986) *Why We Still Need the United Nations* (Berkeley, CA: Institute of International Studies, University of California).

Hinsley, F.H. (1963) *Power and the Pursuit of Peace* (Cambridge University Press).

Imobighe, T.A. (1980) ''An African High Command; the Search for a Feasible Strategy for Continental Defence', *African Affairs,* vol. 79 (April), pp. 241–54.

Inegbedion, E. John (1991) 'Nigerian Foreign Policy and Collective Security in ECOWAS: Peacemaking Intervention in Liberia', paper presented at the 34th annual meeting of the African Studies Association, St. Louis, Missouri, November.

Inegbedion, E. John (1992a) 'Nigeria in Post-Cold War Africa: Continental Leadership or Meddling in Liberia?', paper presented at the 33rd annual meeting of the International Studies Association, Atlanta, Georgia, April.

Inegbedion, E. John (1992b) 'ECOWAS and Intervention in Liberia: Humanitarianism vs. Sovereignty?', *Dalhousie African Studies Seminar Series* (Halifax: Center for African Studies, Dalhousie University), March.

Jervis, Robert (1982) 'Security Regimes', *International Organization,* vol. 36 (spring), pp. 357–78.

Jolly, Richard (1988) 'Poverty and Adjustment in the 1990s', in John P. Lewis, *Strengthening the Poor: What Have We Learned?* (New Brunswick: Transaction Books), pp. 163–75.

Klare, Michael T. (1991) 'Deadly Convergence: The Arms Trade, Nuclear/ Chemical/Missile Proliferation, and Regional Conflict in the 1990s', in Michael T. Klare and Daniel C. Thomas (eds), *World Security: Trends and Challenge at Century's End* (New York: St. Martin's Press), pp. 170–96.

Korten, David C. (1990) *Getting to the 21st Century: Voluntary Action and the Global Agenda* (West Hartford, CT: Kumarian Press).

Korten, David C. (1991) 'The Role of Non-Governmental Organizations in Development: Changing Patterns and Perspectives', in Samuel Paul and Arturo Israel (eds), *Non-Governmental Organizations and the World Bank: Cooperation for Development* (Washington, DC: World Bank), pp. 20–43.

Lewis, Gary P. (1986) 'Prospects for a Regional Security System in the Eastern Caribbean', *International Journal,* vol. 15 (Spring), pp. 167–84.

Liska, George (1968) *Alliances and the Third World* (Baltimore: Johns Hopkins University Press).

Low, Linda (1991) 'The East Asian Economic Grouping', *Pacific Review,* vol. 4, no. 4, pp. 375–82.

MacDonald, Robert (1965) *The League of Arab States* (Princeton University Press).

Mazzeo, Domenico (1984) 'Conclusion: Problems and Prospects of Intra-African Cooperation', in Mazzeo (ed.), *African Regional Organizations* (Cambridge University Press).

McQueen, Matthew (1990) 'ACP Export Diversification: The Case of Mauritius', ODI Working Paper no. 41, (London: Overseas Development Institute), August.

McQueen, Matthew and Christopher Stevens (1989) 'Trade Preferences and Lomé IV: Non-traditional ACP Exports to the EC', *Development Policy Review,* vol. 7, no. 3, September.

Miller, Lynn (1973) 'The Prospect for Order Through Regional Security', in Richard Falk and Saul Mendlovitz (eds), *Regional Politics and World Order* (San Francisco: W.H. Freeman).

Minear, Larry (1984) 'Reflections on Development Policy: A View from the Private Voluntary Sector', in Robert F. Gorman (ed.), *Private Voluntary Organizations as Agents of Development* (Boulder, CO: Westview Press), pp. 13–40.

Mosley, Paul, Jane Harrigan and John Toye (1991) *Aid and Power: The World Bank and Policy-based Lending,* 2 vols (London and New York: Routledge).

Mutharika, B.W. (1981) 'A Case Study of Regionalism in Africa', in Nicol Davidson, Luis Echeverria and Aurelio Peccei (eds), *Regionalism and the New International Economic Order* (New York: Pergamon Press).

NGO Working Group on the World Bank (1989) *Position Paper of the NGO Working Group on the World Bank*, photocopy (Geneva: NGO Working Group Secretariat), December.

Nye, Joseph S. (1987) 'Nuclear Learning and U.S.-Soviet Security Regimes', *International Organization,* vol. 41 (summer), pp. 371–402.

Overseas Development Institute (ODI) (1990) 'Crisis in the Franc Zone', ODI briefing paper (London: Overseas Development Institute), July.

Okolo, Julius Emeka (1985) 'Integrative and Cooperative Regionalism: the Economic Community of West African States', *International Organization,* vol. 39, no. 1 (winter), pp. 121–53.

Organization for Economic Co-operation and Development (OECD) (1991) *Development Cooperation: Efforts and Policies of the Members of the Development Assistance Committee: 1991 Report* (Paris: OECD).

Padelford, Norman J. (1954) 'Regional Organizations and the United Nations', *International Organization,* vol. 8, pp. 203–16.

Paul, Samuel (1991) 'Non-Governmental Organizations and the World Bank: An Overview', in Samuel Paul and Arturo Israel (eds), *Non-Governmental Organizations and the World Bank: Cooperation for Development* (Washington, DC: World Bank), pp. 1–19.

Puchala, Donald (1984) 'The Integration Theorists and the Study of International Relations', in Charles Kegley and Eugene Wittkopf (eds), *The Global Agenda: Issues and Perspectives* (New York: Random House).

Qureshi, Moeen A. (1991) 'Popular Participation and the World Bank', remarks at the 1991 International Development Conference, 24 January.

Review of African Political Economy (1992) issue entitled 'Democracy, Civil Society and NGOs', vol. 55 (November).

Riddell, Roger C. (1990) 'ACP Export Diversification: The Case of Zimbabwe', ODI working paper no. 38 (London: Overseas Development Institute), June.

Rittberger, Volker, Manfred Efinger and Martin Mendler (1990) 'Toward an East-West Security Regime: The Case of Confidence and Security-Building Measures', *Journal of Peace Research,* vol. 27, no. 1.

Roberts, Kenneth (1990) 'Bullying and Bargaining: The United States, Nicaragua, and Conflict Resolution in Central America', *International Security,* vol. 15 (fall).

Salmen, Lawrence F. and A. Paige Eaves (1991) *World Bank Work with Non-Governmental Organizations,* Policy, Planning, and Research Working Paper (Washington, DC: World Bank's Public Sector Management and Private Sector Development Division, Country Economics Department).

Schuh, G. Edward (1987) 'PVO Role in Influencing Agricultural Policy: A View from the World Bank', paper presented at the Quarterly Meeting of the Advisory Committee for Voluntary Foreign Aid, USAID, Washington, DC, June.

Schwartz, Elliot (1978) *Private and Voluntary Organizations in Foreign Aid* (Washington, DC: Special Studies Division, Office of Management and Budget).

Shakow, Alexander (1990) 'The World Bank and Non-Governmental Organizations (NGOs): A Review of Operational Experience', World Bank office memorandum, 14 June.

Shaw, Timothy M. (1989) 'The Revival of Regionalism in Africa: Cure for Crisis or Prescription for Conflict', *Jerusalem Journal of International Relations,* vol. 11 (December), pp. 79–105.

Shaw, Timothy M. and Larry A. Swatuk (1993) 'Third World Political Economy and Foreign Policy in the Post-Cold War Era: Towards a Revisionist Framework with Lessons from Africa', *Journal of Asian and African Affairs* (fall), pp. 1–25.

South Commission (1990) *The Challenge to the South: The Report of the South Commission* (New York: Oxford University Press).

Stevens, Christopher (1990) 'ACP Export Diversification: Jamaica, Kenya and Ethiopia', ODI working paper no. 40 (London: Overseas Development Institute), September.

Swatuk, Larry A. (1994) 'Post-Apartheid Directions for Southern African Regional Integration', in Mark Denham and Mark Lombardi (eds), *Problems Without Borders: Perspectives on Third World Sovereignty* (London: Macmillan).

Taylor, Paul (1990) 'Regionalism: The Thought and the Deed', in A.J.R. Groom and Paul Taylor (eds), *Frameworks of International Cooperation* (New York: St. Martin's Press), pp. 151–71.

The Ecologist (1985) 'The World Bank: Global Financing of Impoverishment and Famine', vol. 15, pp. 1–2.

Theoria (1992) special issue entitled 'The State and Civil Society', vol. 79 (May).

Tovias, Alfredo (1991) 'The Single Market and Labour Mobility', paper presented at United Nations Symposium on 'The Implications of the Single Market Act for Non-Member Countries', Geneva, 27–31 May.

Tow, William (1990) *Subregional Security Cooperation in the Third World* (Boulder, CO: Lynne Rienner).

United States Agency for International Development (USAID) (1982), 'AID Partnership in International Development with Private and Voluntary Organizations', AID policy paper (Washington, DC: USAID).

Wilcox, Francis W. (1965) 'Regionalism and the United Nations', *International Organization,* vol. 10, pp. 789–811.

Williams, Aubrey (1990) 'A growing role for NGOs in development', *Finance and Development* (December), pp. 31–3.

World Bank (1987) *Cooperation between Non-Governmental Organizations (NGOs) and the World Bank: Fifth Progress Report* (Washington, DC: World Bank).

World Bank (1989) *The World Bank Operational Manual,* 'Involving Non-Governmental Organizations in Bank-Supported Activities', operational directive 14.70 (Washington, DC: World Bank).

World Bank (1990a) *Cooperation between the World Bank and NGOs: Progress Report* (Washington, DC: World Bank), 8 March, photocopy.

World Bank (1990b) *How the World Bank Works with Non-Governmental Organizations* (Washington, DC: World Bank).

World Bank (1990c) *A World Bank Response to the NGO Working Group Position Paper on the World Bank* (Washington, DC: World Bank, Strategic Planning and Review Department), 13 March, photocopy.

World Bank (1991a) *Cooperation between the World Bank and NGOs: 1990 Progress Report* (Washington, DC: World Bank, International Economic Relations Division, External Affairs Department), 31 January.

World Bank (1991b) *World Bank Annual Report 1991* (Washington, DC: World Bank).

Yalem, Ronald (1973) 'Theories of Regionalism', in Richard Falk and Saul Mendlovitz (eds), *Regional Politics and World Order* (San Francisco: W.H. Freeman).

Yalem, Ronald (1979) 'Regional Security Communities', in George W. Keeton and George Scharzenberger (eds), *The Year Book of International Affairs 1979* (London: Stevens and Sons).

Part IV   Africa

Adedeji, Adebayo (1977) 'Africa: The Crisis of Development and the Challenge of a New Economic Order', address to the Fourth Meeting of the Conference of Ministers and the Thirteenth session of the Economic Commission of Africa, Kinshasa, February–March.

Adedeji, Adebayo (1990a) *The African Alternative: Putting the People First* (Addis Ababa: ECA).

Adedeji, Adebayo (1990b) 'Economic Progress: What Africa Needs', *Transafrica Forum,* vol. 7 (summer), p. 2.

Africa Recovery (1990) vol. 4, no. 2 (July–September).

Bates, Robert H. (1981) *Markets and States in Tropical Africa: The Political Basis of Agricultural Policies* (Berkeley, CA: University of California Press).

Bratton, Michael (1990) 'Non-Governmental Organizations in Africa: Can They Influence Public Policy?', *Development and Change,* vol. 21, no. 1 (January), pp. 87–118.

Clark, John (1991) *Democratizing Development: The Role of Voluntary Organizations* (West Hartford, CT: Kumarian Press).

Drabek, A.G. (ed.) (1987) *Development Alternatives: the Challenge for NGOs* (New York: Pergamon Press).

Economic Commission for Africa (1989) *African Alternative Framework to Structural Adjustment Programmes for Socio-Economic Recovery and Transformation* (Addis Ababa: ECA), July.

Economic Commission for Africa (1990a) *Economic Report on Africa 1990* (Addis Ababa: ECA).

Economic Commission for Africa (1990b) *African Charter for Popular Participation in Development* (Addis Ababa: ECA).

Ergas, Zak (ed.) (1987) *The African State in Transition* (New York: St. Martin's).

Gereffi, Gary and Donald L. Wyman (1990) *Manufacturing Miracles: Paths of Industrialization in Latin America and East Asia* (Princeton University Press).

Harsh, Ernest (199Oa) 'African Economy Posts Upturn', *Africa Recovery,* vol. 4, (October–December), pp. 3–4.

Harsh, Ernest (1990b), 'Limited Progress on African Debt', *Africa Recovery,* vol. 4, (October–December), pp. 3–4.

Hyden, Goran (1983) *No Shortcuts to Progress: African Development Management in Perspective* (Berkeley, CA: University of California Press).

Ihonvbere, Julius O. (ed.) (1989) *Political Economy of Crisis and Under-development in Africa: Selected Works of Claude Ake* (Lagos: JAD Publishers).

Ihonvbere, Julius O. (1993) 'Economic Crisis, Structural Adjustment and Social Crisis in Nigeria', *World Development*, vol. 21 (January), pp. 141–53.

Institute for African Alternatives (IFAA) (1989) *Alternative Development Strategies for Africa* (London: IFAA).

Joseph, Richard (1990) 'The Challenge of Democratization in Africa', in *African Governance in the 1990's* (Atlanta: The Carter Center of Emory University).

Juma, Omar Ali (1989) 'Closing Address', in IFAA, *Alternative Development Strategies for Africa* (London: IFAA).

Lancaster, Carol (1989) 'Economic Restructuring in Sub-Saharan Africa', *Current History*, vol. 88 (May), p. 538.

Leonard, David K. and D.R. Marshall (eds) (1982) *Institutions of Rural Development for the Poor: Decentralization and Organizational Linkages* (Berkeley, CA: Institute of International Studies, University of California).

'Link National, International Democratization: OAU's Salim' (1990) *Africa Recovery* (July–September).

Lone, Salim (1990a) 'Africa: Drifting Off the Map of the World's Concerns', *International Herald Tribune*, 24 August.

Lone, Salim (1990b) 'Donors Demand Political Reforms', *Africa Recovery* (July–September).

Nelson, Joan M. (ed.) (1989) *Fragile Coalitions: The Politics of Economic Adjustment* (New Brunswick, NJ: Transaction Books).

Nyang'oro, Julius E. (1989) *The State and Capitalist Development in Africa: Declining Political Economies* (New York: Praeger).

Nyang'oro, Julius E. and Timothy M. Shaw (1989) *Corporatism in Africa: Comparative Analysis and Practice* (Boulder, CO: Westview).

OAU (1988) 'The African Position', OAU's Mid-Term Review of the United Nations Programme of Action for African Economic Recovery and Development, *Africa Review*, vol. 2, p. 4.

Obasanjo, Olusegun (1990) 'An African Voice', keynote address delivered at the 1990 International Conference organized by the Third World Education Foundation reported in *FAX* 4, p. 28 (10 July).

Onimode, Bade (ed.) (1989) *The IMF, the World Bank and the African Debt: The Social and Political Impact* (London: Zed Press).

Rodney, Walter (1974) *How Europe Underdeveloped Africa* (Washington: Howard University Press).

Rothchild, Donald and Naomi Chazan (eds) (1988) *The Precarious Balance: State and Society in Africa* (Boulder, CO: Westview).

Rweyemamu, Justinian (1972) *Underdevelopment and Industrialization in Tanzania: A Study of Perverse Capitalist Industrial Development* (Nairobi: Oxford University Press).

Sandbrook, Richard (1990) 'Taming the African Leviathan', *World Policy Journal* (fall).

Shaw, Timothy M. (1988) 'Africa in the 1990s: From Economic Crisis to Structural Readjustment', *Dalhousie Review*, vol. 68 (spring/summer), nos 1–2.

Shaw, Timothy M. (1993) *Reformism and Revisionism in Africa's Political Economy in the 1990s* (London: Macmillan).

South Commission (1990) *The Challenge to the South* (London: Oxford University Press).

'The Prospects for Africa in the 1990s' (1990) *West Africa,* (London) 25 June–1 July.

UNDP and World Bank (1990) *The Social Dimensions of Adjustment in Africa: A Policy Agenda* (Washington, DC: World Bank).

World Bank (1989) *Sub-Saharan Africa: From Crisis to Sustainable Growth. A Long-Term Perspective Study* (Washington, DC: World Bank).

Wunsch, James S. (1990) 'Centralization and Development in Post-Independence Africa,' in James S. Wunsch and Dele Olowu (eds), *The Failure of the Centralized State: Institutions and Self-Governance in Africa* (Boulder, CO: Westview).

Part V   Asia

Alexandrova, Olga (1992) 'Geostrategic Reconstructuring in the Former USSR', *Aussenpolitik,* vol. 4.

Amsden, Alice H. (1989) *Asia's Next Giant: South Korea and Late Industrialization* (New York: Oxford University Press).

Aoki, Takeshi (1992) 'Japanese FDI and the Forming of Networks in the Asia-Pacific Region: Experience in Malaysia and Its Implications', in Shojiro Tokunaga (ed.), *Japan's Foreign Investment and Asian Economic Interdependence: Production, Trade, and Financial Systems* (Tokyo: University of Tokyo Press).

Appelbaum, Richard P. and Jeffrey Henderson (eds) (1992) *States and Development in the Pacific Rim* (Newbury Park: Sage Publications).

ASEAN Centre (1992) *ASEAN–Japan Statistical Pocketbook 1992* (Tokyo: ASEAN Promotion Centre on Trade, Investment and Tourism).

Atkins, Muriel (1989) 'The Survival of Islam in Soviet Tajikistan', *Middle East Journal,* vol. 43 (autumn), p. 4.

Balassa, Bela (1981) *The Newly Industrializing Countries in the World Economy* (New York: Pergamon Press).

Balassa, Bela (1988) 'The Lessons of East Asian Development: An Overview', *Economic Development and Cultural Change*, vol. 36 (April).

Bayalinov, K. (1992) 'Pragmatist Akaev Maneuvers for the Good of Kyrghyzstan', *Current Digest of the Post-Soviet Press,* vol. 44, p. 42.

Benoit, Emile (1971) 'Impacts of the End of the Vietnam Hostilities and the Reduction of the British Military Presence in Malaysia and Singapore', in Asia Development Bank, *Southeast Asia's Economy in the 1970s* (London: Longman).

Bodie, William C. (1992) 'Strategy and Successor States: Report from Kiev', *World Affairs,* vol. 154, no. 3 (winter) .

British Broadcasting Service (BBC) (1993) *World Service News,* 4 January.

British Information Office (1993) 'Turkish Relations with Neighbouring States of the Former Soviet Union', background brief, issue 6/93.

Brown, Lester (1991) 'The Aral Sea: Going, Going, ..., ' *World Watch,* vol. 4 (January–February).

Caldwell, J. Alexander (1974) *American Economic Aid to Thailand* (Lexington: D.C. Heath).

Cantori, Louis and Steven Spiegel (eds) (1970) *The International Politics of Regions* (Englewood Cliffs, NJ: Prentice-Hall).

Cumings, Bruce (1987) 'The Origins and Development of the Northeast Asian Political Economy', in Frederic C. Deyo (ed.), *The Political Economy of the New Asian Industrialism* (Ithaca: Cornell University Press).

Current Digest of the Post-Soviet Press (CDPSP) (1993) '5-State Commonwealth Set Up', *CDPSP*, vol. 45, p. 1.

de la Gorce, Paul-Marie (1992) 'La modernite d'Ankara contre le petrole de Teheran', *Jeune-Afrique,* no. 1626 (5–11 March), pp. 38–39.

Der Spiegel (1992) 'Der Duft des Imam', no. 2, pp. 108–111.

Duffy, Charles and Werner Feld (1980) 'Whither Regional Integration Theory?', in Werner Feld and Gavin Boyd (eds), *Comparative Regional Systems* (New York: Pergamon Press), pp. 497–522.

Economist Intelligence Unit (EIU) (1968) *The Economic Effects of the Vietnamese War in East and Southeast Asia* (London: EIU).

Esman, Milton (1972) *Administrative Development in Malaysia: Institution Building and Reform in a Plural Society* (Ithaca: Cornell University Press).

Gharabaghi, Kiaras (1994) 'Development Strategies in Central Asia in the 1990s: In Search of Alternatives', *Third World Quarterly*, vol. 15, no. 1 (April).

Girling, John L.S. (1981) *Thailand: Society and Politics* (Ithaca: Cornell University Press).

Golub, Roman (1992) 'The Caspian/Khazar Sea', *Environmental Policy Review,* vol. 16 (spring).

Halbach, Uwe (1992) 'World Politics and Indigenous Development in Central Asia', *Aussenpolitik,* vol. 4.

Hawes, Gary (1987) *The Philippine State and the Marcos Regime: The Politics of Export* (Ithaca: Cornell University Press).

Hoeppner, Rolf (1977) 'The Future Course of the RCD: Iran, Turkey, Pakistan', *Aussenpolitik*, vol. 28, p. 2.

Hughes, Helen (ed.) (1989) *Achieving Industrialization in East Asia* (Cambridge University Press).

Hunter, Shireen (1992) 'The Emergence of Soviet Muslims: Impact on the Middle East', *Middle East Insight,* vol. 8 (May–June).

Hyman, Anthony (1993) 'Moving Out of Moscow's Orbit: The Outlook for Central Asia', *International Affairs,* vol. 69, p. 2.

Ibrahim, Yousset M. (1992) 'To Counter Iran, Saudis Seek Ties with Ex-Soviet Muslim Republics', *New York Times,* 22 February, I, 4, p. 5.

International Monetary Fund (IMF) (1992a) *Economic Reviews* (Washington, DC: IMF).

International Monetary Fund (1992b) *Common Issues and Interrepublican Relations in the Former USSR* (Washington, DC: IMF).

International Monetary Fund, *et al.* (1991) *A Study of the Soviet Economy, Vol. 1* (Washington, DC: IMF).

Johnson, Chalmers (1987) 'Political Institutions and Economic Performance: The Government–Business Relationship in Japan, South Korean, and Taiwan', in Frederic C. Deyo (ed.), *The Political Economy of East Asian Industrialism* (Ithaca, NY: Cornell University Press).

Krueger, A.O. (1979) *The Development Role of the Foreign Sector and Aid* (Cambridge, MA: Harvard University Press).

Lapidus, Gail W. and Victor Zaslavsky with Philip Goldman (eds.) (1992) *From Union to Commonwealth: Nationalism and Separatism in the Soviet Republics* (Cambridge, MA: Cambridge University Press).

Mason, Edward S. *et al.* (1980) *The Economic and Social Modernization of the Republic of Korea,* (Cambridge, MA: Harvard University Press).

McBeth, John (1989) 'The Boss System: Manila's Disarray Leaves Countryside Under Local Barons', *Far Eastern Economic Review,* 14 September.

Michalopoulos, Constantine and David Tarr (1993) 'Energizing Trade of the States of the Former USSR', *Finance and Development,* March.

Migdal, Joel S. (1988) *Strong Societies and Weak States: State–Society Relations and State Capabilities in the Third World* (Princeton University Press).

Migranyan (1992) 'Migranyan Looks at Ex-Soviet Republics' Future', *Current Digest of the Post-Soviet Press,* vol. 44, p. 43.

Muscat, Robert J. (1990) *Thailand and the United States: Development, Security and Foreign Aid* (New York: Columbia University Press).

Myint, H. (1971) 'The Economic Impacts of the Ending of the Vietnam Hostilities', in Asia Development Bank, *Southeast Asia's Economy in the 1970s* (London: Longman).

Olcott, Martha (1993) 'Kazakhstan: A Republic of Minorities', in Ian Bremmer and Ray Taras (eds), *Nations and Politics in the Soviet Successor States* (Cambridge, MA: Cambridge University Press).

Onis, Ziya (1991) 'The Logic of the Developmental State,' *Comparative Politics,* vol. 24 (October), p. 1.

O'Toole, Pam (1992) 'Turkey Driven to Diplomacy', *The Guardian,* 16 December.

Olcott, Martha (1992) 'Central Asia's Post-Empire Politics', *Orbis* (spring).

Portnikov, Vitaly (1992) 'Turkmenia: Niyazov Runs Prosperous Autocracy', *Current Digest of the Post-Soviet Press,* vol. 44, p. 42.

Ramazani, R.K. (1992) 'Iran's Foreign Policy: Both North and South', *Middle East Journal,* vol. 46, no. 3 (summer).

Riedel, James (1989) 'Economic Development in East Asia: Doing What Comes Naturally?', in Helen Hughes (ed.), *Achieving Industrialization in East Asia* (Cambridge University Press).

Rodan, Garry (1989) *The Political Economy of Singapore's Industrialization: National, State and International Capital* (London: Macmillan).

Rudner, Martin (1989) 'Japanese Official Development Assistance to Southeast Asia', *Modern Asian Studies,* vol. 23 (February).

Ruehl, Lothar (1992) 'Die Turkei Zwischen Europa und dem Orient', *Europa-Archiv,* vol. 11.

Stubbs, Richard (1974) *Counter-Insurgency and the Economic Factor: The Impact of the Korean War Prices Boom on the Malayan Emergency* (Singapore: Institute of Southeast Asian Studies).

Stubbs, Richard (1989) *Hearts and Minds in Guerrilla Warfare: The Malayan Emergency, 1948–1960* (Singapore: Oxford University Press).

Wade, Robert (1990) *Governing the Market: Economic Theory and the Role of Government in East Asian Industrialization* (Princeton University Press).

Wade, Robert (1992) 'East Asia's Economic Success: Conflicting Perspectives Partial Insights, Shaky Evidence,' *World Politics,* vol. 44, no. 2 (January).

Wade, Robert (1993) 'Managing Trade: Taiwan and South Korea as Challenges to Economic and Political Science', *Comparative Politics*, vol. 25, no. 2 (January).

World Bank (1987) *World Development Report, 1987* (Washington, DC: World Bank).

World Bank (1991a) *World Development Report, 1991* (Washington, DC: World Bank).

World Bank (1991b) *Best Practices in Trade Policy Reform* (New York: Oxford University Press).

World Robert (1993) *World Bank News*, 25 April.

Part VI   The Caribbean and Latin America

Abercrombie, Nicholas, Stephen Hill and Bryan Turner (1980) *The Dominant Ideology Thesis* (London: Allen and Unwin).

Annis, Sheldon (1987) 'Can Small-Scale Development be Large-Scale Policy? The Case of Latin America', *World Development*, vol. 15, supplement (autumn), pp. 129–33.

AVANCSO-IDESAC (1990) 'ONGs, Sociedad Civil y Estado en Guatemala: Elementos para el Debate', unpublished document, Guatemala, March.

Barry, Tom (1986) *Low Intensity Conflict: The New Battlefield in Central America* (Albuquerque: Inter-Hemispheric Education Resource Centre).

Black, David R. and Peter McKenna (1993) 'Canada and Structural Adjustment in the South: The Significance of the Guyana Case', paper presented at the annual meeting of the Canadian Political Science Association, Ottawa, June.

Bowles, Samuel and Herbert Gintis (1987) *Democracy and Capitalism: Property, Community and the Contradictions of Modern Social Thought* (New York: Basic Books).

Bull, Hedley (1977) *The Anarchical Society: A Study of Order in World Politics* (New York: Columbia University Press).

Bull, Hedley and Adam Watson (eds) (1984) *The Expansion of International Society* (Oxford: Clarendon Press).

Burton, John (1985) 'World Society and Human Needs', in M. Light and A.J.R. Groom (eds), *International Relations: A Handbook of Current Theory* (London: Frances Pinter), pp. 7–26.

Caves, G. (1989) *Le Tourisme International: Mirage Ou Strategie D'Avenir?* (Paris: Hatier).

Concertación Centroamericana de Organismas de Desarrollo (1988), 'Memoria – Reunión de organismos no-gubernamentales para la constitutión de la Concertación Centroamericana de Organismos de Desarrollo' (San José, Costa Rica, November), unpublished document.

Cox, Robert W. (1983) 'Gramsci, Hegemony and International Relations: An Essay in Method', *Millennium*, vol. 12, no. 2 (summer), pp. 162–75.

Cox, Robert W. (1987) *Production, Power, and World Order: Social Forces in the Making of History* (New York: Columbia University Press).

Dahl, Robert (1971) *Polyarchy: Participation and Opposition* (New Haven: Yale University Press).

Deere, Carmen Diana (Coordinator) (1990) *In The Shadows of the Sun* (Boulder, CO: Westview Press).

Diaz-Briquets, Sergio, and Sidney Weintraub (eds) (1991) *Migration Impacts of Trade and Foreign Investment, Mexico and Caribbean Basin Countries* (Boulder, CO: Westview Press).

Economist (London), 17 October 1992, 'GATT Lives'.

Erzan, Refik and Alexander Yeats (1992) 'U.S.–Latin American Free Trade Areas: Some Empirical Evidence', in Sylvia Saborio (ed.), *The Premise and the Promise: Free Trade in the Americas* (Washington, DC: Overseas Development Council), pp. 117–46.

FACS (1990) *Fundación Agosto C. Sandino – Diez Años al Servicio del Pueblo Nicaragüense* (Managua).

Fowler, Alan (1991) 'The Role of NGOs in Changing State-Society Relations: Perspectives from Eastern and Southern Africa', *Development Policy Review*, vol. 9, pp. 53–84.

Gayle, Dennis J. (1988) 'Singaporean Market Socialism: Some Implications for Development Theory', *International Journal of Social Economics*, vol. 15, no. 7, pp. 53–75.

Ghils, Paul (1992) *International Social Sciences Journal*, vol. 133, pp. 417–29.

Gill, Stephen (1990a) *American Hegemony and the Trilateral Commission* (Cambridge University Press).

Gill, Stephen (1990b) 'Intellectuals and Transnational Capital', *Socialist Register 1990*, (London: Merlin Press), pp. 290–310.

Gill, Stephen and David Law (1988) *The Global Political Economy: Perspectives, Problems and Policies* (Baltimore: Johns Hopkins University Press).

Gramsci, Antonio (1971) *Selections from the Prison Notebooks* (New York: International Publishers).

Griffin, Winston H. (1990) 'CARICOM Countries and the Caribbean Basin Initiative', *Latin American Perspectives*, vol. 17 (winter), pp. 33–54.

Groom, A.J.R. (1975) 'Functionalism and World Society' in A.J.R. Groom and Paul Taylor (eds), *Functionalism: Theory and Practice in International Relations* (London: University of London Press), pp. 93–111.

Hufbauer, Gary and Jeffrey Scholtt (1992) *North American Free Trade: Issues and Recommendations* (Washington, DC: Institute for International Economics).

Ietto-Gillies, Grazia (1992) *International Production: Trends, Theories, Effects* (Cambridge: Polity Press).

Inter-American Development Bank (IDB) (1992) *Economic and Social Progress in Latin America*, 1992 Report (Washington, DC: IDA).

Inter-Hemispheric Resource Centre (IHRC) (1988a) *Private Organizations U.S. Connections in EL Salvador* (Albuquerque: IHRC).

Inter-Hemispheric Resource Centre (1988b) *Private Organizations U.S. Connections in Guatemala* (Albuquerque: IHRC).

Inter-Hemispheric Resource Centre (1988c) *Private Organizations with U.S. Connections in Honduras* (Albuquerque: IHRC).

International Monetary Fund (IMF) (1993) *World Economic Outlook*, May (Washington, DC: IMF).

International Monetary Fund (1992) *International Financial Statistics Yearbook*, (Washington, DC: IMF).

International Monetary Fund (various), *Direction of Trade Statistics Yearbook*, (Washington, DC: IMF).

Jara, Oscar H. (1987) *Las 'Organizaciones No-Gubernamentales', la Crisis y el Futuro de Centroamérica* (San José: Centro de Estudios y Publicaciones Alforja).

Jones, Roy E. (1981) 'The English School of International Relations: A Case for Closure', *Review of International Studies*, vol. 7, no. 4, pp. 1–13.

Keane, John (ed.) (1988a) *Civil Society and the State: New European Perspectives* (London: Verso).

Keane, John (1988b) *Democracy and Civil Society* (London: Verso).

Kothari, Rajni (1986) 'NGOs, the State and World Capitalism', *Economic and Political Weekly*, vol. 21, no. 50 (13 December), pp. 2177–82.

Krugman, Paul (1992) 'Regionalism vs. Multilateralism: Analytical Notes', paper no. 7, World Bank and CEPR Conference on New Dimensions in Regional Integration, Washington, DC, April.

Laclau, Ernesto and Chantal Mouffe (1985) *Hegemony and Socialist Strategy: Towards a Radical Democratic Politics* (London: Verso).

Lewis, David (1992a) 'Facing Free Trade Challenges and Opportunities for the Caribbean Basin', a memorandum by the Caribbean Basin Technical Advisory Group (San Juan, Puerto Rico), September.

Lewis, David (1992b) 'The North American Free Trade Agreement and Its Impact on Caribbean Economic Transformation: The Case of the Eastern Caribbean', paper presented in St. Vincent, July.

Lipschutz, Ronnie D. (1992), 'Reconstructing World Politics: The Emergence of Global Civil Society', *Millennium*, vol. 21, no. 3, pp. 389–420.

Lipsey, Richard (1992) 'Getting There: The Path to a Western Hemisphere Free Trade Area and Its Structure', in Sylvia Saborio, (ed.), *The Premise and the Promise: Free Trade in the Americas* (Washington, DC: Overseas Development Council), pp. 95–114.

Macpherson, C.B. (1973) *Democratic Theory* (Oxford: Clarendon Press).

Magnusson, Warren and Rob Walker (1988) 'De-centring the State: Political Theory and Canadian Political Economy', *Studies in Political Economy*, vol. 26 (summer), pp. 37–71.

Mahon, Rianne (1991) 'From "Bringing" to "Putting": the State in Late Twentieth-Century Social Theory', *Canadian Journal of Sociology*, vol. 16, no. 2, pp. 119–44.

McBain, Helen (1993) 'Foreign Capital Flows and Caribbean Economic Development', in S. Lalta and M. Freckleton (eds), *Caribbean Economic Development: The First Generation* (Kingston, Jamaica: Ian Randle Publishers), pp. 130–40.

McCarthy, Stephen (1993) 'Technology and Development', *The Courier*, no. 139 (May–June), pp. 60–62.

Meyer, Lorenzo (1984) *Historia de las relaciones entre Mexico y los Estados Unidos* (Mexico, DF: El Colegio de Mexico).

Mitrany, David (1966) *A Working Peace System* (Chicago: Quadrangle Books).

Nelson, Joan (1992) 'Poverty, Equity, and the Politics of Adjustment', in S. Haggard and R. Kaufman (eds), *The Politics of Economic Adjustment* (New Haven: Princeton University Press), pp. 221–69.

Noques, Julio and Rosalinda Quintanilla (1992) 'Latin America's Integration and the Multilateral Trading System', paper no. 5, World Bank and CEPR Conference on New Dimensions in Regional Integration, Washington, DC, April.

Norsworthy, Kent (1989) *Nicaragua: A Country Guide* (Albuquerque: Inter-Hemispheric Education Resource Centre).

North, Lisa and CAPA (1990) *Between War and Peace in Central America: Choices for Canada* (Toronto: Between the Lines).

Organisation for Economic Cooperation and Development (OECD) (1974) *Agricultural Trade with Developing Countries* (Paris: OECD).

Pateman, Carole (1988) 'The Fraternal Social Contract', in Keane, 1988a.

Peterson, M.J. (1992) 'Transnational Activity, International Society and World Politics', *Millennium*, vol. 21, no. 3, pp. 371–88.

Ranis, Gustav and Syed Mahmood (1992) *The Political Economy of Development Policy Change* (Cambridge: Blackwell Publishers).

Rico, Carlo (1992) 'Migration and U.S.–Mexican Relations, 1966-1986', in Christopher Mitchell (ed.), *Western Hemisphere Immigration and United States Foreign Policy* (University Park, PA: Pennsylvania State University Press).

Rivera Urrutia, Eugenio, Ana Sojo and Jose Roberto Lopez (1986) *Centroamérica Politica Económica Y Crisis* (San José, Costa Rica: DEI).

Saborio, Sylvia (ed.) (1992) *The Premise and the Promise: Free Trade in the Americas* (Washington, DC: Overseas Development Council).

Saint-Martin, Jean-Guy (1992) 'Development with Equity and Ecological Security: Strategies and Institutions for the 21st Century', paper presented to the Society for International Development, Rome, 11–12 September.

Sakamoto, Yoshikazu (1991) 'Introduction: The Global Context of Democratization', (special issue on 'The Global Context of Democratization'), *Alternatives,* vol. 16, no. 2 (spring), pp. 119–27.

Segal, Aaron (1991) 'The Caribbean, the European Community and the Caribbean Basin Initiative', paper presented to the Dalhousie University Symposium, 'The Political Economy of Security and Democracy in the South in the 1990s', Center for African Studies, Dalhousie University, Halifax, September.

Segal, Aaron (1992) 'Communist Cuba Struggles to Stay Afloat', *Geonomics,* no. 4.

Serbin, Andres (1982) 'Menage a Trois au Partouze', *Caribbean Affairs* (April–June), pp. 70–80.

Shaw, Martin (1992) 'Global Society and Global Responsibility: The Theoretical, Historical and Political Limits of "International Society"', *Millennium,* vol. 21, no. 3, pp. 421–34.

Smith, Brian H. (1990) *More Than Altruism: The Politics of Private Foreign Aid* (Princeton University Press).

Smith, Carol A. (1990) 'The Militarization of Civil Society in Guatemala: Economic Reorganization as a Continuation of War', *Latin American Perspectives*, vol. 17, no. 4 (fall), pp. 8–41.

Stallings, Barbara (1992) 'International Influence on Economic Policy: Debt, Stabilization, and Structural Reform', in S. Haggard and R. Kaufman (eds), *The Politics of Economic Adjustment* (New Haven: Princeton University Press), pp. 41–88.

The Times of the Americas (1989), special section on the Caribbean Basin Initiative, 13 December.

The Times of the Americas (1991) 'The El Banana War', 7 March.

Torres-Rivas, Edelberto (1989) *Repression and Resistance: The Struggle for Democracy in Central America* (Boulder, CO: Westview Press).

Trejo Reyes, Saul (1984) *La Economia de Mexico* (Mexico, DF: El Colegio de Mexico).

UNCTAD, *Handbook of International Trade and Development Statistics,* various years.

United Nations (1992) *World Investment Report* (New York: UN).

United Nations (1993) *Monthly Bulletin of Statistics* (New York: UN) April.

United Nations Development Program (UNDP) (1992) *Human Development Report* (New York: UNDP).

Vermez, George and David Ronfeldt (1991) 'The Current Situation in Mexican Immigration', *Science* (8 March), pp. 1189–93.

Walker, R.B.J. (1990a) 'Security, Sovereignty, and the Challenge of World Politics', *Alternatives,* vol. 15, pp. 3–27.

Walker, R.B.J. (1990b) 'Sovereignty, Identity, Community: Reflections on the Horizons of Contemporary Political Practice', in R.B.J. Walker and Saul H. Mendlovitz (eds), *Contending Sovereignties: Redefining Political Community* (Boulder, CO: Lynne Rienner), pp. 159–85.

Wood, Ellen (1990) 'The Uses and Abuses of "Civil Society"', *Socialist Register 1990* (London: Merlin).

Wood, Robert E. (1986) *From Marshall Plan to Debt Crisis: Foreign Aid and Development Choices in the World Economy* (Berkeley, CA: University of California Press).

World Bank (1991) *World Development Report* (Washington, DC: IBRD).

World Bank (1992) *World Development Report* (Washington, DC: IBRD).

Worrell, Delisle (1992) 'U.S. Caricom Free Trade', in Sylvia Saborio (ed.), *The Premise and the Promise: Free Trade in the Americas* (Washington, DC: Overseas Development Council), pp. 217–29.

Part VII Conclusion

'Africa: Democracy is Not Enough' (1992) *Africa Confidential,* vol. 33, no. 1 (10 January), p. 24.

African Leadership Forum (1991) *Kampala Document from the Conference on Security, Stability, Development and Cooperation in Africa* (Kampala: OAU/ ECA) (May).

Baskin, Jeremy (1993) 'Corporatism: Some Obstacles Facing the South African Labour Movement' (Johannesburg: Centre for Policy Studies, research report no. 30, April).

Blight, James G. and Aaron Belkin (1993) 'USSR's Third World Orphans: Deterring Desperate Dependents', *Third World Quarterly,* vol. 13, no. 4, pp. 715–26.

Blight, James G. and Thomas G. Weiss (1992) 'Must the Grass still Suffer? Some thoughts on Third World conflicts after the Cold War', *Third World Quarterly,* vol. 13, no. 2, pp. 229–53.

Campbell, Bonnie K. and John Loxley (eds) (1989) *Structural Adjustment in Africa* (London: Macmillan).

Chan, Steve (1992) 'National Security in the Asia-Pacific: Linkages among Growth, Democracy and Peace', *Contemporary Southeast Asia,* vol. 14, no. 1 (June), pp. 13–32.

Clark, John (1991) *Democratising Development: The Role of Voluntary Organisations* (London: Earthscan).

Clarke, Jonathan (1993) 'The Conceptual Poverty of U.S. Foreign Policy', *The Atlantic Monthly,* vol. 272, no. 3 (September), pp. 54–75.

Edwards, Michael and David Hulme (eds) (1992) *Making a Difference: Grassroots Movements for Global Change* (London: Routledge).

Healey, John and Mark Robinson (1992) *Democracy, Governance and Economic Policy: Sub-Saharan Africa in Comparative Perspective* (London: ODI).

Homer-Dixon, Thomas F. (1991) 'On the Threshold: Environmental Changes as Causes of Acute Conflict', *International Security,* vol. 16, no. 2 (fall).

Huntington, Samuel P. (1993) 'Cart Before the Horse', *Financial Mail* (Johannesburg), vol. 129, no. 5 (30 July), p. 39.

Hutchful, Eboe (1988) 'The Violence of Periphery States', *African Journal of Political Economy,* vol. 2, no. 1, pp. 48–74.

Hyden Goran and Michael Bratton (eds) (1992) *Governance and Politics in Africa* (Boulder: Westview).

Klare, Michael T. (1991) 'Deadly Convergence: The Arms Trade, Nuclear/Chemical/ Missile Proliferation and Regional Conflict in the 1990s', in Michael T. Klare and Daniel C. Thomas (eds), *World Security: Trends and Challenges at Century's End* (New York: St. Martin's), pp. 170–96.

Korany, Bahgat (1986) 'Hierarchy Within the South: in search of theory', *Third World Affairs 1986* (London: Third World Foundation), pp. 85–100.

Korany, Bahgat, Paul Noble and Rex Brynen (eds) (1992) *The Many Faces of National Security in the Arab World: Dilemmas of Security and Development* (London: Macmillan).

Korten, David C. (1987) 'Third Generation NGO Strategies: A Key to People-Based Development', *World Development,* vol. 15 (special issue, autumn), pp. 145–59.

Kuhne, Winrich (1991) quoted in Philip van Niekerk, 'Out of Africa. But it May Halt Cycle of Despair', *Weekly Mail* (Johannesburg), 18–24 January, p. 9.

Maree, Johann (1993) 'Trade Unions and Corporatism in South Africa', *Transformation,* vol. 21, pp. 24–54.

Maynes, Charles William (1990) 'America Without the Cold War', *Foreign Policy,* vol. 78 (spring), pp. 5–19.

Moore, Mick (ed.) (1993) 'Good Government?', *IDS Bulletin,* vol. 24, no. 1 (January), pp. 1–79.

Mosley, Paul, Jane Harrigan and John Toye (1991) *Aid and Power: the World Bank and Policy-Based Lending,* two volumes (London: Routledge).

Nelson, Joan M. (ed.) (1989) *Fragile Coalitions: The Politics of Economic Adjustment* (New Brunswick: Transaction).

Nelson, Joan M. (1990) *Economic Crisis and Policy Choice: The Politics of Economic Adjustment in Developing Nations* (Princeton University Press).

Nyang'oro, Julius and Timothy M. Shaw (eds.) (1989) *Corporatism in Africa: Comparative Analysis and Practise* (Boulder: Westview).

Nyang'oro, Julius and Timothy M. Shaw (eds) (1992) *Beyond Structural Adjustment in Africa: The Political Economy of Sustainable and Democratic Development* (New York: Praeger).

Palmer, Ingrid (1991) *Gender and Population in the Adjustment of African Economies: Planning for Change,* Women, Work and Development 19 (Geneva: ILO).

Rathman, Atiq (1992) 'The Informal Sector in Bangladesh: An Appraisal of its Role in Development', *Development and Change* (January).

Rengger, N.J. (1993) 'No Longer "A Tournament of Distinctive Knights"? Systemic Transition and the Priority of International Order', in Mike Bowker and Robin Brown (eds), *From Cold War to Collapse: Theory and World Politics in the 1980s* (Cambridge University Press).

Rothchild, Donald and Naomi Chazan (1988) *The Precarious Balance: state and society in Africa* (Boulder: Westview).

Sandbrook, Richard (1993) *The Politics of Africa's Economic Recovery* (Cambridge University Press).

Shaw, Timothy M. (1992) 'Africa', in Mary Hawkesworth and Maurice Kegan (eds), *Encyclopedia of Government and Politics*, vol. II (London: Routledge) pp. 1178–200.

Shaw, Timothy M. (1993a) *Reformism and Revisionism in Africa's Political Economy in the 1990s: Beyond Structural Adjustment* (London: Macmillan).

Shaw, Timothy M. (1993b) 'Civil Society, the State and African Development in the 1990s: NGOs under SAP Conditionalities', AACC and Mwengo workshop on 'Receding Role of the State in African Development and Emerging Role of NGOs', Arusha, August.

Shaw, Timothy M. and E. John Inegbedion (1991) 'Alternative Approaches to Peace and Security in Africa', in Jorge Rodriguez Beruff, Peter Figueroa and J. Edward Greene (eds), *Conflict, Peace and Security in the Caribbean* (London: Macmillan), pp. 259–83.

Shaw, Timothy M. and Julius Emeke Okolo (eds) (1994) *The Political Economy of Foreign Policy in ECOWAS* (London: Macmillan).

Stallings, Barbara (1993) 'The New International Context of Development', *SSRC Items,* vol. 47, no. 1 (March), pp. 1–6.

Stallings, Barbara (1994) *The New International Context of Development: Obstacles or Opportunities?* (Madison: University of Wisconsin Press).

Swatuk, Larry A. (1993) *Dealing With Dual Destabilisation in Southern Africa: Foreign Policy in Botswana, Lesotho and Swaziland, 1975–1989,* unpublished PhD dissertation, Dalhousie University.

UNDP (1991) *Human Development Report 1991* (New York: Oxford University Press).

UN-ECA (1989) *African Alternative Framework to Structural Adjustment Programmes for Socio-Economic Recovery and Transformation* (Addis Ababa).

Williams, Marc (1993) 'Re-articulating the Third World Coalition: the role of the environmental agenda', *Third World Quarterly,* vol. 14, no. 1, pp. 7–29.

Wurfel, David and Bruce Burton (eds.) (1991) *The Political Economy of Foreign Policy in Southeast Asia* (London: Macmillan).

Index